PETER OF IRELAND,
WRITINGS ON NATURAL PHILOSOPHY

BREPOLS LIBRARY OF CHRISTIAN SOURCES

VOLUME 9

Editorial Board
Professor Thomas O'Loughlin
Dr Andreas Andreopoulos
Professor Lewis Ayres
Dr Lavinia Cerioni
Professor Hugh Houghton
Professor Doug Lee
Professor Joseph Lössl
Dr Elena Narinskaya
Dr Sara Parks

Peter of Ireland,
Writings on Natural Philosophy

Commentary on Aristotle's On Length and Shortness of Life *and the* Determinatio Magistralis

Edited with an Introduction and English Translation by
MICHAEL W. DUNNE

BREPOLS

© 2023, Brepols Publishers n.v., Turnhout, Belgium.

All rights reserved. No part of this publication may be reproduced, stored in a retrieval system, or transmitted, in any form or by any means, electronic, mechanical, photocopying, recording, or otherwise without the prior permission of the publisher.

D/2023/0095/71
ISBN 978-2-503-60568-5
eISBN 978-2-503-60569-2
DOI 10.1484/M.BLCS-EB.5.133299

Printed in the EU on acid-free paper.

Table of Contents

Preface	7
Introduction	9
Life, Longevity and Death	9
Peter of Ireland, Life and Works	10
The *De longitudine* commentary	14
The *Determinatio Magistralis*	33
Principles of the Edition and Translation	35
Text and Translation	37
Bibliography	211
Indices	
Index nominum	215
Index operum	216
Index rerum	220
Index to Introduction	225

Preface

The position of Peter of Ireland within the history of thought is well established due to an increasing number of articles and publications, beginning with the groundbreaking work of Clemens Baeumker in 1920. Thus, Peter's contribution is now acknowledged in terms of the development of Aristotelianism in Southern Italy and beyond. His extant works have been edited and published, but up to now they have remained the preserve of the specialist, as is increasingly the fate of all Latin editions nowadays. We now live in a cultural situation in the Anglo-American world where most University students and lecturers do not have a knowledge of Latin. Students of medieval philosophy, especially undergraduates, are unable to read texts in the original language and are in need not only of introductions to medieval thought in general, but increasingly of translations of medieval philosophical texts. It is hoped that the present work will encourage a better public understanding of the person, historical situation, and works of Peter of Ireland. It is also hoped that it will also encourage others to edit and translate other works of the to date largely unedited *corpus* of medieval Irish thinkers.

I would like to thank the Trustees of the Maynooth Scholastic Trust for the financial assistance received in the preparation of this volume.

I wish to thank Prof. Jean-Michel Counet, UC Louvain, and Luc Peeters of Peeters Publishers, Leuven, for their permission to reproduce the Latin text from the series *Philosophes Médiévaux.*

I would also like to thank my friends and colleagues for their support during the preparation of this volume, but especially Stephen McCarthy for his close reading of the text and many helpful suggestions and also Susan Gottlöber for her constant encouragement. Finally, in acknowledgement of our cordial *disputatio* I wish to dedicate this book to Prof. Andrea Robiglio, *con amicizia.*

Introduction

1. Life, Longevity and Death

> I can see that in times gone by things must have been different.
> In those days people knew (or suspected) that they had death
> inside them like the stone inside a fruit
>
> *Rainer Maria Rilke*, The Notebooks of Malte Laurids Brigge

To people looking in from the outside it can seem that philosophy is primarily concerned with the last of the triad announced in the title of this section and the other two only in reference to and in function of the third. It is this awareness of death, the stone inside the fruit, that marks out human beings precisely as human: I am aware not only that people die but more significantly that I will die. Most civilizations and cultures are full of the symbolism and presence of death which makes our own contemporary Western culture all the stranger because of the absence of death and that we, again quite uniquely, have absolved ourselves from the care of the dead. To some it might seem surprising that the notion of a being-towards-death was not a recent discovery of the wizard of *Being and Time* but is a fundamental realization of all human cultures. The topic of life and death remains a central theme of philosophical speculation but now this speculation is being informed by developments in biotechnology which raises ethical issues regarding both beginning and end of life issues, as well as the possibilities of extending and developing human life through transhumanism.[1]

Turning to that cultural chronotopos which we call the Latin Middle Ages there are certain recurrent ideas, the notion of the human being as *viator*, a being whose short life is marked by the limitations of original sin and death but yet with the anticipation of a future state, of life beyond death. The heart of medieval Christian anthropology is that man is weak, weak in body, weak in understanding, weak willed, thanks to the sin of Adam in which all of his descendants share. That what characterizes human nature as such is weakness is, of course, very different from the conception of human nature in Greek and Roman Philosophy

---

1 For a general survey of the main points under contemporary discussion, gathered under the headings of "The Metaphysics of Life and Death", "The Significance of Life and Death" and "The Ethics of Life and Death", see Luper (2014).

and Medicine.[2] What is important is to learn the true meaning of suffering rather than to seek the prevention of suffering and perhaps even its elimination by means of some secular and profane learning.

A recovery of the ancient paradigm begins with the translation of Arabic medical texts into Latin beginning in the eleventh century, themselves relying on the works of authors such as Galen, and the establishment of medical schools at Montpellier and Salerno in the twelfth century. To be sure, the religious dimension is never absent but it exists side by side with a more optimistic vision of the potential of human life in the here and now. The impact of these Latin translations of medical works from the Arabic, and their reception in the Latin West, is well documented in Peter of Ireland's work. Of course, rich and wealthy clients not only wanted cures for their bodily and psychological ills but also wished to know which products might be anti-aging and which kinds of medicines and practices might actually lengthen life. Then as now, people put their faith in diets and medicines which were a trap for the gullible and parting them from their money.

By the late twelfth century, and throughout the thirteenth, by means of the recovery of the writings of Aristotle (directly from Greek sources, and indirectly through Arabic sources, themselves in turn relying often on Syriac translations from the Greek), there is the rediscovery of what we would recognise today as a "scientific" approach to questions such as length and shortness of life, and particularly in the treatise of that name which was the subject of commentaries by Arabic authors such as Averroes and then many Western authors including Peter of Ireland.

2. Peter of Ireland, Life and Works

Peter of Ireland (Petrus de Hibernia, de Ybernia) was active as a teacher and writer at the University of Naples from perhaps as early as the 1240s until at least the mid-1260s. Born in Ireland sometime towards the beginning of the thirteenth century, the fact of his career taking place in the South of Italy, with its Norman links with Ireland and England, would make his being of Gaelic origin less probable than his being of an Anglo-Irish family. The lack of a University in Ireland meant that, like Richard FitzRalph a century later, he probably left Ireland at around fifteen years of age to pursue his studies abroad. We do not know at which university he studied but the most likely candidate is Oxford. The historical records we do have place him at the world's first state university at Naples as Professor of Logic and Natural Philosophy in the mid part of the thirteenth century.

The initial interest of scholars in Peter of Ireland was mainly due to the fact that he was held to be a teacher of the young Thomas Aquinas at Naples

---

2 See Crisciani (2018), 6.

University from 1239–1244, introducing Thomas to the study of Aristotle and perhaps also to the commentaries of Avicenna and Averroes. However, based upon internal evidence, the surviving works of Peter would seem to date from at least a decade later, and to relate to lectures given in the 1250s and 1260s. Moreover, the testimony of William of Tocco at the time of the process for the canonisation of Aquinas, which identifies Peter as the teacher of the young Thomas, has been questioned (see below) as being perhaps an attempt to complete Thomas' biography by extending the activity of a well-known Professor of the early University of Naples to a decade earlier.

The effect of these doubts regarding Peter's master-pupil relationship has been to focus attention upon the value of Peter's three surviving texts, each found in a single manuscript only, giving us some idea of what must have been a distinguished and productive career.[3] The texts are all *reportationes*, or classroom records of Peter's lectures. Peter must have had an open and enquiring mind. He was aware of contemporary ideas and was one of those who explored and taught the new learning which had arrived with the translations of Aristotle's works and his Arabic commentators (at a time when these works were forbidden to be taught at the University of Paris). To take an important example: at the instigation of the Emperor Frederick II Hohenstaufen, the work of the great Jewish thinker Moses Maimonides was translated into Latin in the 1240s, a result of Jewish-Christian co-operation. This co-operation continued, since we know from Rabbi Moses ben Solomon of Salerno that he met with Peter of Ireland, whom he called "that wise Christian", and some others in the 1250s to discuss the leading doctrines of Maimonides.[4] Peter's approach to philosophy embraces Aristotle's naturalism and involves a search for the truth which seems independent of theology or personal belief. In fact, Peter does not make any references to Scripture or to the Church Fathers, and, whereas Boethius is mentioned, Augustine is not.[5] In terms of his philosophical approach he seems to largely ignore the Christian Neoplatonic tradition.[6]

a. Peter and Thomas Aquinas

The story of the relationship between Peter of Ireland and Thomas Aquinas begins, it would appear, in the early years of Aquinas' life. Having been sent to the Benedictine Abbey of Montecassino at the age of five, Thomas was expelled

---

3 See editions in Dunne (1993), (1996).
4 See Sermoneta, (1969), 45.
5 See McEvoy (1994), 146–58.
6 The exception being the opening of the *De longitudine* commentary, beginning as it does with the *Liber de causis*, or the *Liber de pura bonitate* as Peter terms it, the original title as translated from the Arabic *Kalâm fî mahd al-khayr*. The text is based on the *Elementatio theologica* of Proclus with commentaries by an unknown Arabic author. Peter like many of his contemporaries presumably thought that it was a work of Aristotle although some held it to be by Alpharabi.

together with most of the monks some ten years later under the orders of the Emperor Frederick II, owing to conflict between the Empire and Papacy. Thus it was that Thomas Aquinas, aged about 15, went to the University of Naples to continue his studies.

The University of Naples had been founded in 1224 by Frederick II without seeking Papal approval and so it became the first State University. Frederick wrote in his charter establishing the University:

> We have therefore decided that in the most pleasant city of Naples that there should be the teaching of the arts and all disciplines, so that those who are starved of knowledge will find it in their own kingdom, and will not be forced in their search for knowledge, to become pilgrims and to beg in foreign lands.[7]

He then goes on to order that no student should dare to leave the kingdom and that all students already abroad should return. There are to be doctors and teachers in every faculty and special loans are to be made available to students as well as cheap accommodation.

Universities had been founded as a recognition of previously established or existing schools. Frederick began from scratch and invited scholars and students to come to Naples. One scholar who arrived at Naples to teach was Peter of Ireland, presumably sometime after 1224. Thomas Aquinas, we are told, was a student in the Arts faculty aged between 15 and 20 and it was during this time that he encountered the Dominican Order and made his decision to enter this mendicant order. During his time at the University of Naples we are told by two of Thomas' biographers that Aquinas was taught by Peter of Ireland. Writing some 40 years after the rather early death of Aquinas, both William of Tocco and Peter Calo tell us something about Aquinas' teachers at Naples. William tells us that at Naples, Thomas was educated in grammar and logic by Master Martin and in natural philosophy by Peter of Ireland. Peter Calo varies the story slightly and in view of later discoveries seems to have recorded correctly that since Aquinas soon learnt all that Master Martin could teach him in grammar (Aquinas had had ten years of education with the Benedictines), he was then transferred to Master Peter the Irishman who taught him logic and natural philosophy.

However, Andrea Robiglio has put forward the thesis that when he was a student at Naples, Thomas Aquinas did not have the philosopher Peter of Ireland as professor.[8] This is despite the fact that, as the author notes, many writers accept the historiographical tradition according to which Peter of Ireland was the teacher of Thomas Aquinas in the 1240s. Robiglio quite correctly points out that we have very little evidence concerning Thomas' studies and teachers in the years 1239–1244 when he was a student at the *studium generale* of Naples. Indeed much of what we can say has to be surmised from other sources regarding what would

---

7 Delle Donne (2009), 103. For a discussion relative to the foundation of the University of Naples, see ibid., 101–03.

8 Robiglio (2002) 107–11; 110.

have been normal at the time, namely, that as part of his studies as a student *in artibus* he would have attended lectures in philosophy. Such studies would, as a matter of course, have included logic and the philosophy of nature.

It must be acknowledged that details concerning the early life of any medieval thinker are often largely a matter of conjecture. However, regarding Tocco's information we have to ask if it is possible that Peter was in Naples before 1250 and whether Tocco is a credible witness regarding this. For all its faults, William of Tocco's work is the principal biographical document which we possess concerning Thomas' life. It was, however, written with an eye towards the process of Aquinas' canonization and so emphasized his heroic virtues and miracles associated with him.

To sum up, we can state the following:

1 Peter of Ireland lived in the Naples-Salerno region from around 1250–1265.
2 Peter taught logic and the philosophy of nature.
3 Aquinas probably read Peter in the 1270s and so was influenced by him to some extent.
4 Tocco says that Peter taught Aquinas.

It seems that it is the last point which is at issue. Could Tocco have obtained his information from a reliable source? He could have had it directly from Aquinas — Tocco was 30 when he met Aquinas in 1272–1273. If we choose 1210 as an arbitrary date of birth for Peter — making him 30 when he taught Aquinas and 50 when he spoke before Manfred — Peter could still have been alive when Tocco was in Naples. Thus, it is at least possible that Tocco could have had first hand knowledge and was right in what he wrote. To prove the opposite thesis, that Thomas never had Peter as a teacher is difficult to do. I agree with Robiglio that we cannot be absolutely sure on the basis of what evidence we have. However, one of effects of this debate is that subsequent authors who refer to Aquinas' early career now seem to avoid mentioning Peter of Ireland as if erring on the side of caution. This, however, has the opposite tendency, which is, unfortunately, to completely ignore the historical evidence.

But in fact, it is not only perhaps Peter's influence at the beginning of Aquinas' career that is significant but also his influence at the end of Aquinas' life when he was engaged in his massive project of commenting on all of the works of Aristotle. When writing his own commentary, Aquinas had Peter's commentary on the *Peri Hermeneias* in front of him. Gauthier comments that although Peter's commentary probably dates from 1259–1265 and contains a record of lectures which Aquinas could not have attended, yet:

> It is nonetheless not impossible that he [Aquinas] had in his hands a *reportatio* of the course given by Peter of Ireland; we have noted many similarities

14   INTRODUCTION

between Peter's course and Aquinas' exposition — some of which are quite remarkable.[9]

Indeed, Aquinas sometimes places the authority of Peter's text together with the commentaries of Boethius and Ammonius, something which is in marked contrast to Albert the Great's commentary from around 1260.

3. The *De longitudine* commentary

When the edition of the Commentary of Peter of Ireland (Petrus de Hibernia, fl. 1240–1260) on the *De longitudine et brevitate vitae* was published in 1993,[10] it is fair to say that comparatively little interest had been shown up to then on that text or its medieval reception and indeed that statement could probably be extended to the *Parva Naturalia* as a whole (with some exceptions): these short treatises on Aristotle's natural philosophy seemed somewhat of an embarrassment compared with the great treatises such as the *De anima*. In fact, they seemed to be to a large extent a repetition of themes dealt with elsewhere in the Aristotelian corpus in greater detail and clarity. Indeed, it was their location in the *Opera Omnia* following after the *De anima* which caused some unease. In the intervening years, a reconsideration of the reception history of the *Parva Naturalia*, has led in part at least, as we shall see below, to the reconsideration of the *De anima* as *also* being a work of natural philosophy.[11] As Silvia Donati points out, the subject matter of the *De anima* and the *Parva Naturalia* broadly overlap, the main difference being that the former focuses on the study of the soul and its parts whereas the latter focuses on the operations of the soul, to the physiological processes which accompany the activities of the soul in the body.[12]

As regards the *De longitudine*, some editions of important authors such as St Albert and Peter of Spain existed already but the preparation of the edition of Peter of Ireland opened up a possibility of making a sounding of other thirteenth and fourteenth century authors on their approach to this text of Aristotle, either by literal commentary, commentary and questions or, in the latter stage, merely by questions, and then potentially to move on to editions of these authors' "commentaries" on the entire *Parva Naturalia*. To be acknowledged here is the

---

9 My translation. Gauthier (1989), 68*: *Il n'est pas impossible cependant qu'il [S. Thomas] ait eu en mains une reportation du cours de Pierre d'Irlande: nous avons noté, entre le cours de Pierre et son exposition, plusieurs rencontres, dont quelques-unes assez remarquables.*

10 Dunne, 1993.

11 See Federici Vescovini (2004), 125, where the author points out that in the mid thirteenth century the *De anima* was treated as belonging to Aristotle's natural works. Aristotle makes it clear that the *De anima* and associated works such as the *De animalibus* and *Parva naturalia* are in that part of Natural Philosophy which studies living things composed of matter and form where the soul is the formal principle and general cause of life.

12 Donati (2012), 346.

INTRODUCTION   15

amount of work on this regard has been carried out at Copenhagen under the direction of Sten Ebbesen, predominantly in recent years on the *De somno*.[13]

In fact, Peter of Ireland's commentary was soon recognized as important in shedding a light on the history of the early reception in the thirteenth century of this part of Aristotle's natural philosophy but also of the reception and use of Averroes' *Compendium*,[14] something which reaches its height in the long quotations taken from Averroes by Walter of Burley in his commentary.

As already mentioned, medieval commentaries on Aristotle's *Parva naturalia* have received little if any attention from scholars, something which is especially true of the commentaries on Aristotle's *De longitudine et brevitate vitae* (known in the *translatio vetus* as *De morte et vita*).[15] Yet, as is becoming obvious, such texts are of great interest as records not only of the reception of Aristotle's philosophy of nature but also of how thinkers sought to integrate this new knowledge with already accepted ideas in the fields of natural philosophy and medicine. Some general questions are beginning to become addressed. For example, what was the function and significance of the texts of the *Parva naturalia* in the overall context of University education in the Arts Faculty; how were the same texts treated by lecturers in the "higher" faculties, especially medicine and theology; when and for what reasons did the transition begin from teaching these texts by commentary (and sometimes *quaestiones* as well) to *quaestiones* only. Although we are well aware of the extant manuscripts containing questions and commentaries on this work, until recently the topics treated there have been studied only occasionally, if at all. In many cases, the commentaries on the *De longitudine* reflect a tendency by some masters to deal with such "minor" texts in a cursory fashion; for some the text provided the opportunity to reinforce and revise teaching that had already been done elsewhere (for example, on the *Physics, De anima, De animalibus*); for others again it provided the opportunity to revisit topics and perhaps to deal with some of them in a specific manner which had not been done elsewhere. Thus, scholars are beginning to recognize that commentaries on the *De longitudine* provide important evidence regarding the ways in which medieval thinkers were challenged in making sense of the text of Aristotle by expounding and introducing

---

13 King (2001) gives a systematic treatment of how the investigation into living things in the *De anima* is completed in the *Parva naturalia* and more specifically in the *De longitudine* and the *De iuventute et senectute*, a similar task undertaken by Peter of Ireland some 750 years before.

14 Federici Vescovini (2004), 139, points out that the edition and publication of Peter of Ireland's commentary on the *De longitudine et brevitate vitae*, Dunne (1993), "sheds new light on the knowledge of this treatise at the time of St Thomas and, in particular, on the greater or lesser influence of Averroes' teaching, as well as the coming together of the two ways of teaching a commentary (exposition and question)" (... *una expositio et questiones in Aristotelis librum di Pietro de Ybernia, maestro di san Tommaso ... getta nuova luce sulla conoscenza di questo trattato al tempo di san Tommaso e in particolare sull'influenza maggiore o minore della doctrina di Averroè e sulla mescolanza delle due forme didattiche di commento (l'*exposito e la questio').

15 See Dunne (2003), 320–35; Repici (2007), 283–305.

ideas from elsewhere, both from Aristotle himself but also rather interestingly from other authors particularly in the realm of medical theory.

The commentary of Peter of Ireland is, from those I have examined, one of the most in depth of all of the treatments of the text in either the thirteenth or the fourteenth centuries.[16] Peter of Ireland devotes seven *lectiones* to the text and a total of twenty-two *quaestiones*, making it by far the most extensive analysis of the text to survive from the middle ages. Internal evidence suggests that the text dates from the middle part of the thirteenth century. For example, there is no use of the "new" translations of Aristotle by William of Moerbeke present in the text.

If one looks at the works which Peter quotes, there are extensive quotations from writings by Aristotle, *Physics, De caelo, De generatione et corruptione*, the fourth book of the *Meteorologia, De anima, Parva Naturalia, De animalibus* and also from the available medical authors, Constantine the African, Galen, Haly Abbas, Isaac Israeli, Nicolaus Peripateticus and Al-Razi. It is clear that Peter is making a conscious attempt to reconstruct Aristotle's philosophy of life by looking at and exploring all of the pertinent sources and not just the text of the *De longitudine*. There are the conventional references to *Physics* V, *Meteorologica* IV, the *De generatione*, but Peter is unusual is giving many references to the *De plantis*, and especially in his extended references to the *De animalibus*. In fact, in style and content Peter is quite close to the more extended treatment of Peter of Spain in his *Questiones super libro De animalibus*.[17]

a. The Structure, Approach and Methodology Followed in the De longitudine Commentary

The Prologue

Summary

1 The origin of life.
2 Is life a univocal term? The distinction between the life of the heavens and the life which derives from the soul.
3 The diversity of mortal life, its characteristics and properties.
4 Classification of the different areas which should be investigated in a study of living things; the suitability of natural science in this regard.
5 Scholium: the relation of time to length and shortness of life.

The Prologue to Peter of Ireland's commentary on the *De longitudine* does not deal with Aristotle's text but is, instead, an extended version of what was known as a *divisio scientiae* and is found in other contemporary commentaries. As a literary

---

16 The commentary of Geoffrey of Aspall is certainly a very extensive and detailed commentary but lacks perhaps the clearer focus and structure of Peter's work. See Dunne (2022b).

17 See Navarro Sanchez ed. (2015).

form it serves to give an idea of the nature and subject of the science (*divisio scientiae*) which studies the problem in question — life and death — and the reasons why life is short or long. This science is natural philosophy (*physica*).

The Prologue begins with a long quotation from the *Liber De causis* (a work which was sometimes attributed to Aristotle but many favoured Alpharabi as the author instead). Thomas Aquinas, who in his own work on the *De causis* shows that it is largely a compilation from the *Elementatio theologica* of Proclus, holds that the purpose of Proposition 18 is to show the universal dependence of all things upon the First Being which is God.[18] As the subject matter of Peter's commentary will refer to life, its length or shortness, and its contrary death, it makes sense to examine the ultimate origin of life first of all. Peter, however, is selective in his use of the quotation, he is interested in the dependence of life upon the First Being and excludes those passages in the proposition and commentary which refer to knowledge and understanding (*scientia, intelligentia*); Peter is more concerned with using the *auctoritas* of the *De causis* than with addressing problems of the text such as the mediation of the intelligences in creation. Actually, the terminology found in this section of the text is quite different from that found in the main part of Peter's commentary which remains by and large Aristotelian. With one exception, all of the occurrences of the terms *creo, creatio* are found in the Prologue along with the three occurrences of the Neoplatonic *processio*. Contingent being, life and substance are reduced to their formal causes using quotations from Boethius and Aristotle.

A series of *dubia* follow where the arguments are presented in a very concise fashion; the life of the heavens is discussed in order to exclude it from the enquiry in hand. Life in the sublunary world is varied and manifests itself in different levels of activity: the vegetative, sensitive and rational. Of these three, it is the vegetative soul which is the cause of life in all mortal beings, being as it were the root of life in all living things. Thus, life and death (which is the object of Aristotle's treatise) will be a characteristic of the vegetative soul, a study which falls under the science of natural philosophy, namely an examination of the reasons for the preservation of life in a living thing from a physical point of view.

The Lectures

In Peter's commentary there are a total of seven *lectiones* and twenty-seven *quaestiones*. Peter divides Aristotle's text as follows:

First Part

Lecture 1: i, 464b 19–26 (five questions but undifferentiated in the text)
Lecture 2: i, 464b 26–465a 2 (two questions)
Lecture 3: i, 465a 2–12 (two questions)

---

18 Thomas Aquinas, *Super librum de causis expositio* Prop. 18, 100–04; 103. Proposition 18 of the *Liber de causis* is, in fact, based on Proposition 102 of the *Elements* of Proclus.

18   INTRODUCTION

Second Part

Lecture 4: ii, 465a 13–iii, 465b 4 (four questions)
Lecture 5: iii, 465b 4–iv, 466a 17 (four questions)

Third Part

Lecture 6: v, 466a 18–466b 12 (three questions)
Lecture 7: vi, 466b 12–467a 25 (seven questions)

The text of each *lectio* is discussed according to the following general schema (which is also the same method as that found in Peter's commentary on the *Peri Hermeneias*):

> *Lemma*: the first words of Aristotle's text which the *lectio* discusses.
> *Sententia in generali*: the main purpose and contents of the text of the *lectio*.
> *Ordo et divisio textus*: the text of Aristotle is divided and arranged prior to being explained.
> *Sententia in speciali*: the contents of the subdivisions of the text are explained according to the *divisio textus*.
> *Quaestiones*: the philosophical points of the text are opened out into a wide debate.

This kind of commentary is common in the middle part of the thirteenth century. Clearly, as the text of Aristotle becomes better known and more easily understood, interest will focus on the questions which, by the fourteenth century, begin to stand on their own as a way of fulfilling the obligation of lecturing on the treatise. Although the *Quaestiones* take their start from problems arising from the text itself, they can be wide-ranging, bringing in other texts of Aristotle in order to compare and coordinate different aspects of the topic. There are, for example, frequent references to Aristotle's works on animals (translated from the Arabic and known as the *De animalibus*) which did not normally have a commentary of their own. There are also frequent references to the works of medical authors. However, as we have already pointed out, Peter embraces Aristotle's naturalism: there are no references to religious writings or authors, no moral considerations of sin and death, nor even any existential considerations.

b. General Philosophical Background

The ideas put forward by Aristotle in the *De longitudine*[19] in the overall context of his thought are reasonably straightforward and pose little difficulty for commentators particularly when placed in the context of other works by Aristotle, especially the *De generatione et corruptione*, the *De generatione animalium* and the

---

19 The material in the following section draws upon and updates some of the introduction to be found in Dunne (2002), 153–200.

fourth book of the *Meteorologica*.[20] The very concise nature of the text and some obscure passages did, however, give rise to the usual problems of interpretation. In general, we can say that Aristotle explains the coming to be and passing away of substances as being primarily due to the matter out of which the substance is formed. Thus, with regard to life, it is the material conditions that underlie life which are focussed upon in the *De longitudine et brevitate vitae*, especially the role of the hot and the moist.

Differences in length and shortness of life are noted by Aristotle in respect of certain comparisons: between certain species, different regions, but also between individuals of the same species and in the same locality. A living being is highly structured and unified in such a way that the four elements and the accompanying qualities are arranged in a certain way. Where there is a balance between the elements then the individual continues to exist for a certain amount of time. There is, however, a natural instability in all composite substances, as is pointed out in the *De longitudine*: "opposites destroy each other".[21] For Aristotle, the elements tend not towards complexity but towards simplicity. Unless they are equally balanced the hot and the cold will be changed into each other.[22] Again, a nature is maintained so long as the correct proportion of heat and moisture within it is maintained;[23] this balance cannot, however, be maintained and then things pass away. Passing-away can, however, as we shall see, be "postponed" by a number of factors.

Again, all stable substances are compounds of the moist and the dry. The decay of living beings, i.e., the process of aging and death, consists in their becoming dry and cold.[24] As the vital heat diminishes, the ability to draw in moisture from the environment lessens; it begins to dry out as well as getting colder. Length of life will depend upon the preservation of vital heat and inner moisture; shortness of life will be due to something becoming colder and so drying out.[25] Aristotle himself distinguishes between two kinds of moisture, one

---

20 Repici (2007), although focussing on the first three chapters of the *De longitudine*, is an invaluable examination and contextualisation of Aristotle's text and is a very useful source for recent bibliography relating to the text. Repici's article goes a long way to rectifying the situation which had obtained and which she herself mentions, namely, that up to now the *De longitudine* had not been the object of a specific study but is merely mentioned, if at all, in the context of an overall treatment of the *Parva naturalia*. An important contribution to changing this situation is *Vita longa. Vechiaia e durata della vita nella tradizione medica e aristotelica antica e medievale* (2009). However, one notes that in Bydén and Radovic (2018), in a text of 14 chapters running to 368 pages, there is but one reference to the *De longitudine*. That notwithstanding, Chapter 1 "Introduction: The Study and Reception of Aristotle's *Parva naturalia*", 1–50, shows that this book is an invaluable guide to the historical reception of the *Parva naturalia* from Antiquity to the present day and provides a very comprehensive bibliography.

21 *De longitudine* iii, 465b 3.

22 See *De generatione et corruptione* II vii, 334b 23–24.

23 See *Meteorologica* IV ii, 379b 35.

24 *De longitudine* v, 466a 19–20.

25 *De longitudine* v, 466a 29 ff.

20 INTRODUCTION

which evaporates easily and another "fatty" moisture which is more resistant to drying up, be this due to the action of heat or of cold.[26] Thus, plants live longer than animals because they have an oiliness which allows them to better retain their moisture and be resistant to cold.[27] Similarly aquatic animals do not live as long as land animals because their moisture is not as "fatty".[28]

The four elements cannot produce life on their own; something must act from outside, be this the vital heat or heat used as an instrument of the soul. Vital heat informs matter so as to perpetuate the species. It is considered to be "more divine" than the four elements.[29] Thus, whatever is hotter will live for longer and hence sexual difference will be a factor, Aristotle holding that the male lives longer than the female.[30] The eternal process whereby life is transmitted and the species preserved is something which is immanent, individuals producing individuals.[31] And yet, the persistence of species points to a natural good end within the sublunary world where life or existence continues throughout change and in an ordered fashion.[32]

As already mentioned, the two active qualities, the hot and the cold, will be transformed into each other unless they are equally balanced,[33] a nature is maintained for so long as the correct proportion of heat and moisture is maintained;[34] destruction follows when what should be kept in place gets the upper hand, as it were. Destruction, or passing-away, is the natural and inevitable outcome of material necessity.[35]

Therefore, from the existence of the four elements it follows that there must be coming-to-be and passing away, for the reason that none of them is eternal, since contraries act upon each other and are mutually destructive.[36] Composite substances can never be eternal when they contain contrary elements.[37]

Destruction can, however, be staved off only for as long as the dominating quality is reinforced from outside: "the environment either works with or works against composite substances ... ensuring that they exist for a greater or lesser period of time than nature warrants".[38] Thus, one cause of length or shortness of life will be environmental factors. One environmental factor to be taken into

---

26 *De longitudine* v, 466a 23.
27 *De longitudine* vi, 467a 6 ff.
28 *De longitudine* v, 466b 33 ff.
29 See *De caelo* II iii, 286a 9.
30 *De longitudine* v, 466b 14 ff.
31 See *Metaphysics* XII iii, 1070a 28.
32 *De anima* II iv, 415a 26–b 7.
33 See *De generatione et corruptione* II vii, 334b 23–24.
34 See *Meteorologica* IV iii, 379b 35.
35 *De longitudine* ii, 465a 12 ff.
36 *De caelo* II iii, 286a 32.
37 *De longitudine* iii, 465b 29.
38 *De longitudine* iii, 465b 27 ff.

INTRODUCTION 21

account is the sun's annual motion as the moving cause of the elements and of change in general.

The root of life is the nutritive soul,[39] an active cause over and above the four elements and the elemental qualities. Freudenthal argues[40] that Aristotle's hylomorphic and biological notions of soul are here complementary in that one can speak of a certain equivalence between vital heat and the nutritive soul; one is the "active" formal cause and the other is the "active" material cause. Life involves the presence of heat, the lack of heat being a sign of, or a cause of death.

Freudenthal argues for the importance of vital heat as connected with the root of life, namely, the nutritive soul.[41] For Aristotle, heat acts upon matter, warming it, informing it, digesting or "cooking" it. Heat is also regarded as a factor in the cohesion of inanimate substances. It is heat as a physiological agent which brings about plant and animal reproduction. Heat is also a factor in certain higher functions associated with the animal soul such as perception.

The physiological account of vital heat as informing matter is also accompanied by a psychological account of the origin of life as due principally to the soul.[42] Thus, the material efficient cause is accompanied by the formal cause of life in the nutritive soul. Nonetheless, Aristotle holds that all of the functions deriving from the soul (except that of the *nous*) hinge upon vital heat as the underlying factor. The well-functioning of activities such as perception and memory thus depend upon the quality of the heat (as with Empedocles,[43] Aristotle regards the blood as the seat of perception). Within the blood (as in the seed of animals) there is *pneuma* or *spiritus* (a concept which Aristotle derived from medical sources), something which is analogous to the substance of the stars. It is not our place to discuss it here, but it would be a very interesting study to assess how Aristotle's philosophy of biology impacts upon his philosophy of mind.

For Aristotle, both heat and cold are active powers which, acting upon the passive powers (the moist and the dry), bring together things of the same kind and eliminate what is foreign.[44] Heat establishes a stable proportion between the moist and the dry and ensures that a substance acquires its proper form or nature.[45] In terms of reproduction, the vital heat contained in the semen acts upon the *catamenia* (the menstrual fluid), informing the matter and producing an offspring which resembles the (male) parent, while lack of heat produces a female

---

39 See *De anima* II iv, 416a 6–9.
40 Freudenthal (1995), 3.
41 Freudenthal (1995), 3.
42 See *De anima* II iv, 416a 9–15.
43 For Empedocles see, for example, Theophrastus, *Sens.* 10 = DK 31 B 107:
   [For] it is out of these [i.e. the elements] that all things are adjusted and assembled,
   And it is by them that they think and feel pleasure and pain.
   ἐκ τούτων <γὰρ> πάντα πεπήγασιν ἁρμοσθέντα καὶ τούτοις φρονέουσι καὶ ἥδοντ᾽ ἠδ᾽ ἀνιῶνται.
44 See *De generatione et corruptione* II ii, 329b 26 ff.
45 See *Meteorologica* IV ii, 379b 25 ff.

and is ultimately responsible for deficient forms.[46] Thus, sexual differentiation is traced to a variation in vital heat. The spontaneous generation of living things in matter is also traced to the action of the vital heat, in this case the heat of the sun acting upon putrefying matter. The role of the moist is to bind the substance together, for if a substance loses moisture, i.e., becomes dry, it starts to fall apart. A substance decays if the heat in the surrounding air masters the substance's own heat and so it ultimately becomes cold (and dry). Thus, moisture and natural heat are the causes of cohesion, while decay is a form of drying. Nonetheless, individuals cannot be composed of the moist on its own, some kind of limit must be imposed by the dry — any melting or dissolving involves something becoming moist. Thus, all stable substances are compounds of the moist and the dry. The decay of living beings, i.e., the process of aging and death, consists in their becoming dry and cold.[47] If life is associated principally with heat, aging and death will be primarily associated with cold. As the vital heat diminishes, its ability to draw in moisture from the environment lessens,[48] and it begins to dry out as well as getting colder.

This theory also allows for a difference in resistance to decay, i.e., a difference in length and shortness of life. Length of life will depend upon the preservation of vital heat and inner moisture; shortness of life will be due to something becoming colder and so drying out.[49] Aristotle distinguishes between two kinds of moisture, one which evaporates easily and another "fatty" moisture which is more resistant to drying up, be this either due to the action of heat or of cold.[50] Similarly, aquatic animals do not live as long as land animals because their moisture is not as "fatty".[51] It seems that Aristotle has in mind the nature of olive oil which does not dry or solidify when affected by either heat or cold.[52] He states in the *De longitudine* (466a 24–25) that the reason why fat does not easily decay is that it contains air and that air among the other elements is closer to fire and that fire itself does not decay. Thus, it would seem that the internal heat of the fat itself preserves it from decay given that fat is a result of the concoction of blood and that some heat remains after the process. This hot air, it seems, would be close to the *pneuma* or *spiritus*.

---

46 See *De generatione animalium* IV i, 765b 2 ff.; 766b 31 ff.; IV x, 767b 6 ff.

47 *De longitudine* iv, 466a 19–20.

48 See *Meteorologica* IV i, 379a 24. As Freudenthal (1995), 156, notes Galen held the opposite point of view, namely that the body's vital heat is nourished by its radical moisture, so that death ensues when the moisture has been entirely consumed. This was also the view of Avicenna and so passed into medieval medicine being found, for example, in the work of Peter of Ireland.

49 *De longitudine* v, 466a 29 ff.

50 *De longitudine* v, 466a 23.

51 *De longitudine* v, 466b 33 ff.

52 See *Meteorologica* IV vii, 383b 34. Freudenthal (1995), 179, mentions that the most important feature associated with oil and the olive tree is longevity and a "divine" power of growth.

INTRODUCTION 23

As is well known, Aristotle held that in the sublunary world there is an eternal persistence of plant and animal species despite the passing material instantiation of individuals of the species, namely the individual plants and animals themselves:

> For this is the most natural of all functions among living creatures [...] namely, to reproduce one's kind, an animal producing an animal, and a plant a plant, in order that they may participate in the immortal and the divine inasmuch as this is possible. For every creature aspires to this and this is the goal for the sake of which all natural functions occur. [...] Since, then, they cannot participate continually in the immortal and the divine, since no perishable being can remain numerically one and the same, they share in this in the only way that they can, some to a greater and some to a lesser extent. What survives is not the individual itself but something similar to it, which is not numerically one but is so according to the species.[53]

Nonetheless, it would seem that there is no material necessity whereby life should emerge out of matter itself, nor again why the species themselves should persist throughout eternity. The theory of the four elements and the four elemental qualities cannot account for this.[54] What then brings about this teleology in nature?

The four elements cannot produce life on their own — something must act from outside, be this the vital heat or heat used as an instrument of the soul. Vital heat informs matter so as to perpetuate the species. It is considered to be "more divine" than the four elements, i.e., something connected with immortality and everlastingness.[55] Thus, whatever is hotter will live for longer and so the male lives longer than the female.[56] The eternal process whereby life is transmitted and the species preserved is something which is immanent, each individual producing an individual,[57] and not owing anything to a Platonic world of transcendent forms. And yet, the persistence of species points to a good within the sublunary world where life or existence continues throughout change and in an ordered fashion. In this way the individual in the baton-race of existence shares for a moment in something divine.

In conclusion, Aristotle in the treatise *De longitudine et brevitate vitae* establishes the following: a material explanation for the persistence of individual substances; an explanation of the material substrate required for life; that the basic functions of life (the nutritive soul) depend upon certain material conditions both internal (in terms of the constitution of the body) and external (environmental) factors. Aristotle also offers an explanation for sexual differentiation which is

---

53 *De anima* II iv, 415a 26–b 7.
54 This, of course, implies a rejection of the notion of material necessity present in someone such as Democritus.
55 See *De caelo* II iv, 286a 9.
56 *De longitudine* v, 466b 14.
57 See *Metaphysics* XII iii, 1070a 28.

24   INTRODUCTION

material rather than formal. Since Aristotle cannot account for the breakdown of life through his notion of soul, it must be due to material conditions — the quantity of vital heat present at the beginning of life is gradually consumed.[58] Death, then, is not due to the form but rather to material causes following from the basic instability of matter itself. The perfection of form and longevity coincide in the fact that the male lives longer than the female,[59] but why then do some plants live longer than human beings (466a 1–9), and the elephant longer than human beings? Thus, the kind of perfection which a human being enjoys as the possessor of mind must be set aside when considering length of life — here, various material factors such as size, location, sex, bodily composition, etc., count for more when compared with form.

It is hoped that this now puts us in a position to read Peter's commentary and to see his achievement in perspective.

c. The Content of the Commentary

Peter begins the first lecture by stating that the entire text is divided into three parts, and stating that the First Part runs from 464b 19 to 465a 12. The First Part is subdivided into two main parts: the First Part of the First Part, running from 464b 19–26 and corresponding to Lecture 1; the Second Part of the First Part (464b 26 to 465a 12) is further subdivided into two parts (corresponding to Lectures 2 and 3). From the *divisiones textus* given later on in the text, the Second Part runs from 465a 13 to 466a 17 (subdivided into two parts corresponding to Lecture 4 and Lecture 5), and the Third Part of the text runs from 466a 18 to 467a 25 (subdivided into two parts corresponding to Lecture 6 and Lecture 7). These divisions of the text correspond roughly to the modern chapter divisions found in Bekker but Peter's dividing of the text is presented as not being arbitrary but always as being motivated by a logical justification on the part of Aristotle.

Aristotle begins the *De longitudine* by stating that we need to consider why some living things have a short life and some a long life, and not just the particular causes but why in general we see that some live for a longer time and some for a shorter time. Again, as he points out, it is not clear whether length and shortness of life in animals and plants is from one and the same cause. The first problem arising from the text in Peter's literal exposition is why Aristotle speaks first of all of the life of animals,[60] when he already states that he wants to look at all living things and this includes plants. As Peter comments, plants only have the most basic level of soul, the vegetative, and so have a hidden life, or life in a certain qualified sense. Thus, speaking somewhat legally, Peter states that in hidden matters one has to use witnesses and so Aristotle refers first of all to those

---

58 See *De iuventute* i, 479b 1.
59 *De longitudine* v, 466b 15, vi, 467a 30.
60 See below, 53.

in whom there is clearly life. The next point is that Aristotle wishes to look at the complete length of life and, as Peter notes,[61] to each living thing there is assigned a minimum length of time in which the functions of life can mature and be exercised. This complete length of life is mentioned by Aristotle to exclude the question of the accidental ending of life from the consideration of length and shortness of life. Finally, after length and shortness of life is examined in animals, Aristotle will look at this with regard to plants.

We now move on to the Questions. Here in the First Lecture these are not so well defined and isolated from each other as they are later on in the text but we can identify four topics.

The first question arises regarding what Aristotle says in chapter 5 of the text, at 466a 18, that every animal is hot and moist. This seems to anticipate what will be discussed in Lecture 6, question 1, and one is initially tempted to think that the material here is out of place. However, Peter has already pointed out that Aristotle wishes to first of all deal with those universal principles which determine length and shortness of life. Peter will do the same by examining the role of the hot and the moist in animal life and later proceeding to examine the role of the *virtus spiritualis*. The fact that Peter is aware of and uses not only Aristotle's physiological theories in this section but also those of medical authorities such as Galen and Rasis indicates that he more than likely also studied medicine. Indeed, the faculty of medicine offered the only possibility to have further training in natural philosophy after the Arts degree. Peter is certainly confident enough to make an authoritative assertion regarding the movement of the heart in cases of apoplexy.[62]

Since warmth and moisture are clearly essential to life, Peter says that life will be found in living things when the hot predominates over the moist as well as the other contraries.[63] Here, however, with regard to the dominance of one elemental quality over another, Peter introduces a problem based on the notion of degrees of heat and cold which serves to illustrate his indebtedness to the medical writings of Arabic authors, diffused above all through the translations of Constantine the African. The notion of the degrees of heat or cold is usually found in discussions of the properties of medicines and how to rebalance a temperament or complexion which through illness has become too hot or too cold.[64] Peter enters into a long discussion of the different types of heat and humidity where again it will be necessary to clarify some terms.

First of all, vital heat is the heat by which something is said to be alive and its centre is in the heart or its analogue. It is vital heat which is the source of all

---

61 See below, 53.

62 See below, 65.

63 See below, 55.

64 Constantine the African, *De gradibus medicinarum* II, f. lxxxv^{ra}, speaks about this where he says that the grades of heat or coldness are judged with respect to a healthy human complexion. The fourth degree is the most extreme and causes lasting damage.

life activity. It is described by Aristotle as being analogous to the same kind of heat as that of the heavens and to be related to *spiritus* or *pneuma*. This heat is not the same as elemental heat or fire. Furthermore, vital heat cannot reach the kind of heat as that of the fourth degree (as it would destroy a living thing) but is normally temperate.

An objection is made regarding certain animals which are cold to the extreme (certain venomous animals and those "which are born from the earth"): such cold should extinguish life.[65] Peter introduces a distinction, a different kind of heat, namely constitutional heat (*calor complexionabilis*) which is the same as the heat of the elements and so is not the same as the vital heat by which a thing is said to be alive. Thus, coldness to the fourth degree and vital heat can coexist in the bodily constitution of cold-blooded animals because they do not have the same mode of being. There are also two kinds of humidity, the elemental watery kind and another which is airy and which serves to nourish vital heat, nutrimental humidity (*humidum nutrimentale*).

The next objection[66] comes from the commentary or *Compendium* of Averroes where the Commentator refers to the elemental qualities (the hot, the dry, the cold and the moist) as being responsible for coming to be, growth, decrease, etc. Peter replies with another quotation from Averroes where the latter speaks of two kinds of heat and which Peter interprets as being the same distinction he has made above between vital and constitutional heat.

It is not my intention to look at every point raised in the text but mainly those which might help the reader to understand the general principles being used or assumed in the text. The last long section of Lecture 1 deals with the important notion of *spiritus*.[67] Peter uses the word *spiritus* thirty-seven times and its cognate, *virtus spiritualis*, twenty-two times. An English reader will normally read the word "spirit" in a moral or religious sense but the Latin word is much richer, including, of course, the notion of breath and, here in the way Peter uses it, a physical or biological meaning. Aristotle never clearly explained what he meant by this *pneuma* but used the term to indicate that which sustains life from the beginning to the end. Some indications as to its nature are given: it is to be found in semen and the *spiritus* contains the originative vital heat which characterizes all living things; it causes movement without itself undergoing any change; like ether it acts as an intermediary between an immaterial mover and a material object. Thus, the immaterial soul moves the spirits, and the spirits in turn cause change, thereby moving the limbs of the body or initiating the movement which is the growth of the embryo. In terms of sensation, just as the spirits transmit to the parts of the body the movements caused by the soul and thereby produce change and movement, so in the reverse direction it transmits to the soul the movement of the alteration caused in the sense organs by the movements of the external stimuli.

---

65 See below, 57.
66 See below, 59-61.
67 See below, 63-73.

Sensation for Aristotle arises from the heart, the seat of the *anima sensitiva*. Hence, any movement in the sense organ must be communicated to the heart. It seems clear that the senses of touch and taste are connected to the heart; so also are the others, though not so obviously or directly. Thus, Peter writes that there are passages (*pori*) which from the eyes run to the veins around the brain, and similarly from the ears a passage connects to the back of the head.[68] This is confirmed by Aristotle in the *De generatione animalium* where he says that smell and hearing are said to be passages full of connatural spirits, connecting with the external air, and terminating at the veins which surround the brain but which come from the heart.[69] In pulsation, the blood is infused with spirits by the action of vital heat.

The discussion continues with regard to the differences between plant and animal life and that the power of movement is from the sensitive soul and is only to be found in animals.[70] The role of the heart is affirmed as the principle and foundation of life.[71] Peter, following Aristotle, rejects the opinion of the medical authors such as Galen who maintained instead that the origin of sensation is in the brain.

The vegetative soul gives rise to the most basic and simple form of life, namely, nutrition, growth and reproduction and, consequently, the means which are required to carry out its functions will be correspondingly simple. Its functions of generation and nutrition can be sufficiently accomplished by means of natural heat which seems to be the same heat as that found in fire, i.e., *calor complexionalis*. The sensitive soul being more complex and "noble" has functions which are likewise more complex and higher than those carried out by the vegetative soul, namely sensation, cognition and locomotion, and so requires not only natural heat but also *spiritus*.

The next part of the text albeit interesting is also puzzling. Peter refers to lower animals who do not have the powers of cognition and locomotion and who are produced from earth directly under the action of the sun, presumably the belief in the spontaneous generation of life under the conditions of heat and moisture from matter such as dung. Peter is interested, as was Aristotle before him, in those living things which seem on the borderline between plant and animal life. Peter gives the example of the possibility of plant life making a transition to animal life in the case of certain birds which, it seems, arise from wood. The reference is to the Barnacle Geese, which are so named because of the belief that certain barnacles found attached to wood washed up on the beach look like a developing goose's beak and neck. Both Vincent of Beauvais (*Speculum Naturale*, XVII, 40) and Bartholomeus Anglicus (*De proprietatibus rerum*, IV, 2) defend the notion and explain how certain environmental conditions cause the plant life of the branch

---

68 See below, 65. See also *De partibus animalium* II x, 656b 17 ff.
69 See *De generatione animalium* II vi, 744a 2.
70 See below, 67.
71 See below, 71.

on which the barnacles are hanging as a kind of fruit to develop into animal life and so into adult birds. What is perplexing is that whereas Albert the Great rejects the legend from first-hand experience, Peter's "employer", Frederick II had also done so and again on the basis of the evidence. Frederick, in fact, had sent messengers north to get examples of these barnacles and stated that they were shellfish like any other and had nothing in common with birds.[72] Why did Peter oppose the view of the Emperor? Perhaps it was an attachment to tradition or the example was just too useful for the point he was making.

Further points made in the rest of the text concern the origin of the spiritual power (which Peter suggests is not from any particular division of the soul but is from the soul as such in animals) and then the question of what we might call the body-soul relationship. As regards the latter, Peter quotes the *Quaestiones* of Nicholaus Peripateticus stating that it is wonderful how a bodily substance moves at once because of some affection existing in the soul.[73] For Peter, the different affections of the soul are communicated by the intellect to the movements of the heart and then the heart in turn communicates its motion to the *spiritus*, these vital energies or impulses. The spirits obey the heart, the heart the intellect and the intellect obeys the rational soul. This psychosomatic thesis is illustrated with the example of the scholar whose overuse of the intellectual powers results in an imbalance of the bodily humours negatively affecting his digestion and causing him to be phlegmatic! A discussion follows of the manner in which the heart emits the spirits into the body through the arterial system and the manner in which this is affected by soft or hard arteries. Some negative remarks on the sexual behaviour of women with soft arteries and a full pulse are noted (originating in Urso of Salerno (1936) *Aphorism*, 24). Further negative comments about women, inspired by Aristotle's teaching on reproduction will be seen below in Lecture 7, q. 2.

The Second Lecture raises the problem of the connection between health and disease and length and shortness of life and deals with two questions: are animals healthy by nature and what is the nature and function of sleep? The first problem is inspired by the statement of Constantine the African that health naturally inheres in an animal. This, however, is opposed to the fact that the health of an animal is constantly changing due to the constant flux of the four elements out of which all bodies are composed. The solution is provided by using Aristotle's distinction between what is a nature, natural and according to a nature; and then by distinguishing between health as a *habitus* and *secundum actum*.

Turning to the question of sleep, Peter notes that Aristotle in the *De generatione animalium* regards sleep as a kind of intermediate state between living and non-living. On the other hand, sleep is not like death but seems to be a middle state between life and death. Waking is a state which occurs in virtue of sensation as it is sensation which manifests life. Do plants then sleep or not? A plant has

---

72 See Haskins (1924), 321; Frederick II, *De arte venandi* I, 99, 120.
73 See below, 69.

natural functions which if they tire out surely require rest, if not in themselves at least due to the fact that their instruments or organs tire or weaken. Peter's solution is that sleep is a consequence of sensation and its function is to give rest to the senses; hence it is only applied to animals and human beings. The animal power, which has its seat in the brain and whose operations are sensation and consciousness, requires repose when it exceeds the period during which it is able to perform its functions. Those functions associated with the basic form of life, the vegetative soul, cannot rest because if they did life would cease and thus plants do not sleep.

In the Third Lecture Peter begins his exposition of the text of Aristotle by making a number of important points arising from what he regards as the central part of the text. For Aristotle length and shortness of life differs according to the diversity of living things; according to substance and accident, genus and species, number and place. Two reasons are given for length of life in the commentary of Averroes: the predominance of active qualities over the passive; the relative proportion of active qualities to each other and passive qualities to each other. These ideas are drawn, as Averroes himself acknowledges, from the fourth book of the *Meteorologica*.

Two issues are raised: why does Aristotle not examine length and shortness of life with regard to time when he does so here in relation to place; and, secondly, while considering the difference in length of life between a man and a horse, the role of heat and moisture is examined and then the effect of a cold environment. With regard to the first question, Peter points out that Aristotle wishes to examine the complete length of life, which an animal has according to nature, and that this differs from place to place. Time is the measurement of something that is determined not by the passage of time itself but by the internal principles of a body such as the hot and moist. In the second of these two rather short questions Peter clarifies which kind of moisture contributes to length of life especially that which is found abundantly in a human being. In fact, even among human beings, the sanguineous (as opposed to the phlegmatic, choleric or melancholic) live longer than all others because blood has more airy and oily humidity which is not negatively affected by external heat or cold. Finally, it is pointed out that living things in cold and dry regions are short-lived because the cold congeals and thickens the vital energies (*spiritus*) and the dry consumes the moisture. The environment transforms what it contains into its own temperament (*crasis*) and so in northern regions there is not so much vegetation because the prevalence of cold congeals the moist and extinguishes the heat that is the cause of life.

In the Fourth Lecture, the text of Aristotle discusses the role of fire and water as active elements with earth and air as passive elements and the role of each in generation and corruption. Different forms of corruption are discussed: those which have their own particular type of corruption such as knowledge, health and sickness, as well as accidental corruption and its relation to the soul. In passing, Peter mentions the *Dator formarum* as the giver of forms but does not elaborate

30   INTRODUCTION

any further with respect to its role in terms of the intellect and illumination theory.[74]

Question 1 examines the nature of fire as an active element and Peter points out that fire is the form of the elements and has more of universal form, the universal form being light. One possible influence here might be the *De luce* of Grosseteste.

The second question asks whether such things as health and sickness have their own forms of corruption? Peter answers that they have their own causes, similar to corruption, which destroy each other as distinct from corruption which destroys both them and their subjects.

The third question asks how can the corruption of ignorance by recollection and the openness to be taught (*docibilitas*) be explained in terms of first qualities. The answer which Peter gives draws upon Averroes and Costa ben Luca and examines the physical composition of the brain in terms of remembering and recollecting.

Finally, Question 4 asks whether the soul can be said to be destroyed in its very being along with the corruption of the body. Here Peter draws heavily upon Avicenna in order to defend the immortality of the soul.

In Lecture Five Peter turns to the second part of what he identified as "chapter 1" in his division of the text in the previous lecture. In Lecture Four Peter examined the ways in which something is destroyed *per se* and *per accidens*; here he will examine the reasons why every thing that is destroyed per se is destroyed by its contrary. In the course of his exposition of the text, Peter concentrates upon a curious phrase that has not survived in the modern editions of the Greek text. (Perhaps it is an interpolation from an ancient commentary? We have to await the edition in the *Aristoteles Latinus* series to resolve the problem.) It does not help, as Peter notes, that he had two variant readings in the manuscripts available to him and he chooses the second reading: *mox enim cum posito/ponitur inest contrarium passibili materie* (it was the fourth word which gave rise to the different readings among which I have also found "*potencia*" and "*ponat*" and I am sure that there are more). In any case Peter regards the text as meaning that it is impossible that there is not a contrary in something which has matter. He advises us to pay attention to the word "*positum*" since position means location and arrangement. Thus, as soon as the matter is arranged and is located according to place and part, then it is impossible that it will be without some kind of opposition; it will have a contrary

---

74 The *Dator formarum* or Giver of Forms is the spiritual Intelligence associated with the sphere of the moon. In Avicennian terms its functions are those of a separate Agent Intellect which illuminates all human minds and enables the reception of forms. Initially our minds do not have any ideas but our intellect, the *intellectus possibilis*, acquires a certain preparation in order to receive the appropriate idea from the *Dator formarum* which corresponds to the sensitive representation of things. We do not retain these ideas but must constantly turn to the *Dator formarum* for the appropriate idea on the occasion of experience.

which acts, and inasmuch as it is passible (i.e., capable of being acted upon), it will be acted upon and so it will change and be destroyed.

The first question of Lecture Five asks whether corruption *per se* derives from contraries? Peter gives the answer in the affirmative through an examination of and analysis of movement.

Question 2[75] deals which a doubt which arises from the text and which raises the question as to whether there is opposition (*contrarietas*) among the heavenly bodies just as there is in those bodies which are found below the sphere of the moon. Peter's answer is that there can be no such opposition found in the heavenly bodies because their perfect circular motion excludes such a possibility. This is further excluded through an examination of the difference between material and formal opposition.

Question 3[76] puts forward three *dubia*: a) how something which is an accident acts upon something passible, namely, how the heat of the body acts upon its subject and destroys it; b) how is natural heat destroyed by the heat of the environment, since they are the same kind of heat (elemental) they cannot be contraries; c) heat would not seem to destroy humidity and so not be responsible for ending life. The answer is based upon an examination of the hot and moist, finishing with introducing the notion of respiration as responsible for refrigeration.

Question 4 asks should animals be cooled down more by water more than by air; and where does the heat of the heart derive from? The rather detailed discussion ends by concluding that the accidental heat of the heart, arising from friction in the heart itself and from the accidental heat of the spirits or vital energies hastens the consumption of the humidity which is the nourishment of innate heat. Thus, these two kinds of accidental heat destroy innate heat in the same way that the greater flame destroys the lesser. To conclude, Peter says that the innate heat of the heart needs to be cooled down.

The order and division of the text of Aristotle in Lecture 6 brings us to the second chapter which is divided into two parts, which will be the basis for *lectio* 6 and *lectio* 7. The subject of the sixth lecture is the intrinsic causes of length and shortness of life and begins with the *lemma*, "We must grasp that an animal is hot and moist by nature". During his exposition of the text, Peter discusses: the role of airy fat in length of life; the need for both quantity and quality in the hot and moist; that the loss of semen from the body causes animals to be short-lived.

Question 1 asks whether every animal is indeed hot and moist? Peter responds by using the examples of the *melancholica* as well as the *narchotica* (animals which are slow moving such as lizards, etc.). Question 2 discusses whether fatty things are not liable to decay. Question 3 discusses whether the emission of semen causes an animal to age quickly and consequently to die. There is then a discussion of the different views put forward.

---

75 See below, 129.
76 See below, 133.

32 INTRODUCTION

The final Lecture 7 divides the second part of the second chapter into three parts which deal with the following:

a the aging effect of work on male animals (but not on females!);
b the beneficial effect of a warm climate;
c the third part is divided into two:
    i why plants live longer than animals;
    ii the comparison of plants to insects.

Appropriately, Lecture 7 has seven questions:

Question 1: why should work and toil cause males to age quickly and not females also? The role of heat.

Question 2: Is the female of a colder nature than the male? The reason for the distinction of male from female.

Question 3: Do those who live in warm regions live longer than those in cold regions? The case of cold-blooded animals.

Question 4: The role of watery humidity in shortening life.

Question 5: The role of blood in length of life.

Question 6: The cause of the greater length of life in plants; that they can continually renew themselves.

Question 7: Some matters relating to plants, among which is the function of the root, and the role of the natural power in nutrition.

The final lecture of Peter's commentary is quite detailed and rich in its treatment of certain matters which now serve as a conclusion to the investigation into the causes of length and shortness of life. Certain differences among living things that affect length and shortness are pointed out such as sexual difference and difference in location (for instance, whether an animal lives in a hot region or a cold region, is a land animal or an aquatic one). The question of the longevity of plants or trees is addressed: plants live longer than animals because they are less watery and their moisture is not easily dried up. A comparison is made between plants and insects since both have parts when cut which can live on; the latter, however, are only capable of living for a short time. Again, plants have the source in every part of producing a new part in the place of the old and so live longer than animals who cannot renew themselves when they lose a part.

Both Questions 1 and 2 look at the differences between men and women in terms of heat and moisture. Since women are naturally colder than men, exercise and work operate to their advantage warming them up because in their case a lack of heat leads to indigestion and the production of residues, which as contraries destroy the body. Males, on the other hand, are naturally warmer and if their heat is increased by exertion and work, this has the effect of consuming natural humidity and so inducing old age. This leads into a discussion of the nature of reproduction and the reasons given by Aristotle in the *De generatione animalium*, IV i, for the difference between male and female. The views of Anaxagoras, Empedocles and Leophantes are recounted and Aristotle's rejection of their views. Focusing on the

nature of the sperm itself the discussion leads to the explanation as to why women are "changed" males owing mainly to a lack of heat in the process of generation. Questions 3, 4 and 5 develop some points made in Aristotle's text regarding the effect of the environment on the moisture which is an essential component of life. The final two questions deal with matters related to plant life and how its ability to constantly renew its parts enables it to live longer than, for example, mammals. A unique quotation from Ibn Zaur, undocumented elsewhere, is given where the shoot or stalk is described as a *filius naturae*.[77]

In the last paragraph of the text, Peter makes a threefold division of "sense", namely, animal, rational and natural. Interestingly, he explains magneticism by the notion of a natural sense whereby the magnet "senses" the iron, and draws it to itself by "choice" since it intends or reaches out to the iron in a natural way. It is again, by this natural sense that a natural thing "feels" what is compatible or compatible with its needs and draws in what nourishes its life. Thus, says Peter, concluding his work, the drawing in of food does not happen because of the sensation that a rational or sensitive soul has but it happens because of the natural sense. With this last observation, which we may take to be his attempt to explain what we do now in terms of stimulus, tropisms, etc., and the natural force of magneticism, our text is concluded.

4. The *Determinatio Magistralis*

The first text of Peter of Ireland to have been edited and printed, the *Determinatio magistralis*,[78] is also his most accessible.[79] It is also the one we can date with the greatest accuracy, namely to around 1260. This was the date when King Manfred of Sicily (1258–1266), who is addressed in the text by Peter of Ireland, brought the University back to Naples from Salerno and it is probable that this *Determinatio* was associated with a public event related to the re-foundation of the University. The text shows Peter at the centre of the cultural life of the court and to be recognised as a highly respected academic.

The text is also of interest for the history of the reception of Aristotelian natural philosophy and the thought of Averroes. It deals with the question of purpose and nature in a way which is both "physical" (scientific) and metaphysical. It is not just confined to matters of anatomy and physiology but looks at some central philosophical questions such as the problem of evil.

There was a tradition of monarchical interest in philosophy in this southern kingdom under the Hohenstaufen. King Manfred's father, the Emperor

---

77 See below, 197

78 The Latin text first appeared in Baeumker (1920), 41-49; reprinted in Dunne (1996), 246-50.

79 See Dunne (2014), 49–64, where a more expanded treatment of the points mentioned here can be found. The text has also been studied by Weijers (2002), 216–17, and has been examined and partially translated into French by Imbach (1996), 106–09.

Frederick II, had encouraged the translation work of Michael Scot. This was not just a matter of patronage but Frederick II had a real engagement with the exchange of philosophical ideas, a familiarity with scholastic terminology and a not uncritical admiration for Aristotle especially when it came to hunting with birds.[80]

King Manfred's question to the Professors of the University of Naples as to "Whether the bodily organs are made on account of their functions or whether the functions happen because of the organs" probably had its origin in the work he was then engaged in, namely, the editing and completion of his father's great work, the *De arte venandi cum avibus*. However, it may well be that the question had already established itself as normal introductory material in the university curriculum.[81]

Peter determines that the answer to the question is not to be found in Natural Philosophy but rather in Metaphysics and somewhat concisely refers to Aristotle's doctrine of a natural providence, as not perhaps concerned so much with the survival of the individual but rather the eternal survival of the species. However, does not the problem of natural evil, the fact that in order to live some animals kill and eat other animals, contradict the notion of providence in nature. Peter remarks[82] that the difficulty of the problem led some people (e.g., the Cathars) to posit two principles in things, a principle of good and a principle of evil.

However, evil cannot exist on its own, since it is a privation and, as Peter concludes, it is not possible for evil to be separated from the good but it must always be found with it.[83] However, if "everything which is, insofar as it is, is good", what then of the preying of one animal upon another? Peter comments[84] that in the universe some things exist for the sake of others, even to be the food of others, as plants for animals, and animals for other animals. Animals which have curved claws and which eat raw meat fight with all other animals because their

---

80 See Frederick II, *De arte venandi cum avibus*, 3–5: *In scribendo etiam Aristotilem, ubi oportuit, secuti sumus. In pluribus enim, sicut experientia didicimus, maxime in naturis quarundam avium, discrepare a veritate videtur. Propter hoc non sequimur principem philosophorum in omnibus, raro namque aut nunquam venationes avium exercuit, set Nos semper dileximus et exercuimus. De multis vero, que narrat in Libro animalium, dicit quosdam sic dixisse, set id, quod quidam sic dixerunt, nec ipse forsan vidit, nec dicentes viderunt, fidesque certa non provenit ex auditu.* ("In writing We have also followed Aristotle when this seemed opportune. However, on some matters We are of the opinion, on the basis of our own experience that as far as the nature of some birds are concerned that Aristotle deviated from the truth. Because of this We did not follow the Prince of the Philosophers in everything since he never, or only rarely, practiced hunting with birds, whereas We have always loved and practiced it. For Aristotle narrates many things in his book *On Animals* saying that other people said them. However, that which others held, he himself perhaps did not see nor was it seen by those others — certainty is not gained through hearing").

81 See Albertus Magnus, *Quaestiones super de animalibus* (composed c. 1258) I, q. 2: "Whether a variety of organic parts is necessary to an animal", 16–17.

82 See below, 201-203.

83 See below, 203.

84 See below, 205.

life is sustained through eating other animals. Thus, the universal nature (*natura universalis*) arranges everything to offer assistance, and especially to assist and sustain humanity. And so, Peter writes, if an individual of one species is sustained by means of another individual of another species or genus, this is not against the order of nature, but everything has been established because of the good of order and out of the care of the One who orders. The good of the order of the universe is found according to a greater or lesser extent, inasmuch as the lesser exists for the more perfect, *vilius propter nobilius, imperfectius propter perfectius, materia propter formam et propter motorem.*[85]

The examples given by Peter include birds of prey, namely, the falcon, the eagle and the sparrow hawk. This is no coincidence since, as already mentioned, at the time Manfred was engaged in editing and completing his father's work, the *Art of Hunting with Birds.*[86] The body exists for the soul; therefore, the nature of the soul determines its activities, and these activities determine the kind of body which an animal must have to carry out those activities. The lion has a greedy soul (*anima gulosa*) and so has a large mouth and sharp claws; the bird of prey has an angry soul and has a hooked beak and claws to grasp its prey. Nature has given to each creature the appropriate body and bodily activities in accordance with its soul.[87]

Peter concludes[88] that it is clear therefore that "the limbs and organs of an animal are in function of their activities"; an organ without a function is only called an organ in an equivocal manner. That a bird of prey has a sharp beak and claws is not something which arises out of any material necessity or by chance, but they have these in virtue of a determinate end of their activities. Thus, his solution to the problem: the organs and powers are for the sake of the activities and not the other way around.[89]

The text, though somewhat brief, is a very good example of its genre and an important historical witness to the kind of philosophy being taught and debated at Naples around the middle of the thirteenth century.

5. Principles of the Edition and Translation

The Latin text of the *De longitudine* commentary which is presented here is substantially the same as that edited and published in 1993 and indicated in the footnotes by L = Louvain (Peeters) editions of 1993. The annotations by the editor in those editions have not reproduced here; for the full *apparatus criticus*

---

85 See below, 206.
86 The examples of the birds given by Peter are to be found in Frederick II's text as well as some notable parallel texts on the physiology of birds of prey. See Frederick II, *De arte venandi cum avibus*, 22–25. On the role of Manfred as editor see, ibid., lxxvi–vii; 1139.
87 See below, 207.
88 See below, 209.
89 See below, 209.

36   INTRODUCTION

and the *apparatus fontium* the reader is directed to that edition. The text of the *Determinatio Magistralis* follows Baeumker's edition (1920).

The text of Aristotle which was supplied in the original 1993 edition of the *De longitudine* commentary and reproduced here was constructed from that which appeared in the edition of the commentary of Peter of Spain, an edition of the *vetus* text translated by James of Venice.[90] Some small changes were also made to that edition of Aristotle's text to reflect the text as quoted by Peter. An English translation of this Latin text and the lemmata in his commentary have been provided.

The guiding principle of the translation is that it has endeavoured to be as faithful to the text as possible while using the traditional Scholastic terminology in English. It has been done so as to enable those who wish to follow the text in the original Latin to do so in as clear a fashion as possible. However, the intention of the translation is also to make it clearly readable in English and to "flow" naturally as far as possible. For this reason sometimes the translation of the same Latin word may vary from time to time so as not to repeat the same word twice in the same phrase or sentence by choosing a clearly related synonym. This will not prove too difficult to follow I think and is standard practice for any translation which aims to be legible and comprehensible.

Medieval Latin transliterations of Arabic and Hebrew personal names have been rendered in the English translation by their standard English transliterations, e.g., Ibn Sīna, etc.

---

90 See Volume III of the *Obras Filosóficas* of Peter of Spain, 405–11.

Text and Translation

Magistri Petri de Ybernia

Expositio et Quaestiones in Aristotelis librum
De Longitudine et Brevitate Vitae (c. 1258–1265)

Ex Cod. Vaticano lat. 825 ff. 92ra–102rb

Master Peter of Ireland

Exposition and Questions on Aristotle's work
"On Length and Shortness of Life"

⟨Prohemium⟩

Sicut habetur in libro *De Pura Bonitate: res omnes habent essenciam propter ens primum et res uiue sunt mote per essenciam suam propter uitam primam*, et hoc est sicut dicit ibi commentator, *quia omnis causa dat aliquid suo causato*, unde *ens primum dat causatis suis esse et uita prima dat causatis suis motum*. Vnde dicit quod *uita est processio procedens ab ente primo, quieto* et *sempiterno*. Et quamuis ens primum det causatis suis esse et *uita prima dat hiis que sub ipsa sunt uitam*, non tamen eodem modo, quia *ens primum dat esse per modum creacionis, set uita prima non dat uitam per modum creacionis, set per modum forme*.

Quod potest intelligi dupliciter: quod uita sit in uiuentibus per modum forme et non per modum rei create; non enim forma est creata, sicut iam ostendetur. Vnde potest sic intelligi quod uita non exit in esse per uiam creacionis, set per uiam per quam exit forma, scilicet per infusionem et utroque modo uiuum[1] est.

Quod patet hoc modo: *omne enim esse est a forma*; esse uiuencium est esse; ergo esse uiuencium est a forma. Set *uiuere uiuentibus est esse*; ergo uiuere est a forma; set uiuere est uita; ergo uita est a forma.

Item, argumentum Aristotilis est: *uiuere uiuentibus est esse; set nichil est causa esse nisi substancia*; ergo substancia est causa uiuere; set uita est causa uiuere; ergo uita est substancia; set non materia, non compositum; ergo forma.

Quod autem forma non sit creata, patet: quia omne quod est creatum est hoc aliquid; forma non est hoc aliquid; ergo

---

1 uiuum: unde L.

Prologue

As is held in the book *On Pure Goodness*:[1] "all things have their essence on account of the First Being and living things are moved through their essence on account of the First Life".[2] And this is, as the commentator[3] says there, "because every cause gives something to what it has caused", so "the First Being gives existence to those it has caused", and the First Life gives movement to those it has caused. Thus, the commentator says that "life is a procession proceeding from the First, Unchanging and Everlasting Being". And although the First Being gives existence to those it causes and "the First Life gives life to those under it", they do not however do so in the same way, because "the First Being gives existence by way of creation but the First Life does not give life by way of creation but by way of form".[4]

This can be understood in two ways: that life is in living things by means of form and not by means of a created thing, for form is not created as will now be shown. Thus, it can be understood as follows that life does not come into existence by way of creation, but in the way through which form comes into existence, namely through infusion, and by each way it is alive.

This is clear in the following way: "for all being is from form";[5] the being (*esse*) of living things is to be (*esse*); therefore the being of living things is from form. However, "to live in living things is to be";[6] therefore, to live is from form; but to live is life; therefore life is from form.

Again, the argument of Aristotle is: "to live in living things is to be; but nothing is the cause of being except substance";[7] therefore, substance is the cause of living but life is the cause of living; therefore life is substance; but not the matter or the composite, therefore form.

However, that form is not created is clear: because everything which is created is a certain thing; form is not a certain thing; therefore, it is not created. Indeed,

---

1 The book *On Pure Goodness* (*Kalâm fî mahd al-khayr*), was the title originally given to it in its Arabic source, it was later renamed *The Book of Causes*. Peter uses both titles here in the Prologue. It was long believed to be a work of Aristotle but some people at least had their doubts attributing it instead, e.g., to Alfarabi among others. With the translation of the *Elementatio theologica* of Proclus by Moerbeke in 1268, Thomas Aquinas, while not the first to question the authenticity of the text, was able to identify Proclus as the major source.

2 *Liber de causis* XVII (XVIII).

3 Not Averroes who is normally referred to as the Commentator, but the commentator on the propositions of the *Liber de causis*.

4 *Liber de causis* XVII (XVIII).

5 Boethius, *De Trinitate* ch. 2.

6 Aristotle, *De anima* II iv, 415b 13.

7 Ibid.

non est creata. Quod autem forma non sit hoc aliquid, patet, quia omne quod est hoc | aliquid est id quod est; forma non est id quod est; ergo non est hoc aliquid.

Probatio assumpcionis: id quo est unumquodque quod est, non est id quod est; forma autem est ⟨quo est⟩ unumquodque quod est; ergo forma non est id quod est. Immo uidetur quod ita debeat formari: id quo est unumquodque quod est, non est id quod est; forma est quo est unumquodque quod est, ergo non est id quod est.

Item, quod forma non sit hoc aliquid patet per Aristotilem in principio secundi *De Anima*: ibi enim dicit quod *forma est secundum quam unumquodque est hoc aliquid*, nam forma non est creata set infusa, uita uero infusa et non creata.

⟨Questiones⟩

Set dubitabit aliquis, cum dicat Aristotiles uitam esse celi et uitam esse in istis mortalibus, utrum uniuoce sumatur uita utrobique?

Quod autem non uniuoce, potest abstrahi ex uerbis Aristotilis: uita enim que in mortalibus est, omnino est ab anima; Set ostenditur hoc modo quod uita celi non sit ab anima: uita celi non est penosa nec laboriosa; omnis uita que est ab anima est penosa et laboriosa; igitur ⟨uita celi⟩ non est ab anima. Probatio maioris extrahitur ibidem ex uerbis Aristotilis: Omnis uita in uiuente habente unum solum motum qui est ei naturalis, (et non potest illi uiuenti inesse necessario uirtus prohibens ipsum ab inclinacione sua naturali) est sine labore et pena; talis est uita celi, ergo est sine labore et pena. Assumpcio illius sillogismi sic ostenditur: Quia omnis uita que est ab anima inest alicui habenti motum naturalem cui potest inesse uirtus necessario prohibens ipsum a sua inclinacione naturali, igitur omnis talis uita est cum labore et pena.

that form is not a certain thing is clear because everything which is a certain thing is something which is; form is not that which is; therefore it is not a certain thing.

Proof of the assumption: that by which something is what it is, is not that which is; form, however, is that by which something is what it is; therefore, form is not that which is. Or rather it seems that it should be constructed as follows: that by which something is what it is, is not that which is; form is that by which something is what it is, therefore it is not that which is. [8]

Again, that form is not a certain thing is clear from Aristotle at the beginning of the second book of the *De Anima*: for there he says that "form is that according to which something is a certain thing",[9] for form is not created but infused; life, on the other hand, is infused and not created.

Questions

However, someone might raise the question, since Aristotle says that there is life in the heavens and life in these mortals, can the term "life" be understood univocally in both cases?

That it cannot be understood univocally can be drawn from the words of Aristotle: the life which is in mortals is entirely from the soul. However, it can be shown in this way that the life of the heavens is not from the soul: the life of the heavens is neither difficult nor wearisome;[10] all life that comes from the soul is difficult and wearisome; therefore the life of the heavens is not from the soul. The proof of the major premise can be obtained from the words of Aristotle in the same place: All life in a living thing, having only one movement which is natural to it (and there cannot be necessarily in that living thing a power impeding it from its natural inclination), is without pain and toil; such is the life of the heavens, therefore it is without pain and toil. The assumption of this syllogism can be shown in this way: Because all life which is from the soul inheres in something which has a natural motion and in which there can be necessarily a power impeding it from its natural inclination, all such life is, therefore, with pain and toil.[11]

---

8 The argument seems to be based on the expression by Boethius, "existence differs from that which is" (*diversum est esse et id quod est*) and is found in a number of works by Boethius but also in the *De Trinitate*, ch. 2, cited by Peter above.

9 Aristotle, *De anima* II i, 412a 8–9.

10 Aristotle, *De caelo* II i, 284a 14–15.

11 This alludes to Aristotle's famous distinction between the material composition of the heavens which is ether and which has no opposition, whereas the soul informs a body in the sublunary world which is composed of the four elements of earth, air, water and fire and their attendant elemental qualities, all of which are opposed to the other (hence the source of the pain and toil) and have a different natural place, e.g., earth has an inclination to go downwards and fire to go upwards. This is the source of the fundamental instability of material bodies in the sublunary world.

44 TEXT AND TRANSLATION – PROHEMIUM

69   Item, patet quod non eodem modo influit in celum motor celi et anima in suum mobile, quia motor celi non influit in suum motum secundum partem et partem; set anima influit in suum motum secundum partem et partem, quia in unam partem corporis influit motum secundum unam partem eius et in aliam secundum aliam partem, et similiter diuersificatur uiuere quod est ab anima secundum diuersitatem membrorum; patet ergo quod non uniuoce dicitur uita inesse celo et mortalibus.

     Vnde, credendo quod uita celi non sit processio sui motus a primo motore separato, ⟨s⟩et a motore coniuncto, necesse est ponere duplicem motorem primi mobilis, coniunctum et separatum.

     Viuere ergo quod est ab anima dicitur multipliciter: quod testatur Aristotiles in libro *De Anima* dicens: uiuere dicto multipliciter, et⟨si⟩ secundum unumquodque alicui inest ipsum uiuere dicimus, ut intellectum, ⟨sensum⟩, motum secundum locum uoluntarie, secundum alimentum, crementum, detrimentum. Ex quo patet quod non solum animalia uiuunt, set eciam plante: habent enim potenciam et principium motus in se, secundum quem per alimentum sussipiunt crementum et detrimentum. Sic ergo concludit Aristotiles quod plante uiuunt. Vnumquodque enim uiuit in fine quousque accipiat alimentum, et cum non possit sucipere alimentum, non amplius natum est uiuere. Et ita potencia uegetatiua in mortalibus est causa uite. Vnde alibi dicit Aristotiles quod uegetatiua est communissima potencia anime, secundum quam inest uiuere omnibus uiuentibus. Ista enim potencia potest separari ab omnibus aliis in mortalibus, alie uero nullo modo ab ista: quedam enim

Again, it is clear that the mover of the heavens[12] and the soul do not influence what they move in the same way because the mover of the heavens does not influence what it moves according to one part and another. However, the soul influences what it moves according to one part and another because in one part of the body the soul influences what it moves according to one part of it and in another part of the body according to another part, and similarly the life which is from the soul is diversified according to the diversity of the organs. Therefore, it is clear that life cannot be said to be univocally in the heavens and in mortals.

Thus, by believing that the life of the heaven is not a procession of its own motion from the first separated mover but from a conjoined mover, it is necessary to posit a twofold mover of the *primum mobile*, one that is conjoined and one that is separate.[13]

Therefore, life which is from the soul is spoken of in many ways, which is shown by Aristotle in the book *On the Soul*, saying: Living is said in many ways and if any one of the following are in something we say that it is living, such as understanding, sensation, voluntary movement according to place, and movement in the sense of nutrition, growth and decay.[14] From which it is clear that not only animals are alive but so also are plants, for they have the power and origin of movement in themselves according to which they receive growth and decrease by means of nutrition.[15] In this way, therefore, Aristotle concludes that plants are alive.[16] For, in short, anything lives for as long as it gets food[17] and when it cannot get food, it is not destined to live for very long. Thus, it is the vegetative power which is the cause of life in mortals. Thus, elsewhere Aristotle says that the vegetative power is the most common power of the soul, according to which life is in all living things.[18] This power can be separated from all others in mortal things but no other power can be found separated from it.[19] For some animals live by vegetation and sensa-

---

12 The Mover or Intelligence which moves one of the heavenly spheres and whose influence is not diversified because of elemental opposition and dispersion which is, on the contrary the situation of the soul trying to bring its influence on this or the other part of the material body.

13 Avicenna and Algazel assigned two movers to each heaven, a conjoined mover or soul, and a separated mover or Intelligence. The Intelligences impart motion to the heavens whereas the soul is the substantial form of the heavens. Thinkers such as Aquinas identify the Intelligences with Angels but there is no sign of such an identification here. Peter seems to reject the emanationist theory that life is a procession from the First Separate Mover (God) but instead assigns two movers to the *primum mobile*. The *primum mobile* ("first moved") is the outermost sphere of the geocentric universe and which moves around the earth every twenty-four hours carrying the inner spheres with it.

14 Aristotle, *De anima* II ii, 413a 22–25.

15 Ibid., 413a 26–27.

16 Ibid., 413a 26.

17 Ibid., 413a 30–31.

18 Ibid., 413a 32–413b 2.

19 Ibid., 413a 31–32.

46 TEXT AND TRANSLATION – PROHEMIUM

70 animalia uiuunt | uegetacione et sensu et non habent motum
uoluntarium secundum locum, sicut sunt animalia que uiuunt
per adherenciam, et hec non sunt perfecta animalia, immo sunt
medium inter animalia perfecta et plantas. Viuunt enim per
adherenciam sicut plante, set addunt aliquid super uitam plante: uita enim plante non est nisi uita occulta, set sensus est
illustracio uite, sicut habetur ab Aristotile in principio primi *De
Vegetabilibus*. Primus autem sensus, scilicet tactus, separabilis
est ab omnibus aliis, set alii omnes nequaquam separantur ab
ipso. Maxime autem dicitur uiuere quod habet in se omnem
causam uite, scilicet intellectum, sensum, motum secundum
locum et cetera. Vnde dicitur in *6 Principiis* quod racionale
animancius est bruto.

Ex predictis ergo patet quod ista passio "mors et uita"
sequuntur animam uegetabilem secundum quod est actus
corporis. Set ista passio "sompnus et uigilia" per se ⟨con⟩comi-
tantur animam sensibilem ut est actus corporis. "Memoria"
uero et "reminiscencia" sequuntur animam racionabilem ut est
actus corporis organici. Et sicut subiecta passionum ordinantur,
et ita ordinantur passiones eorumdem, et sicut subiecta et
passiones, ita sciencia subiectorum et passionum. Sciencia ergo
de uegetabilibus et de passione concomitante ipsam ⟨animam
uegetabilem⟩ debet antecedere scienciam de naturis animalium
et scienciam de passione concomitante ipsam ⟨animam sensibi-
71 lem⟩; ille autem sciencie debent antecedere | scienciam de ani-
ma et scienciam de passione concomitante animam racionalem,
ut est actus corporis.

Ex hiis patet quod sciencia ista supponitur physice.

Et si aliquis obiciat: Omnis physica est de corpore solum
mobili, in genere uel in specie; uita autem non est ali⟨quo⟩
modo corpus; non ergo ista sciencia continetur sub ista; si
enim subiectum non est sub subiecto, neque sciencia sub sciencia; et ita non erit sub physica.

Et dicendum ad hoc quod non sequitur, si subiectum non
sit sub subiecto, quod sciencia non sit sub sciencia. Ex parte
affirmacionis tenet: si subiectum sub subiecto, et sciencia sub

tion but do not have voluntary movement according to place, such as are those animals which live by adhesion.[20] These, however, are not complete animals but rather are an intermediary between complete animals and plants. For they live by adhesion just like plants but add something on to the life of plants: indeed, the life of a plant is nothing but a hidden life but sensation is a clear indication of life, as Aristotle says in the beginning of the first book of *On Plants*.[21] The first sense, namely touch, can be found on its own apart from all the others but none of the others can be separated from touch.[22] Something is said to be living to the greatest extent which has in itself the complete cause of life, namely understanding, sensation, motion according to place, and so on. Whence it is said in the book *On the Six Principles* that the rational animal is more animated than the brute.[23]

Therefore, from what has been said it is clear that this attribute "death and life" follows the vegetative soul inasmuch as it is the act of a body. However, this attribute "sleeping and waking" in itself accompanies the sensitive soul inasmuch as it is the act of the body. Moreover, "memory and reminiscence" follows the rational soul inasmuch as it is the act of an organic body.[24] And just as the subjects of the attributes are arranged, so also are the attributes of the same subjects arranged, and just as the subjects and the attributes are arranged, so also is the science of the subjects and the attributes.[25] Therefore, the science of the vegetative things and of the attribute accompanying this vegetative soul should come before the science of the natures of animals and the science of the attribute accompanying the sensitive soul. Indeed, those sciences must come before the science of the soul and of the science of the attribute accompanying the rational soul, inasmuch as it is the act of the body.

From the above it is clear that this science falls under natural philosophy.

And someone might object that all of natural philosophy is concerned with the body only inasmuch as it is moveable, either in genus or species, but life is not in any way a body; therefore, this science does not come under natural philosophy; for, if a subject is not under a subject then neither is a science under a science; and thus it will not be under natural philosophy.

With regard to this, it should be said that it does not follow that if a subject is not under a subject, that a science is not under a science. The affirmative part is valid: if a subject is under a subject, so also is a science under a science. For it is the

---

20 Nicholas of Damascus (Pseudo-Aristotle), *De plantis* I i.

21 Ibid.

22 See Aristotle, *De anima* II ii, 413b 4–7.

23 Anonymous, *Liber de sex principiis* II, 29, *De passione*.

24 Aristotle, *De anima* II iv, 416a 27–28.

25 Here we have a typical *divisio scientiae* where a justification is given for locating this particular theme under a certain branch of science, in this case that the study of length and shortness of life falls under Natural Philosophy.

sciencia: eiusdem enim sciencie est cognoscere ⟨subiectum⟩ et proprias passiones illius subiecti. Vnde quamuis uita non sit corpus neque a corpore proprie loquendo, saluatur tamen per ea que sunt in corpore, ut per calidum et humidum et cetera; et quia physice per se est considerare causam saluacionis uite in uiuente, propter hoc sciencia de uita et de eius opposito ad ipsam pertinet. Alio tamen modo considerando uitam secundum eius causam efficientem primam, non pertinet ad physicam considerare secundum quod sic diffinitur in libro *De Causis*: uita est processio procedens ab ente primo, quieto et sempiterno. Sic ergo patet de quo sit ista sciencia, quia de passione ⟨con⟩comitante ipsam animam uegetabilem in corpore, de qua demonstrat[2] aliam passionem, scilicet longitudinem et breuitatem. Vnde proprie intendit in hac sciencia inquirere causam longitudinis et breuitatis uite. Omnia autem mensurantur periodo, non tamen eodem, sicut habetur in physicis, quia quedam mensurantur reuolucione que fit una die, quedam autem reuolucione que attenditur secundum reuolucionem lune, quedam autem secundum reuolucionem solis; et ita quedam uiuunt per unam diem, quedam per plures, quedam per mensem, et sic deinceps. Etsi causa huius diuer|sitatis longitudinis et breuitatis uite sit diuersitas reuolucionum corporum supercelestium, tamen hanc diuersitatem non attendit hic primo et per se, set diuersitatem que attenditur secundum principia materialia uiuentis, secundum tamen quod regulatur a superioribus.

---

2 demonstrat: demonstrant L.

task of the same science to know both the subject and the proper attributes of the same subject.[26] Thus, whereas life is not a body nor, properly speaking, from a body, yet it is preserved by those things which are in a body, such as by means of the hot and moist, etc. And because it is the task of Natural Philosophy in itself to examine the cause of the preservation of life in a living thing, for this reason the science of life and its opposite will pertain to it as well. However, another way of examining life with regard to its First Efficient Cause is not appropriate for Natural Philosophy to examine, according to what is defined in the book, *On Causes*: "Life is a procession, proceeding from the First, Unchanging and Everlasting Being".[27] Thus, it is clear what this science is about, since it is about the attribute which accompanies the vegetative soul in the body, about which Aristotle demonstrates another attribute, namely, length and brevity. Thus, Aristotle specifically wishes in this science to investigate the cause of length and shortness of life. For everything is measured according to a certain length of time[28] which is not the same, as is held in Natural Philosophy since some are measured by the revolution [of the heavens] which occurs in a day; some, however, [are measured] according to the revolution which follows upon the revolution of the moon; some, however, [are] according to the revolution of the sun. And so some live for a single day, some for more than one, some for a month, and so on. And even if the cause of this diversity of length and shortness of life is the diversity of the revolutions of the heavenly bodies, yet that diversity is not the one which Aristotle considers here first and foremost, but what is the diversity which arises according to the material principles of a living thing, according, however, as this is regulated by the heavenly bodies.

---

26 See Aristotle, *Metaphysica* IV ii, 1004b 4–17.

27 *Liber de causis* XVII (XVIII).

28 Aristotle, *De generatione et corruptione* II x, 336b 12–16.

⟨Lectio 1⟩

1. [Bekker 464b 19] De eo autem quod est esse alia quidem longe uite, alia uero [20] breuis, et de uite tota longitudine et breuitate considerandum. Principium autem intentionis necessarium est primum exponere de ipsis. Non autem manifestum est, utrum una et eadem causa sit omnibus animalibus et plantis, hec quidem esse longe uite, alia uero breuis; et [25] plantarum quidem alie breuem, alie uero multo tempore habent [26] uitam.

De eo autem quod est longe uite, et cetera [i, 464b 19]. Hiis uisis, sciendum est quod liber iste diuiditur in tres partes, in quarum prima notificat in uniuersali de quibus in secunda specialiter prosequitur in tractatu. Et patet ordo et multiplicacio: pluribus enim modis non potest aliquid considerari nisi in uniuersali et in speciali, et notificacio in uniuersali naturaliter debet antecedere notificacionem eiusdem in speciali. Et terminatur prima pars ibi: *Oportet autem accipere quid corruptibile*, et cetera [ii, 465a 13].

Prima pars subdiuiditur in duas partes principaliter, in quarum prima enumerat in uniuersali quid de causis longitudinis et breuitatis uite; in secunda parte ostendit diuersos modos secundum quos possunt diuersificari cause longitudinis et breuitatis uite, quia[1] prius est cognoscere si sint cause diuersitatis uite secundum longitudinem et breuitatem quam cognoscatur qualiter et quot modis diuersificetur uita secundum illas causas. Propter[2] hoc prima pars antecedit secundam: questio enim "si est" naturaliter antecedit questiones istas "quid est" et "qualiter est". Et terminatur prima pars ibi: *Amplius autem utrum eadem sint que sunt longe*, et cetera [i, 464b 26].

---

1 uite, quia: uite. Quia L.
2 causas. Propter: causas, propter L.

First Lecture

Text (464b 19–26)[1]

The reasons why it is that some indeed have a long life, and some have a short life, and the causes of complete length and shortness of life, are to be considered. Indeed, the necessary beginning of our intention is first of all to explain about these. For it is not clear whether one and the same cause is to be found in all animals and plants, that indeed of the former some have a long life and some, on the other hand, a short one; again, some plants indeed live for a short time while others live for a long time.

Division of the Text

The reasons why some have a long life, etc. Having seen the above, it should be noted that this book is divided into three parts, in the first of which Aristotle recounts in general about those things which in the second part he continues with in particular in his treatment. And the order and the development [of the treatment] is clear: a thing cannot be considered in many ways except in general and in particular, and recounting in general naturally must come before recounting the same in particular. And the first part finishes there: *It is necessary, however, to understand what is corruptible,* etc.

The first part is subdivided into two main parts; in the first Aristotle enumerates in general about the causes of length and shortness of life; in the second part he shows the different ways according to which the causes of length and shortness of life can differ. This is because knowing if there are causes of the diversity of life according to length and shortness comes before knowing how, and in how many ways, life is diversified according to those causes. For this reason the first part comes before the second: for the question "is it?" naturally comes before these questions: "what is it?" and "in what manner is it?". And the first part ends here: *And furthermore, whether they are the same which are long-lived,* etc.

---

1 It should be kept in mind that the text of Aristotle presented here is a literal translation of the Latin translation, itself a literal translation from the Greek made by James of Venice (died after 1147). James' method of translation was a literal one, translating the Greek word for word and preserving in Latin the word order of the origin text which he had, itself the product of many centuries of transcribing. The result was generally good and reliable but at times confusing for the Latin mind. The Latin text as presented here is an attempt to reproduce the Latin text which Peter had before him. The English translation is a literal translation of that Latin text. Its awkwardness is deliberate in order to give the reader some sense of what a challenge it posed for Masters of the middle decades of the Thirteenth Century.

Illa pars secunda diuiditur secundum duplex opus sapientis: est enim duplex opus sapientis non mentiri de quibus nouit et manifestare mencientem. Et terminatur prima pars illius secunde partis ibi: *Preter hec autem sunt et hanc habencia differenciam*, et cetera [i, 465a 2].

⟨Expositio Littere⟩

Dicit ergo, *De eo quod est*, et cetera [i, 464b 19].

Hic queritur quare hic tangat Aristotiles in principio de longitudine et breuitate uite animalium, cum non intendat hic solum de longitudine et breuitate uite animalium, set generaliter omnium uiuencium?

Et solucio huius questionis patet, quia plantis non inest pars anime, set pars partis anime, cum non habeant uitam nisi secundum quid, quia uitam occultam: sensus enim est illustracio uite, sicut predictum est. Quia[3] ergo oportet in occultis apertis uti testimoniis, propter hoc tangit ea in quibus est uita per manifestacionem; consequens enim tangit ea in quibus est uita occulta.

Dicit enim: quedam animalium sunt *longe uite*, quedam *breuis uite, et de tota longitudine* [i, 464b 19–20], id est de causis longitudinis uite, *considerandum*, et de tota breuitate, id est integre breuitatis. Et bene dicit "de tota longitudine", quia, sicut dicit Aristotiles, determinatum[4] est tempus cuilibet accioni in quo maiori uel in quo minori compleri non potest illa accio, ut percussioni cordis determinatum est tempus in quo minori compleri non potest, sicut uult Aristotiles in 5 *Physicorum* et in libro *De Celo et Mundo*; ita eciam determinatum est tempus secundum naturam deductioni uite in quo minori inpossibile est uitam durare. Vnde, sicut dictum est, omnia mensurantur peryodo suo; ante terminum peryodi sui fixum a natura potest secundum accidens finiri uitam; ad differenciam talis finictionis | uite, dicit: "totam longitudinem": non enim est tota longitudo uite cum finitur ante terminum prefixum sibi a natura.

Principium autem intencionis ⟨necessarium⟩ est primo exponere de ipsis, et cetera [i, 464b 21–22]. Ibi determinat de quibus intendit primo determinare, dicens quod est principium sue intencionis primo exponere *de ipsis*, id est de causis longitudinis

---

3 est. Quia: est, quia L.

4 Aristoteles, determinatum: Aristoteles: determinatum L.

The second part is divided according to the twofold task of the wise man: for it is the twofold task of the wise man not to deceive about those things which he knows and to expose falsehood.[2] And the first part of this second part ends here: *Besides these, however, are those having this difference,* etc.

Literal Explanation of the Text

Therefore, he says: *The reasons why it is,* etc.

At this point the question arises as to why Aristotle alludes here at the beginning to the length and shortness of life of animals when he does not intend to consider here only the length and shortness of life in animals, but generally the length and shortness of the life of all living things?

And the solution to this question is clear because in plants there is not a part of the soul but a part of a part of the soul,[3] since they do not have life except in a qualified way since it is a hidden life. This is because sensation is the indication of life, as has already been said.[4] Since, therefore, in hidden things it is necessary to use clear witnesses, because of this Aristotle touches upon those in whom there is clearly life. Subsequently he deals with those in whom there is a hidden life.

For he says: some animals have *a long life,* some have *a short life,* and [that which is] *concerning the complete length,* that is concerning the causes of length of life, *is to be considered, and* concerning complete *shortness,* that is concerning complete shortness of life. And well he says "concerning complete length" since, as Aristotle says, the amount of time is fixed for any action under which and beyond which an action cannot be completed, just as there is a certain minimum amount of time under which a heart beat cannot be completed, as Aristotle states in Book V of the *Physics* and in the book, *On the Heavens and Earth.*[5] So also a minimum amount of time is fixed according to the nature of the extent of life under which it is impossible for life to last. Thus, as has been said, all things are measured by their own period of time;[6] it is possible for life to be ended accidentally before this period of time as fixed by nature; and to distinguish this from such an accidental ending of life Aristotle says "complete length". For there is not a complete length of life if it is ended before the term already fixed for it by nature.

Indeed, the necessary beginning of our intention is first of all to explain about these, etc. Here Aristotle states what things he intends to speak about first, saying that it is the beginning of his intention to first explain *those things,* that is, the caus-

---

2 Aristotle, *De sophisticis elenchis* i, 165a 24–27.

3 Nicholas of Damascus, *De Plantis* I ii.

4 Above in the Prologue, 47.

5 See Aristotle, *Physica* V i, 224a 35; *De caelo* II vi, 288b 30–289a 1.

6 See above, 49.

et breuitatis uite. Et redit causam quare debet exponere de ipsis, dicens: quia non est manifestum *utrum una et eadem causa sit omnibus animalibus ⟨et plantis⟩* [i, 464b 23], quare quedam sunt longe uite, alie uero breuis uite.

Et quia aliquis posset dubitare utrum sit reperire istam diuersitatem in plantis sicut in aliis animalibus, dicit quod sic, dicens: *Plantarum enim alie quidem breuem uitam alie uero multo tempore habent uitam* [i, 464b 24–26].

⟨Questiones⟩

Hic posset aliquis dubitare, cum omne uiuens sit calidum et humidum, sicut patet per uerbum Aristotilis consequens, ubi dicit quod *omne animal est calidum et humidum* [v, 466a 18]; si hoc, tunc ergo caliditas et humiditas si⟨n⟩t per dominium in quolibet uiuente; si igitur aliquid uiuens dicatur frigidum in 4 gradu, eius caliditas, cum dominetur, erit ultra gradum; talis autem caliditas omnino repugnaret uite; ex quo uidetur quod si aliquid dicatur frigidum in 4 gradu, non erit uiuens, aut, si sit uiuens, non erit frigidum in 4 ⟨gradu⟩. Quid est ergo quod dicitur, quod quedam uiuencia sunt in 4 gradu?

Item, si calidum uitale non incendatur[5] usque ad 4 gradum, set sit temperatum, quomodo uiuens recipit denominacionem ab eo quod minus dominatur? Omnis enim complexio debet denominari a dominante.

Item, si caliditas uitalis sit temperata et frigiditas sit in modo ultimi gradus, cum omnis qualitas existens in modo ultimi gradus sit destructio sui contrarii temperati, tunc ergo est eleuacio [non] talis frigiditatis, non possibilis[6] erit caliditas in eodem subiecto: omnia enim habencia frigiditatem sic eleuatam erunt breuis uite; si enim uita saluetur per calidum et humidum, sicut ea quorum humidum de facili desiccatur sunt breuis uite, sicut ostendetur consequenter, ita | et ea quorum calidum de facili

---

5 incendatur: intendatur L.
6 possibilis: possibile L.

es of length and shortness of life. And he gives the reason why he must deal with those things, saying: *for it is not clear whether there is one and the same cause in all animals and plants*, because of which some have a long life and others have a short life.

And since someone might wonder if this diversity is to be found in plants just as in other animals, he says it is so, stating: *Some plants indeed live for a short time while others live for a long time.*

Questions[7]

Here somebody might raise some doubts:

[1.] Since every living thing is hot and moist as it clear from what Aristotle says below, where he says *every animal is hot and moist*; then, if this is so, heat and humidity are in any living thing by being dominant. Thus, if any living thing is said to be cold in the fourth degree,[8] its heat, since it dominates, will be said to be above any grade; however, such heat would be completely counter to life. From this it seems that if something is said to be cold in the fourth degree it will not be alive, or if it is alive, then it will not be cold in the fourth degree. What, therefore, is meant when it is stated that some living things are in the fourth degree?

[2.] Again, if vital heat[9] does not become hot as far as the fourth degree but is temperate,[10] in what way can a living thing be identified by that which dominates less? For every complexion must be identified by that which dominates.

[3.] Again, if vital heat is temperate and coldness exists in the mode of the highest degree, since every quality which exists in the mode of the highest degree leads to the destruction of its temperate contrary, therefore there will be an increase of such coldness and it will not be possible for heat to exist in the same subject, for all things which have such elevated coldness will be short of life. For if life is preserved by heat and humidity just as those whose humidity is easily dried up are short-lived, as will be shown below, so also those whose heat is easily cooled and

---

7 It seems that Peter here is anticipating possible questions, rather than ones which were put forward. This section is a bit confusing where the division into actual questions is not as clear as in the other lectures.

8 The distinction in contemporary medicine between degrees of heat and cold, etc., can be traced back to the translations of Constantine the African of Arabic medical authors, they being in turn influenced by the writings of Hippocrates and Galen. The basis of ancient and medieval medicine to curing an imbalance in the body which causes sickness is to treat the patient with some medicine which outweighs the ill effect and brings the patient back to a balance of the humors which is regarded as healthy. For example, onion and garlic would be regarded as hot to the fourth degree and could help a patient who is phlegmatic.

9 The heat produced by the heart and associated with life.

10 See above, 25–26.

infrigidatur et congelatur erunt breuis uite: magis enim operatur ad uitam caliditas quam humiditas, eo quod caliditas est per
modum agentis, humiditas passibile et materiale.

Oppositum tamen huius uidemus in quibusdam terre
nascentibus, que non sunt breuis uite, etsi sint frigida in ultimo
gradu et ultra; et eodem modo uidemus de quibusdam animalibus uenenosis.

Ad ista dicendum quod, cum dicitur: Omne uiuens et est
calidum et humidum, id non intelligitur de calido complexionabili: calor enim complexionabilis est calor elementorum siue
ignis, et ab isto calore non dicitur esse uiuens calidum; set alius
est calor qui dicitur calor celestis, de quo dicit Galenus quod in
unaquaque re est calor per cuius presenciam obseruatur res et
per eius absenciam corrumpitur. Igitur duplex est humidum:
unum quod est continuacio parcium terrestrium, de quo dicit
Aristotiles quod siccum terminatur per humidum, et utrumque
utrique fit sicut colla, et in eodem libro in fine innuit idem
dicens quod terra pura lapis non fit. Item, dicit in 2 *De Generatione*: nisi esset humidum, utique s⟨c⟩inderetur terra; humidum
enim facit ad eius parcium commoracionem. Est et aliud humidum quod est magis aereum, et de tali humido dicit Aristotiles
consequenter in hoc libro quod *non oportet esse cito desiccabile*
[v, 466a 23], cum autem per frigiditatem, que est aeris siue aeree
nature, de tali humido facit Aristotiles mencionem in 4 *Metheororum*, dicens quod ambiguissime nature se habet oleum, eo
quod si esset aque, coagolaretur a gelido, si terre, magis coagolaretur a calido: non autem a neutro coagolatur, et impinguatur
ab | utroque. Causa autem perfecta est, quia est aeris. Quod
ergo dicitur: omne[7] uiuens calidum esse et humidum, non
intelligitur illud de calido complexionabili nec de humido
aqueo, quod facit commoracionem corporis, set intelligitur de
calido uitali, quod est calidum celeste magis, et de humido
aereo, quod est pabulum siue fundamentum, id est calidum
consumit tale humidum, naturaliter humido finito finitur et

---

7 omne: esse L.

congealed will be short-lived. For heat works more in respect of life than humidity because heat exists in the manner of an agent, whereas humidity exists as capable of being acted upon and material.

[Against] However, we see the opposite of this in some which are born from the earth and which are not short-lived even if they are cold to the final degree and beyond; and we see the same regarding certain venomous animals.

[Solution] With regard to these, it should be stated that when it is said that "every living thing is hot and humid", this is not to be taken to be constitutional heat since constitutional heat is the heat of the elements, namely of fire, and from this heat no living thing is said to be hot; but the heat which is said to be the heat of the heavens is heat of another kind. With regard to this heat Galen says[11] that it is that by whose presence a thing is preserved and by whose absence a thing is corrupted. Therefore, moisture is twofold: one which is coextensive with the earthy parts, of which Aristotle says that the dry is bounded by the moist and each one becomes like a glue to the other.[12] Moreover, in the same book, at the end, Aristotle says the same, stating that pure earth does not become a stone.[13] Again, Aristotle says in the second book of *On Generation*: unless there is moisture, earth will always break up; for moisture causes its parts to stay together.[14] Moreover, there is another humidity which is more airy, and concerning this humidity Aristotle says later on in the same book that "it should not be easily liable to dry up", namely through coldness which is airy or of an airy nature. Aristotle makes mention of such moisture in the fourth book of the *Meteorologica*, saying that "oil has a most ambiguous nature, because if it were watery it would be solidified by cold, if earthy it would rather be solidified by heat; it is not, however, solidified by either of them and is thickened by both".[15] The cause is, however, complete "because it is airy".[16] Therefore, when it is said "every living thing is hot and moist" that is not to be taken to refer to constitutional heat, nor to watery humidity which keeps the body together, but is to be taken to refer to vital heat, which is rather the heat of the heavens, and to airy moisture which is its food or foundation, that is, the heat

---

11 See Galen's *Method of Medicine* XI, 8, 753K, where he talks about putrefaction due to external heat, whereas "each and every living thing is increased, strengthened, made health and lives when governed by its own heat". Peter's use of this absence of heat in Galen implies that when an organism's internal heat is missing, that is when putrefaction can occur. See Galen, *Method of Medicine*, 140–41.

12 Aristotle, *Meteorologica* IV iv, 381b–382a 1.

13 Pseudo Aristotle, *Meteorologica vetus* IV xiii, i.e., Avicenna, *De mineralibus seu de congelatione et conglutatione lapidum*, incipit.

14 Aristotle, *De generatione et corruptione* II viii, 335a 1–4.

15 Aristotle, *Meteorologica* IV vii, 383b 20–25.

16 Ibid., IV vii, 383b 25.

ipsum. Vnde dicitur: Quod nobiscum oritur, nobiscum moritur. Et quia inpossibile est consumpcionem huius humidi ex toto prohibere, propter hoc inpossibile est uitam[8] perpetuari; tamen eius consumpcionem retardari contingit[9] per humidum nutrimentale, sicut retardatur consumpcio humidi substancialis licinii per humidum oleoginosum, tamen necessarium ad ultimum finitur. Quanto ergo humidum tale est magis uiscosum, tanto magis resistit consumpcioni, et quanto plus est in quantitate, tanto in longiori tempore consumitur, et quanto minus, in minori uel in breuiori, et sic accidit quedam esse naturaliter breuis uite et quedam longioris. Ex hiis patet quare denominantur uiuencia a calido et humido, et quod opera calidi naturalis et humidi magis per manifestacionem sunt in uiuente. Digestio celebratur per calidum et humidum. Est enim digestio compleccio a naturali et proprio calore, et cetera; uiuunt autem uiuencia in fine usquequo alimentum suscipiunt. Item, necesse est alimentum dequoqui, sicut habetur in 2 *De Anima*; decoctionem[10] autem necessarium est fieri a calore. Ex hoc patet quod non est inconueniens omne uiuens dici calidum et humidum, quamuis quedam uiuencia sint naturaliter frigida in 4 gradu. Frigida[11] | enim non dicuntur in substancia secundum naturam, set quod dicantur calida, hoc est a calore naturali actu operante in corpore sicut in uino, non faciunt contrarietatem quod sit calidum in natura, frigidum secundum actum uel quod sit siccum in uirtute et humidum in substancia. Frigidum ergo in 4 gradu non repugnat calido uitali secundum compleccionem in eodem; et tamen, si sint in eodem, non tamen eodem modo essendi, quia frigiditas est in eo ut uirtus, set calor uitalis est sicut passio et actus; utrumque ergo potest dici inesse per dominium secundum diuersum modum; denominacio tamen debet fieri ab eo cuius opera magis sunt manifesta.

Tamen id uidetur esse contra Commentatorem super librum istum: dicit enim quod quicquid attribuitur animali de generacione et corrupcione, augmento et diminucione, sompno et uigilia, attribuitur ei racione caliditatis, frigiditatis et

---

8 uitam: uita L.
9 contingit: conueniat L.
10 *Anima*; decoctionem: *Anima*, decoctionem L.
11 gradu. Frigida: gradu, frigida L.

consumes such humidity and when this humidity finishes naturally so does the heat. Thus, it is said "what is born with us, dies with us".[17] Moreover, for this reason it is impossible for life to be extended forever because it is impossible to completely prevent the consumption of this humidity. However, it happens that its consumption is delayed by means of nutrimental humidity, just as the consumption of the substantial humidity of the lampwick can be delayed by means of oily humidity, but of necessity it finishes in the end. Therefore, the more viscous this humidity is, the more it resists consumption, and the greater its quantity, the longer it takes to consume, and the less its quantity, the more it is consumed in a lesser or shorter time, and in this way it happens that some things are naturally shorter lived and some are longer lived. From the above it is clear why living things are defined by heat and moisture and that the workings of natural heat and moisture are more clearly shown in a living thing. Digestion takes place by means of heat and moisture.[18] For digestion is an achievement by natural and proper heat, and so on;[19] living things live as long as they can take in food.[20] Again, it is essential that food is cooked, as is held in the second book of *On the Soul*, but cooking must happen by means of heat.[21] From this it is clear that it is not inconsistent to say that every living thing is hot and moist, even if some living things are naturally cold in the fourth degree, for they are not said to be cold in substance according to nature. However, those that are said to be hot, this is from the natural heat in act working in the body, just as in wine. There is nothing against something hot in nature being cold in act or that something that can be dry in power yet moist in substance. Therefore, something cold in the fourth degree is not hostile to vital heat according to the temperament in the same thing; and yet, if they are in the same thing, they are not in the same mode of existing, because coldness is in it as a power, and vital heat, on the other hand, is in it as potency and act. Each one, therefore, can be said to inhere by predominance in different ways; nevertheless, naming something should occur with reference to that whose actions are more obvious.

[A further doubt] This, however, seems to be against the Commentator on this book: for Ibn Rushd says that whatever is attributed to an animal concerning generation and decay, growth and decrease, sleep and waking, is attributed to it by

---

17 A common saying I presume. The source, however, seems to be Maurus Servius Honoratus, (1881) *In Vergilii carmina comentarii. Servii Grammatici qui feruntur in Vergilii carmina commentarii*; VI, 362: me fluctus habet quia secundum philosophos corpus solum nostrum est, quod nobiscum oritur, nobiscum perit.

18 Aristotle, *Meteorologica* IV iii, 381b 7–9.

19 Ibid., IV ii, 379b 18.

20 Aristotle, *De anima* II ii, 413a 30–31.

21 Ibid., II iv, 416b 27–29.

humiditatis et siccitatis, et ita uult[12] quod racione qualitatum elementorum sit generacio, augmentacio et diminucio et cetera.

Set ⟨si⟩ hoc, tunc per eandem causam fiet saluacio uite.

Propter hoc dicendum sicut uult Aueroys in commento *Super Metaphysicam*, dicens quod duplex est calor in uiuente, ut credo, unus qui se habet ad id quod generatur sicut artifex se habet ad metallum: ignis enim non dat formam nec speciem ipsi metallo, set mundificat ipsum a superfluitatibus que non apte sunt recipere formam, et ipsum preparat ut fiat necessitas ad recipiendum formam ab artifice, sicut calor complexionabilis est preparans et disponens in uiuente ipsum alimentum ut sit aptum ad recipiendum speciem uiuentis. Calor autem uitalis, qui est calor celestis, est dans speciem et inprimens, quod ita se habet sicut artifex.

Signum huius est quod dicit Galenus, quod, si esset nutriens presens ossi et carni et esset[13] totum habilitatum ut reciperet speciem ossis, si[14] tunc statim oppilaretur uia que est inter epar et ipsum os,[15] non conuertetur ipsum nutriens in speciem membri. Patet ergo differencia inter calorem qui est causa uite et eius | duracionis siue deduccionis in tempore secundum maius et minus. Patet eciam quod uita stat per calidum et humidum, et patet per quod humidum.

Patet eciam solucio ad id quod obicitur communiter contra hoc secundum uerbum Aristotilis in secundo *De Anima*, dicens quod ex eisdem ex quibus fimus, augmentamur et nutrimur; fimus autem ex calidis, frigidis, humidis, siccis; ergo nutrimur et augmentamur ex eisdem; set nutrimentum est causa continuacionis uite: uiuunt enim uiuencia omnia in fine usquequo alimentum possint recipere. Non ergo stat uita per calidum et humidum solum, set per alia.

Ad quod dicendum quod alia est nutricio uiuentis in uita, et alia uite in uiuente. Viuens[16] enim in uita equaliter potest nutriri ex siccis sicut ex humidis, et ex humidis sicut ex aliis; nisi enim aliud esset nutrimentum ossis quam carnis, non esset os aliud a carne. Set[17] uita in uiuente nutritur solum per calidum et humidum et saluatur. Et quod dicit Aristotiles quod ex hiis

---

12 uult: uniuersaliter L.

13 et esset: et ⟨non⟩ esset L.

14 si: set L.

15 os] + et L.

16 uiuente. Viuens: uiuente: uiuens L.

17 carne. Set: carne; set L.

reason of heat, coldness, humidity and dryness, and so he holds that it is by reason of the elemental qualities that there is generation, growth and decrease, etc. [22]

However, if this is the case, then life would be preserved by means of the same cause.

[Solution] For this reason it should be answered, as Ibn Rushd states in his *Commentary on the Metaphysics*, [23] saying that heat in a living thing is twofold, as I also hold, one which is constituted in respect of that which is generated in the same way as a craftsman is in relation to the metal. For the fire gives neither the form nor the species to the metal but purifies it from the impurities which are not fit to receive the form, and it prepares the metal so that it becomes necessary for it to receive the form from the craftsman; just as constitutional heat prepares and disposes the food in a living thing so that it will become disposed so as to receive the species of a living thing. Vital heat, however, which is the heat of the heavens, gives and impresses the species, because it is constituted just like the craftsman.

A sign of this is what Galen says, that if the food were present to both bone and flesh, and if it were completely adapted so as to receive the form of bone, if then suddenly the passage which is between the liver and this bone were to be blocked then the food will not converted into the species of the organ. Therefore, the difference is clear between the heat which is the cause of life and its duration or shortening in time to a greater or lesser extent. It is also clear that life continues by means of heat and moisture, and it is clear by what kind of moisture.

[Another objection] The solution is also clear to that which is commonly objected against this, according to what Aristotle says in the second book of *On the Soul*, saying that we grow and are nourished from the same things from which we arose. [24] Now we arise from hot, cold, wet and dry things, [25] therefore we are nourished and fed by the same things. However, food is the cause of the continuation of life, for all living things live for as long as they can take in food. [26] Therefore, life does not continue only through the hot and the moist but also by means of other things.

[Solution] To this it must be replied that the nourishment of a living thing in life is one thing and the nourishment of life in a living thing is another. A living thing in life can equally be nourished by dry things as much as by moist things and by moist things just as by other things; for if nothing else would be the nourishment of bone than flesh, then bone would not be different from flesh. Life, however, in a living thing is nourished only by the hot and moist and is preserved. And what Aristotle says, that we are nourished by those things from which we arise, he

---

22 Averroes, *Compendium de causis longitudinis et brevitatis Vitae*, 129.
23 Averroes, *Commentarius super Metaphysicam*, XI (Lambda) comm. 18, ed. Ven., vol. VIII, f. 305r.
24 Aristotle, *De generatione et corruptione* II viii, 335a 10–11.
25 Aristotle, *De anima* II iii, 414b 7–8.
26 Ibid., II ii, 413a 30–31.

nutrimur ex quibus fimus, intelligit de nutricione uiuentis in uita, et non de alia.

Posset aliquis iterum dubitare utrum eadem esset causa uite in plantis et animalibus?

Et uidetur quod sic per hoc quod dictum est secundum Aristotilem quod uegetatiua potencia est euidentissima potencia anime, secundum quam inest uiuere omnibus uiuentibus. Si igitur uiuere sit potencia uegetabilis in plantis et animalibus, uidetur quod eadem sit causa uite in ipsis, quia potencia uegetabilis.

Set contra hoc est quod in animalibus habentibus cor est uita a uirtute spirituali, sicut patet per uerbum Algezel quod uirtutes mo|tiue et uiuificantes sunt fixe in corde et discurrunt mediantibus arteriis in quamlibet partem corporis, et acquirunt sibi uitam propriam et innatam. Illud idem ab Aristotile habetur in 16 *De Animalibus*, dicens quod cor apparet priusquam alia membra in actu, et uirtus spiritualis remanet ultimo in corde, et accidit omnibus membris mortificari priusquam cordi, ac si natura procederet uia circulari; sic ergo a uirtute spirituali in habentibus cor est uita. Cum ergo in uegetabilibus non sit cor nec spiritualis uirtus, uidetur quod non sit ab eodem causa uite in plantis et in animalibus. Quod uirtus spiritualis non sit in plantis patet per hoc quod dicit Aristotiles in principio secundi capituli *De Vegetabilibus*, dicens quod non habet planta spiritum, licet Anaxagoras dixerit eam habere, et si non habet spiritum, sequitur quod non sit in ea uirtus spiritualis: uirtus enim spiritualis dicitur quia est generans uel operans per spiritum.

Si propter hoc dicatur quod, quamuis in habentibus cor uita sit a uirtute spirituali tamquam a causa inmediata, tamen non est ab ipsa tamquam a causa prima, set ab eo a quo est uirtus ipsa spiritualis, uel cum queritur a qua parte anime procedit ista uirtus, si tu dicas quod ⟨ab⟩ anima uegetabili, et si hoc, tunc habetur propositum, scilicet quod ab eadem causa prima sit uita in animalibus et plantis.

Quod autem uirtus spiritualis non sit ab anima uegetabili, patet, cum non sit uirtus spiritualis in plantis, et tamen habent animam uegetabilem.

Item, uirtus spiritualis operatur motum cordis localem;[18] moueri autem localiter non est opus potencie uegetatiue: eius

---

18 localem: localis L.

understands about being a living thing in life, and not about the other source of nourishment.

[Another question] Again, someone might wonder whether there is the same cause of life in plants and animals?

And it seems that this is so because of what is said according to Aristotle that the vegetative power is the most evident power of the soul by which living is in all living things.[27] If, therefore, living is the vegetative power in plants and animals, it seems that the same power is the cause of life in these, as it is the vegetative power.

[1.] However, against this is that life is from the spiritual power in animals which have a heart, as is clear from what Al-Ghazālī says,[28] that the motive and life-giving powers are located in the heart and circulate by means of the arteries into every part of the body and acquire for themselves their own and inborn life. The same is held by Aristotle in the sixteenth book of *On Animals*,[29] saying that the heart appears in act before any other organ and that the spiritual power remains until the end in the heart, and it happens that all other organs die before the heart, as if nature proceeds in a circular way.[30] Therefore, it is the case that life in those who have a heart is from the spiritual power. Since, therefore, there is neither a heart nor a spiritual power in plants, it seems that the cause of life in plants and animals is not from the same thing. That the spiritual power is not in plants is clear from what Aristotle states at the beginning of the second chapter of *On Plants*,[31] saying that plants do not have spirit, even if Anaxagoras said that they had, and if they do not have spirit it follows that there is no spiritual power in them, for a power is said to be spiritual because it generates or operates by means of spirit.

[2.] If, because of this, it were said that even if life in those which have a heart is from the spiritual power as from an immediate cause, yet it is not from this as from a first cause but from that from which the spiritual power exists, or if it is asked from what part of the soul does this power proceed, if you were to say that it is from the vegetative soul, and if so, then we have what was proposed, namely, that life in animals and plants is from the same first cause.

[3.] However, that the spiritual power is not from the vegetative soul is clear since although there is no spiritual power in plants, they still have a vegetative soul.

[4.] Again, the spiritual power brings about the local motion of the heart. Self-movement locally is not the action of the vegetative power; for it consists in two

---

27 Ibid., II ii, 413b 1–2.
28 Algazel, *Metaphysica* II, 5.
29 Aristotle, *De generatione animalium* II vi, 741b 15 ff.
30 Ibid., II vi, 741b 22.
31 Nicholaus of Damascus, *De plantis* I ii.

enim sunt tantum duo opera, scilicet generare et alimento uti; moueri autem localiter non est aliquod istorum operum.

Item, cum uirtus spiritualis non insit nisi animali, est ergo uirtus spiritualis in animali in eo quod est animal, uel in eo quod est aliquod animal. Virtus ergo illa debetur anime que est actus animalis in | eo quod est animal; ergo erit illius partis sensitiue anime uel partis intellectiue; non intellectiue, quia inuenitur uirtus spiritualis ubi non est reperire partem intellectiuam anime; sic ergo uidetur quod uirtus spiritualis sit partis sensitiue.

Set contra: uirtus motiua, credo, non operatur nisi apprehensiua[19] precedente; cor autem mouetur sine apprehensione precedente, quod patet in apoplexia et in consimilibus egritudinibus.

Item, ab alia uirtute numero est determinacio finis motus qui fit a uirtute motiua sensitiua et exercetur ipse motus, sicut patet cum aliquis uult ire ad ecclesiam: uirtus ⟨con⟩cupiscibilis determinat finem motus qui est ad ecclesiam, et hoc est in corde; uirtus autem existens in musculis et neruis facit motum ad acquirendum finem illum. Inperium enim uirtutis inperantis nichil aliud est quam determinacio finis, sicut ostensum est alias. Istam autem diuersitatem in motu cordis non inuenimus: non enim contingit in corde inuenire unam uirtutem determinantem finem motus et aliam uirtutem facientem ipsum motum; et sic ista uirtus faciens motum in corde non est a uirtute sensitiue partis anime.

Solucio. Sicut uult Aristotiles in libro *De Animalibus*, in animalibus habentibus sanguinem, cor est principium et fundamentum uite. In aliis autem non habentibus sanguinem, ut in quibusdam animalibus et plantis, est aliquid proporcionale cordi, quod est in medio sicut cor in animali. Quare autem cor sit principium omnium uirtutum, patet per Aristotilem in eodem libro, ubi dicit quod cor est | principium consimilium membrorum, uidelicet omnium neruorum tam sensitiuorum quam motiuorum, et omnium uenarum. Vnde et instrumenta sensuum mediantibus neruis siue poris colliganciam habent cum corde, quamuis instrumenta quorundam sensuum col⟨l⟩igentur cum ipso mediantibus neruis siue poris transeuntibus per cerebrum; propter quod dicunt medici sensum habere

---

19 apprehensiua: apprehensione L.

FIRST CHAPTER – TEXT AND TRANSLATION   65

actions only, namely, to generate and to make use of food; self-movement locally is neither of these actions.

[5.] Again, since the spiritual power is only to be found in an animal, the spiritual power is in an animal insofar as it is an animal, or is in it insofar as it is a certain animal. Therefore, that power is due to the soul, which is the act of an animal insofar as it is an animal; therefore, it will be of that sensitive part of the soul or of the intellectual part. It is not of the intellectual part because the spiritual power is to be found where we do not come across the intellectual part of the soul; in this way, therefore, it can be seen that the spiritual power is of the sensitive part.

[Against] However, against this: the motive power, I hold, does not act without a preceding perceptive power; the heart, however, is moved without any prior perception as is clear in apoplexy and in similar ailments.

Again, the determination of the end of the motion which arises from the sensitive motive power and [that which] carries out this movement are from numerically distinct powers, as is clear when someone wants to go to the church: the concupiscible power determines the end of the movement which is to go to the church, and this is in the heart; but the power existing in the muscles and the nerves causes the movement which aims at that end. The direction of the power that directs is nothing other than the determining of the end, as has been shown elsewhere. [32] We do not find this diversity in the movement of the heart; for it does not happen that we find in the heart one power determining the end of the movement and another power making this movement; and thus this power which causes movement in the heart is not from the power of the sensitive part of the soul.

[Solution] The solution: as Aristotle says in the book *On Animals*, [33] the heart is the source and foundation of life in animals that have blood. However, in others that do not have blood, such as in some animals and in plants, there is something corresponding to the heart, which is in the middle just like the heart. Why it is that the heart is the source of all of the powers is clear from Aristotle in the same book, [34] where he says that the heart is the source of all of the organs similar to it, namely of all of the sensitive as well as the motor nerves, and of all of the veins. So it is that all of the instruments of the senses have a link to the heart by means of nerves or pores; even if some of the instruments of the senses have a link to the heart by means of nerves or pores which pass through the brain; for this reason the medical authorities say that sensation arises from the brain. Similarly, it is clear

---

32 See ibid., II, iv.

33 Aristotle, *De animalibus* XIII (*De partibus animalium* III, iv, 666a 6–8, 11–13). See also, *De generatione animalium* V, ii, 781a 21–23; *De somno et vigilia* ii, 456a 3–6.

34 *De partibus animalium* III, iv, 665b 15; *De generatione animalium* II vi, 742b 35–36.

ortum a cerebro. Similiter patet quod uirtus naturalis habet ortum a corde, eo quod uene, mediantibus quibus discurrit uirtus naturalis, ab ipso habent ortum, etsi per manifestacionem illa uirtus sit magis in epate. Eodem modo in hiis uiuentibus, que non habent sanguinem, ortum habent uirtutes ab hiis que sunt in hiis proporcionalia cordi.

Sciendum ergo quod in corde aut in eo quod est proporcionale cordi est calor naturalis originaliter, quo mediante uiuificatur quelibet pars ⟨in⟩ uiuentibus. Et propter hoc dicit Aristotiles quod cordi accidit tardius mors quam alicui alii membro et prius accidit ei uita, ac si natura circulariter esset operans, ut, sicut naturaliter incipit uita a corde, ita naturaliter terminetur in ipso. Et sic intelligendum de proporcionale cordi.

Sciendum ergo quod, quanto anima nobilior et perfectior, tanto indiget pluribus mediis et perfectioribus quibus uniatur cum corpore, et quanto est minus nobilis, tanto paucioribus; quia ergo uegetabilis anima est sicut terrena, non indiget pluribus mediis quibus uiuificet corpus, immo se ipsa unitur corpori et corpus uiuificat mediante calore naturali. Sunt enim duo opera eius, sicut dictum est, generare et alimento uti, que sufficienter possunt expleri mediante calore naturali. Plura enim sunt opera partis sensitiue ipsius anime et nobiliora, cum sit et uegetans et cognoscitiua et motiua secundum locum; et loquor de ipsa secundum quod est in animalibus perfectis. Vnde non sufficit ad hoc ut perficiat corpus et utatur ipso sicut organo quod sit medium solum calore naturali, set de necessitate exigitur spiritus mediante cuius claritate et illustracione perficiatur cognicio; et similiter mediante eius irradiacione uel irradiacionis resultacione perficiatur econtrario motus secundum locum. In animalibus autem inperfectis non est necessarium sic esse. In plantis tamen contingit eleuare complexionem alicuius habentis ortum a terre nascentibus in tantum quod in eo generatur spiritus et fit sensibile, ut | patet in auibus oriuntibus a quibusdam arboribus. Sicut[20] ergo anima sensibilis addit supra uegetabilem, ita et perfectioribus mediis indiget.

Viso ergo quare uirtus spiritualis non in⟨est⟩ uegetabilibus secundum ueritatem, nisi dicatur proporcionaliter, sicut dicitur in ipsis esse aliquid proporcionale cordi, respondendum est ad

---

20 arboribus. Sicut: arboribus, sicut L.

that the natural power arises from the heart because the veins by means of which the natural power circulates begin from the heart,[35] even if by the evidence that power would be, rather, in the liver. In the same way, in those living things that do not have blood, the powers arise from those things that correspond to the heart in them.

One should know, therefore, that in the heart (or in that which corresponds to the heart), lies the origin of natural heat, by means of which every part in a living thing is made alive. And because of this, Aristotle says[36] that death comes later to the heart than to any of the other organs and that life comes to it before [any other organ], as if nature were acting in a circular manner, so just as life naturally begins from the heart, so also it naturally ends in the heart. And the same should be understood with regard to that which corresponds to the heart.

Therefore, one should know that the more noble and perfect a soul, the more it requires many and more perfect means through which it is united to the body, and to the extent that it is less noble, the fewer the means required. Therefore, because the vegetative soul is like an earthy soul, it does not require many means by which it gives life to a body, rather it unites itself to the body and gives life to the body by means of natural heat. For there are two actions of the vegetative soul, as has been said, to generate and to make use of food that can sufficiently be carried out by means of natural heat. There are more actions of the sensitive part of the soul and more noble, since it is both vegetative and cognitive as well as locomotive; and I refer to that sensitive part inasmuch as is in the higher animals. Thus, in order that it completes the body and uses it as an organ, the medium of natural heat alone is not enough, but of necessity spirit is required by means of whose clarity and enlightenment cognition is completed; and similarly by means of its illumination or as a result of its illumination, locomotion is, on the other hand, completed. In the imperfect animals, however, it is not necessary for this to be the case. In plants, on the other hand, it happens that the constitution of some which have their origin from the earth is elevated, arising in such a way that spirit is produced in them and they become sensitive, as is clear in birds which arise from certain trees.[37] Therefore, just as the sensitive soul adds more to the vegetative soul, so it also requires more perfect means.

[Another question] Having seen, therefore, why that spiritual power is not truly in plants, unless this is said in a proportional manner, as when it is said that there is something in plants which corresponds to the heart, we have to reply to

---

35 Aristotle, *De respiratione* xx, 480a 11–12.

36 Aristotle, *De animalibus* XIV (*De generatione animalium* II vi, 742b 35–36); see also, *De iuventute et senectute* iii, 468b 28.

37 A reference, presumably, to the legend of the barnacle geese who were believed to begin life as shellfish before becoming birds.

id quod querebatur cuius partis anime sit ista uirtus spiritualis, utrum partis sensibilis uel uegetabilis uel intellectiue?

Dicendum secundum medicos quod ista diuisio non est sufficiens, immo dicunt quod ista uirtus non est alicuius partis anime, set anime secundum se. Vnde dicunt quod motus cordis et pulmonis non est a parte sensitiua anime nec ab intellectiua nec a uegetatiua, set tamen est animalis, quia ab anima.

Et propter hoc cessant omnes obiecciones que facte sunt, nisi[21] incideret questio difficilior quam facit Aueroys in capitulo de uirtute informatiua, ubi querit de obediencia spirituum ipsius anime in suis apprehensionibus. Mirum enim est quomodo res corporea mouetur statim propter affectum aliquem existentem in substancia incorporea, cum non apprehendant affectus generatos ex diuersis apprehensionibus.

Et istud sciendum quod non est in obediencia spirituum inmediate, set prouenit ex obediencia intelligentie mouentis cor diuersimode eo quod cognoscit diuersos affectus anime generatos ex diuersis apprehensionibus; cor[22] autem motum operatur ad motum spirituum. Et ex hoc accidit quod illi qui multum cogitant et habent uarios affectus, quod debilitatur uirtus digestiua in eis propter assuetudinem et uehemenciam motus spirituum; cum enim uehementer et frequenter mouentur spiritus per corpora, ex motu continuo et uehementi super|calefiunt, et supercalefacti dissoluunt poros corporis, et per dissolutos exeunt, et sic accidit debilitacionem fieri uirtutis digestiue in qualibet parte corporis. Et hac eadem causa accidit quod scolares magis incurrunt reuma quam aliqui alii, eo quod spiritus animales propter continuam cogitacionem continue mouentur in cerebro, et propter continuum motum supercalefiunt, et ita supercalefacti sunt causa dissolucionis et fluxus humorum. Ista ergo obediencia spirituum non debetur ipsis spiritibus inmediate, set intelligencie primo cognoscenti diuersos affectus anime in suis apprehensionibus, et per intelligentiam cordi et per cor ipsis spiritibus.

Quidam tamen philosophi attribuunt cordi per suas compressiones mouere spiritus, sicut cum folles comprimuntur, emittunt quod continetur in illis. Set hoc patet omnino esse

---

21 sunt, nisi: sunt. Nisi L.

22 apprehensionibus; cor: apprehensionibus, cor L.

that which was asked: which part of the soul does the spiritual power belong to, is it the sensitive part, or the vegetative, or the intellectual?

[Solution] It must be answered according to the medical authorities[38] that this division is not sufficient. In fact, they say that this power does not belong to any part of the soul, but to the soul as such. Thus, they say that the movement of the heart and lungs is not from the sensitive part of the soul, nor from the intellectual or vegetative parts, but rather it is proper to an animal because it is from the soul (*anima*).

And for this reason all objections which have been made cease, unless the more difficult problem arises which Ibn Rushd makes in the chapter on the informative power,[39] where he investigates the obedience of the vital energies[40] to the soul itself in its own perceptions. For it is extraordinary how a corporeal thing moves at once because of a certain desire existing in an incorporeal substance, since they [the vital energies] do not grasp the dispositions generated from the different perceptions.

And this should be known, that this characteristic not lie immediately in the obedience of the vital energies but it arises out of the obedience of the understanding which moves the heart in different ways because it knows the different dispositions of the soul which are generated from various apprehensions, the heart then moves to move the vital energies. Moreover, because of this it happens that those who think a lot, and have various affections, that their digestive power is weakened because of the habitual and violent movement of the vital energies. For when the vital energies are violently and frequently moved about the body by a continual and forceful motion, they become overheated from the continual and violent movement; and having become overheated they destroy the pores of the body; and they escape through the destroyed pores. In this way it happens that a weakening of the digestive power can occur in any part of the body and for the same reason, it happens that scholars are more likely to suffer from rheum than any others because the animal energies are continually being moved in the brain because of the constant thinking. Again, because of the continual movement the animal energies become overheated, and being overheated in this way they are the cause of the destruction and flux of the humors. Therefore, this obedience of the vital energies is not immediately due to the vital energies themselves but to the understanding, which first knows the different affections of the soul in its perceptions, and through the understanding to the heart and by the heart to the vital energies themselves.

However, some philosophers state that it is the heart which is responsible for the movement of the vital energies by means of its compressions, just as when a bellows is compressed it emits what is contained in it. However, it is clear that this

---

38 See Costa ben Lucca, *De differentia spiritus et animae* II, 130; III, 137; Haly Abbas, *Pantechne* IV, c. xix.

39 See Nicholaus Peripateticus (Ps. Averroes), *Quaestiones* VI, 130, l. 4 ff.

40 The term "spiritus" is used to indicate the imperceptible communicators of information from the sense organs to the brain and the communication of movement from the brain to the limbs. It presumably corresponds to what we now call nerve impulses.

falsum; set quia illi qui habent cor naturaliter depressum, naturaliter sunt discolorati. Set constat quod, si ⟨per⟩ compressionem cordis transmitterentur spiritus ad exteriora corporis, naturaliter omnes habentes cor depressum essent bene colorati, cuius oppositum uidemus. Item, uidemus quod illi, qui habent cor naturaliter depressum, habent pulsum paruum, curtum et profundum. Item, per experienciam possumus uidere quod dicunt falsum: si enim ponat aliquis manum super cor et alteram super arteriam, simul inueniet depressionem cordis et arterie, et eleuacionem. Istud patet similiter per uerbum Haly in commento *Super Tegni*, dicentis quod corde delatato, delatantur et omnes arterie, et ipso compresso comprimuntur. Ex hiis patet quia per dilatacionem cordis mandatur spiritus per arteriam ad uiuificandum quamlibet corporis partem, et per compressionem reuertuntur ad cor. Et hoc est quod dicit Rasis testante Auensoreth[23] | quod homo tardus ad motum hebetis ingenii est. Motus enim fit ex distensione neruorum facta ex spiritibus transmissis ad ipsos a corde. Vnde, cum spiritus sint cordi ad distendendum neruos, significatur quod cor sit tardum in suis motibus secundum diastolem et sistolem, et tarditas motus significat supertarditatem anime in suis inquisicionibus. Et significacio horum est duricies arterie. Dura enim arteria caret humiditate que habilitat ad motum. Vnde per contrarium mollis arteria cum lato pulsu significat superflexibilitatem cordis in omne genus motus secundum diastolem et sistolem. Humiditas enim est ductilis in omnem formam; flexibilitas autem cordis in omnem motum significat flexibilitatem anime in uarios affectus et multimodos, et ex hoc significatur quod mulieres habentes arterias molles et pulsus latos sunt flexibiles ad luxuriam.

Ex hiis patet quomodo quedam solum mediante calore naturali uiuunt, sicut illa de quibus dicit Aristotiles quod ⟨non⟩ habent animam perfectam, set partem partis anime sicut uege-

---

23 Auensoreth: Almansoris L.

is completely false because those who have a heart which is naturally depressed, are naturally pale. Yet it is evident that if the compression of the heart were to send the vital energies to the outer parts of the body,[41] then all those who have a naturally depressed heart would have a good colour, but we see the opposite. Again, we see that those people, who have a naturally depressed heart, have a deficient, short and deep pulse. Again, we can see by experience that what they say is false: for if one places one hand on the heart and the other on the artery, we will find the depression and elevation of the heart and the artery at the same time. Similarly, this is clear from what Ali ibn al-'Abbas writes in his commentary on [Galen's] *Art of Medicine*[42] where he says that when the heart dilates the arteries too are dilated, and when the heart is compressed, they are as well. From what has been said, it is clear in what way the vital energies are sent out by means of the dilation of the heart through the artery to give life to every part of the body, and by means of compression they return to the heart. And this is what al-Rāzī, quoting Ibn Zur'a,[43] states:[44] a man who is slow with regard to movement is dull-witted. For movement occurs through the distention of the nerves and which happens because of the vital energies that are transmitted to them from the heart. Thus, since the vital energies are in the heart in order to distend the nerves, this means that the heart is slow in its movements in respect of diastole and systole, and slowness of motion is a sign of a greater slowness of the soul in its investigations. And what this points to is a hardness of the artery, for a hard artery is lacking in the moisture that aids movement. Thus, on the contrary, a soft artery with a full pulse points to a greater flexibility of the heart in every kind of movement according to diastole and systole. For the humidity is malleable in every kind of form, and the flexibility of the heart towards all movements indicates a flexibility of the soul in various affections and in many ways, and from this it means that women who have soft arteries and full pulses are easily inclined towards lust.[45]

From the above, it is clear how some live by means of natural heat alone such as those of whom Aristotle says[46] that they do not have a complete soul but a part of

---

41 See Nicholaus Peripateticus (Ps. Averroes), *Quaestiones* VI, 131, l. 20–24.

42 See Nicholaus Peripateticus, *Quaestiones* VI, 131, l. 20–24; Haly Abbas, *Pantechne* IV, c. v.

43 Abū 'Alī 'Īsā Ibn Zur'a Ibn Yuhannā (943–1008), latinized as Avenzoreth, was born in Baghdad and belonged to a Syrian Orthodox Christian family. He was a physician and a philosopher, a student of Yahadi ibn Adi (893–974). According to Starr (2006), Ibn Zur'a was best known to later Arabic philosophers as a translator from Syriac to Arabic. His translation of the *Sophistici elenchi* was used by Avicenna and Averroes may have used his translation of the *Compendia* of Nicholaus of Damascenus. Part of a lost commentary by John Philoponus on Galen's *On the Uses of the Parts of the Body* appears to survive in the translation made by Ibn Zar'a. See also, Haddad (1971).

44 See Nicholaus Peripateticus (Ps. Averroes), *Quaestiones* VI, 132, l. 11–12; *Liber Almansoris* II, 170.

45 See Nicholaus Peripateticus (Ps. Averroes) (1973) *Quaestiones* VI, 133, l. 1–2.

46 Ps. Aristotle (Nicholaus Damascenus) (1989), *De plantis* I, ii, 524, l. 52.

tabilia; quedam autem non solum uiuificantur ab anima mediante calore naturali, set mediante spiritu, sicut animalia; et quod non equiuoce dicantur habere uitam sensibilia et uegetabilia: magis enim et minus non faciunt equiuocacionem, nec occultum, nec manifestum.

a part of the soul, such as plants. Some, however, are not only made alive by the soul through natural heat but also through spirit, such as the animals. It is also clear that sensitive and vegetative beings cannot be said to have life in an equivocal manner: for they do not make an equivocation, neither to a greater or lesser extent, neither hidden, nor open.

86 ⟨Lectio 2⟩

[464b 26] Amplius autem, utrum eadem sunt que longe uite et que secundum naturam sana sunt eorum autem que[1] secundum naturam subsistunt sana aut diuisa sint esse longe uite et esse sanum et que sunt breuis uite aut egrotantia aut que secundum quasdam egritudines immutantur egrotantia naturam corpora breui uite, secundum [30] quosdam nichil prohibet et egrotantem esse longe uite. De somno autem et uigilia dictum est prius; sed etiam de egritudine et sanitate in quantum confert philosophie. Nunc [465a 1] autem circa causas hec quidem longe uite, illa uero breuis, [2] sicut dictum est prius, speculandum.

Amplius autem, utrum sint eadem que sunt longe ⟨uite⟩ et que secundum naturam sana, et cetera [i, 464b 26–27]. Hic incipit secunda pars huius partis prohemialis.

Que diuiditur in duas partes, sicut dictum est, secundum duplex opus sapientis: primo remouet mendacium et consequenter ostendit ueritatem. Et prius est exstirpare uicium quam inferre[2] uirtutem.

Dicit ergo quod *amplius* oportet considerare *utrum sunt eadem que sunt longe uite et ea que* [sunt] *secundum naturam sana sunt eorum*, id est de numero eorum, *que secundum naturam subsistunt* [i, 464b 27], et hoc est prima pars questionis; et incipit secunda pars ibi: *Aut diuisa* ⟨...⟩ *que sunt breuis uite aut egrotancia*, et cetera [i, 464b 27–28]. Et est sentencia Aristotilis talis: utrum eadem sunt que sunt breuis uite et egrotancia. Est ergo questio talis: utrum conuertibilia sint esse sana et esse longe uite, et esse egra et esse breuis uite. Et incipit soluere istam questionem ibi: *Aut secundum quasdam egritudines*, et cetera [i, 464b 28], id est, solucio. Dicit ergo quod egrotancia corpora secundum naturam *secundum quasdam egritudines inmutantur breui uita* [i, 464b 28–29], id est secundum quasdam egritudines egrotantia fiu⟨n⟩t breuis uite, *secundum* autem *quasdam nichil prohibet egrotancia esse longe uite* [i, 464b 29–30]. Et quia aliquis posset dubitare quod, cum eius intencio sit hic

1 sana sunt eorum autem que: sunt sana. Eorum autem L.
2 inferre: inferri L.

Second Lecture

Text (464b 26–465a 2)

Furthermore, are they the same that are long-lived and those that are healthy according to nature, indeed of those who according to nature subsist as healthy, or are they different to those who are long-lived and healthy and those who are short-lived or diseased, or those diseased bodies which according to some illnesses change nature to be short-lived, and regarding others there is nothing to prevent those who are diseased also to be long-lived. Sleep and waking have already been spoken about; and also regarding illness and health inasmuch as these relate to philosophy. Now, however, as we have already mentioned, we will investigate the causes of some being long-lived while others are short-lived.

Furthermore, are they the same that are long-lived and those that are healthy according to nature, etc. Here begins the second part of this introductory part.

This is divided into two parts, as was said above, according to the two-fold task of the wise man: firstly he removes falsehood and then he shows the truth.[1] Again, one should first eradicate vices before introducing virtue.

Literal Explanation of the Text

Therefore, Aristotle says that *furthermore* it is necessary to consider *are they the same that are long-lived and those that are healthy according to nature, of those,* that is the number of those, *who according to nature subsist.* And this is the first part of the investigation. And the second part begins there: *Or are they different who are short-lived or diseased,* etc. And the thought of Aristotle is the following: are they the same that are short-lived and diseased? Therefore, the problem is this: are being healthy and long-lived, and being sick and short-lived, interchangeable? And Aristotle begins to solve this problem here: *Or according to some illnesses,* etc., that is, the solution. Therefore, he says that bodies that are diseased according to nature *are changed to a short life by some illnesses,* that is, according to some illnesses become short-lived, however, *regarding others there is nothing to prevent those who are diseased also to be long-lived.* And since someone might wonder, given that Aristotle's intention here is to explain a certain property which accompanies the soul

---

1 See Aristotle, *De sophisticis elenchis*, 165a 24–27.

determinare de quadam passione que concomitat animam in
corpore quod | similiter esset eius intencio ⟨determinare de
omnibus passionibus que concomitant animam in corpore⟩,
dicit quod non, quia *de sompno et uigilia dictum est alibi, et eciam
de egritudine et sanitate, in quantum confert physice* et *philosophie.*
Set *nunc* est intencio *circa causas* propter quas *hec quidem* dicun-
tur *esse longe uite, alia uero breuis* [i, 464b 31–465a 1]; et hoc est
quod determinat usque ad illum locum: *Preter autem et hanc
habencia,* et cetera [i, 465a 2].

⟨Questiones⟩
⟨1⟩

Primo dubitatur hic de hoc quod ipse supponit quod alica
secundum naturam sunt sana [i, 464b 26–27].

Et uidetur quod sic, per auctoritatem Constantini dicentis
quod sanitas naturaliter ⟨in⟩est animali, et ita sequitur quod
sanitas sit disposicio secundum naturam.

Set hic contra hoc obicitur communiter quia ⟨si⟩ sanitas
insit animali naturaliter, cum sanitas et egritudo sint contrarie,
non contingeret in alterutrum permutacionem ⟨fieri⟩, sicut
habetur in *Predicamentis* quod si alica si⟨n⟩t contraria, contingit
in alterutrum permutacionem fieri, nisi alterum insit naturaliter; tunc enim tantum alterum et non alterutrum contingit inesse. Sic ergo si sanitas inesset naturaliter uel secundum naturam,
non contingeret egritudinem inesse.

Istud patet per Aristotilem ibidem: si omnia animalia essent
sana, non essent egritudo; set si sanitas insit naturaliter omni
animali non esset egritudo aut duo contraria inessent eidem.

Quod autem non sint alica sana secundum naturam, uidetur
per Aristotilem in 5 *Physicorum* ubi inquirit utrum eadem sit
sanitas | que acquiritur post egritudinem cum illa que erat ante,
et utrum eadem sanitas maneat in corpore mane et sero, et
ostendit Aristotiles quod non. Cum enim corpora sint in continuo fluxu et in continua deperdicione, tunc cum corporibus
motis moueantur omnia que sunt in ipsis secundum fluxum et
uariacionem corporum, necesse est quod uarientur disposicio-
nes et habitus eorum, et ita non est necesse penitus eandem
esse sanitatem mane et sero, sicut non remanet idem corpus

in the body, that it would also be his intention to explain all of the properties which accompany the soul in the body. Aristotle says it is not his intention, because *sleep and waking have been spoken about; and also regarding illness and health inasmuch as these relate to natural science and philosophy*. However, *now*, the intention is *regarding those causes* on account of which *these* are said *to be long-lived, while others are short-lived*. And this is what Aristotle explains down to this point: *Besides, however, and those having this*, etc.

Question One

Here, first of all, one could raise a doubt concerning what Aristotle presupposes, that some *are healthy according to nature*.

And this seems to be the case, according to the authority of Constantine [the African], who says that health is naturally in an animal. Thus, it follows that health is a natural disposition.

[An Objection] However, here it is commonly objected against this: if health were to be naturally in an animal that because health and sickness are contraries, it would not happen that one would change into the other, as is held in the *Categories*,[2] that if some things are contraries, it happens that one changes into the other, unless one of them inheres naturally; for then it happens that only one and not the other is present. So, therefore, if health were present naturally or according to nature, it would not happen that illness would be present.

This is clear from what Aristotle says in the same book:[3] if all animals were healthy, there would not be sickness; but if health were to be naturally in every animal there would not be sickness, otherwise there would be two contraries in the one thing.

[2.] However, it seems that there are some which are not healthy by nature, according to what Aristotle says in the fifth book of the *Physics*,[4] where he investigates whether the health which is gained after sickness is the same as that which was before, and whether it is the same health which stays in a body morning and evening. And Aristotle shows that this is not so. For since bodies are in continual flux and in continual loss, then given that when bodies are moved everything which is in them is moved too by the flux and change of the body, it is necessary that their dispositions and habits are changed as well. And thus it is not necessary for the same health to be present within in both the morning and evening, just as the body does not remain the same within. Aristotle proves this by means of a

---

2 Aristotle, *Praedicamenta* x, 13a 19–20.
3 Aristotle, *Praedicamenta* xi, 14a 8–9.
4 See Aristotle, *Physica* V, iv, 228a 7–20.

penitus. —Istud ostendit per inconueniens manifestum: si ita esset quod remaneret una et eadem disposicio in mane et in sero, quamuis sint in continuo fluxu, tunc ergo, si ex toto deficiat sanitas et iterum accipiat corpus sanitatem, quare non acciperet illam eandem quam habebat prius? Set si accipiat illam eandem quam habebat prius, sequeretur quod unius disposicionis numero essent diuerse generaciones numero, quod est contra Aristotilem in 7 *Topicorum*, ubi dicit quod quarum generaciones sunt eedem, et ipsa sunt eadem; ergo quarum generaciones sunt diuerse, et ipsa sunt diuersa. Si ergo per eandem inmutacionem numero non procedent in esse sanitas que est post egritudinem et illa que est ante, non erit eadem ista sanitas et illa. Quod autem sint diuerse mutaciones, patet, quia tria exiguntur ad hoc ut sit unus motus numero, scilicet quod sit unum mobile numero et quod sit una species numero ⟨et unum tempus numero⟩. Vnde si non sit unum tempus necessario non erit unus motus. Non est autem unum tempus nisi sit continuum. Cum igitur sic sanitas non habeat permanenciam set sit in continua subcessione quemadmodum et tempus, non potest dici uere quod alica sint sana secundum naturam.

Istud confirmat Galenus in *Tegni*, ubi dicit quod omnibus hiis sensu diiudicatis et secundum naturam rerum; periculum enim esset | sempiterne passionis inreppere dogma; quasi diceret: etsi alica dicantur sana, hoc non est nisi secundum iudicium sensus; set secundum iudicium intellectus omnia inueniuntur egra. Istud probat Aristotiles in secundo *Celi et Mundi*, dicens quod mollificacio omnis et debilitas existens in animalibus est accidens preter naturam; et istud est propter generacionem animalium que componuntur ex contrariis quorum sunt diuersa loca; in animalibus enim non inuenitur alica pars que sit in proprio loco, et ex hoc accidit festinacio mortis. Vnde duas causas tangit ibi, unam secundum mutuam accionem et passionem contrariorum ex quibus generatur uiuens; aliam causam

clear inconsistency: if it were so that one and the same disposition remained in the morning and in the evening, even though they are in continual flux, then therefore, if health were completely absent and the body gained health again, why would it not gain the same health that it had previously?[5] However, if it gained that same health which it had previously, it would follow that there would be various numerically distinct productions of one numerically distinct disposition, which is against Aristotle in the seventh book of the *Topics*,[6] where he says that those whose productions are the same are also the same. Therefore, those whose productions are diverse are also not the same. If, therefore, by the same numerically distinct change the same health does not come to be after sickness as that which is there previously, then the former health and the latter will not be the same. However, that there are diverse changes is clear since three things are required so that there will be one numerically distinct movement, namely, that there be one numerically distinct thing which is moved, and one numerically distinct species, and one numerically distinct time.[7] Thus, if there is not one time, of necessity there will not be one movement. However, there is only one time if it is a continuum. Since, therefore, health does not have permanency in this fashion but is in continual succession just like time, it cannot be said truly that there are some who are healthy by nature.

[3.] Galen confirms this in the *Art [of Medicine]*[8] where he says that when all these cases have been decided by sensation and by the nature of things then there is the danger that the conviction of an enduring attribute could creep in; almost as if he said: even if some are said to be healthy, this is only according to the judgement of sensation, yet according to the judgment of the intellect all are found to be sick. Aristotle proves this in the second book of *On the Heavens*,[9] saying that all weakness and infirmity existing in an animal is an accident aside from nature, and this is because of the production of animals who are made up of contraries which belong to different regions. For no part is to be found in an animal which is in its proper region and as a result of this the hastening of death occurs. Thus, Aristotle touches upon two causes here: the first according to the mutual acting and being acted upon of the contraries from which a living thing is produced; he refers to the

---

5 Ibid., 228a 10–13.
6 Aristotle, *Topica* VII i, 152a 1–3.
7 See Aristotle, *Physica* V iv, 228b 1–2.
8 Galenus, *Tegni* III, 74.
9 See Aristotle, *De caelo* II vi, 288b 12 ff.

tangit propter hoc quod dicit quod nulla pars animalis est in suo proprio ubi, ⟨set naturaliter mouetur⟩ ad ipsum. Patet ergo quod nullum animal naturaliter est sanum.

Quod est concedendum.

Et respondendum ad auctoritatem Constantini dicentis quod sanitas est disposicio inherens animali secundum naturam, dicendum quod non sequitur quod, si aliquid insit secundum naturam, quod insit naturaliter. Quod patet per Aristotilem in principio secundi *Physicorum* ubi distinguit inter id quod est natura et id quod est naturale et id quod est secundum naturam, dicens quod natura est principium motus et status, et cetera; naturale quod habet in se naturam; secundum naturam proprie dicitur esse quod non est natura nec habet in se naturam, est tamen ex intencione nature, ut operacio que inest rei naturali per naturam, sicut igni ferri sursum. Hoc enim nec est natura nec habet in se naturam, inest tamen secundum | naturam, non tamen naturaliter, sicut patet per Auicennam super eundem librum dicentem quod id quod naturaliter inest alicui secundum naturam inest et non potest non esse, ut igni calefieri. Aliquid ergo inest secundum naturam, et illud potest non inesse secundum naturam. Sic ergo dicendum de sanitate quod inest secundum naturam, non tamen sic[ut] quod insit naturaliter.

Ex hoc patet solucio ad illud quod dicitur in *Predicamentis* quod si unum contrariorum naturaliter insit, reliquum non contingit inesse eidem: illud est uerum, set falsum est sanitatem naturaliter inesse, nec inplicat Aristotiles ipsam inesse naturaliter per hoc quod dicit: *quedam secundum naturam esse sana.*

Ad hoc ⟨quod⟩ obiciebatur de uerbo Aristotilis in 5 *Physicorum*, dicendum, sicut uult ibidem, quod sanitas dicatur dupliciter, scilicet secundum actum et secundum habitum; nichil autem inpedit unum habitum numero esse multos actus nume-

second cause[10] inasmuch as he says that no part of an animal is in its proper region, but is naturally moved towards it.[11]

[Conclusion] Therefore, it is clear that no animal is naturally healthy; which one must concede.

[Responses]

[1.] And in response to the authority of Constantine, who says that health is a disposition naturally inhering in an animal according to nature, it must be said that it does not follow that if anything inheres according to nature, that it inheres naturally. This is clear from what Aristotle states at the beginning of the second book of the *Physics*[12] where he distinguishes between that which is natural and that which is according to nature, saying that "nature" is the principle of movement and rest, etc.; "natural" what has a nature in itself; "according to nature" strictly speaking is neither "nature", nor has a nature in itself, but is from the intention of nature, as an activity which is in a natural thing by nature, such as fire to be carried upwards. For this is neither nature nor does it have a nature in itself, rather it is in it according to nature but not naturally, as is clear from Ibn Sīnā[13] on the same book who says that that which is naturally in something according to nature is in it and cannot not be, such as fire makes heat. Therefore, something is in it according to nature, and cannot not be in it according to nature. Therefore, one should say the same regarding health, which is present according to nature; it is not, however, because of this that health is present naturally.

[2.] From this the solution is clear to that which was said in the *Categories*,[14] that if one of the contraries is naturally present, then the remaining one should not be present in the same thing, that is true, but it is false that health is naturally present, nor does Aristotle imply that health is naturally present because of what he says that "some according to nature are healthy".

[3.] With regard to that which was objected concerning what Aristotle says in the fifth book of the *Physics*,[15] it should be said, as Aristotle himself says there, that health is said in two ways,[16] namely, according to act and according to habit; for

---

10 See ibid., II vi, 288b 18–19; and below, Lecture 4, question 1.

11 The Aristotelian doctrine that each of the elements has their own natural place and a natural tendency to move towards this place, for example, earth has a tendency to move downwards and fire upwards. An element can only be out of its natural place if held there by some kind of violence which can be felt if an earthy object is lifted up high or something filled with air is held under water. A composite material body is made up of different elements which naturally tend to disaggregate and so every material body is naturally unstable.

12 Aristotle, *Physica* II I, 192b 21–22; 34–193a 1.

13 Avicenna, *Sufficentia* I vii, f. 17va.

14 Aristotle, *Praedicamenta* xi, 14a 8–9.

15 See Aristotle, *Physica* V vi, 228a 7–20.

16 Ibid., 228a 13–16.

ro, set non est necesse quod unus actus numero sit unus habitus numero; dicendum ergo quod non est eadem sanitas penitus secundum actum illa que est mane et sero, set tamen unus est habitus. Vnde multe sanitates secundum actum consti(t)uunt unum habitum. Vnde etsi sanitas secundum actum non sit manens set successiua, quemadmodum et tempus, non tamen sanitas que est habitus est successiua, set permanens.

Ad aliud quod querebatur, utrum eadem sit sanitas que est post egritudinem et ea que est ante, potest dici quod eadem est habitualiter. Inpossibile est enim ex toto sanitas[3] separari a corpore, manente uita: set cum ex toto destrueretur, separetur sanitas in qualibet parte corporis secundum actum et habitum, sequeretur de necessitate mors, eo quod nichil esset in corpore per quod posset fieri reductio iterum in sanitatem. Subiacent ergo alique particule disposicioni | sanitatis in omni egritudine; aliqua[4] pars conualescit per quam disposicionem sanam existentem habitualiter fit reuersio ab egritudine secundum actum dominantem ad sanitatem secundum actum. Vnde, sicut malum non potest esse ex toto inpermistum bono, set econtrario bonum[5] contingit, sic egritudo numquam posset esse ex toto inpermista sanitati, nec similiter econtrario in istis mortalibus. Vnde non est ex toto simile de bono et malo et sano et egro.

Set contra hoc potest obici de hoc quod dicunt auctores medicine quod in corpore senis non est alica particula quin malefiat, et ita cum malefaccio sit egritudo, innuitur inpermista sanitati. Istud potest intelligi dupliciter: si enim hoc uerbum "malefiat" significat id quod significat infieri,[6] sic uerum; si autem infactum[7] esse, sic falsum.

Si quis dubitabit utrum senectus sit egritudo, id potest ostendi per diffinicionem egritudinis que potest haberi racione opposicionis per diffinicionem sanitatis: qui enim bene diffinit, contraria significat, ut habetur in *Topicis*; cum ergo sanitas sit commensuracio calidorum, frigidorum, siccorum et humidorum ad intra, uel ad continens ad intra, id est ad principium intra quod est natura, principium dico operacionum membrorum consimilium mediante complexione; ad continens, id est ad animam que est principium operacionum membrorum orga-

---

3 sanitas: sanitatem L.
4 egritudine; aliqua: egritudine aliqua L.
5 bonum: bene L.
6 infieri: in fieri L.
7 infactum: in factum L.

there is nothing to stop one numerically distinct habit from being many numerically distinct acts. However, it is not necessary that one numerically distinct act is one numerically distinct habit. Therefore, it should be said that according to act there is not the same health internally which is in the morning and the evening, yet however it is one habitus. Thus, many instances of health according to act constitute one habitus.[17] Thus, even if health according to act is not permanent but successive, just like time, yet health which is a habitus is not successive but permanent.

[4.] As regards what was also queried, whether the health, which is after sickness and that, which is before sickness is the same, it can be said that it is the same in a habitual manner. For it is impossible for health to be completely separated from a body while life remains, but when it is completely destroyed then health is separated from every part of the body according to act and habit, and death occurs of necessity, because there would be nothing in the body through which a restoration of health could occur again. Therefore, some small parts of health underlie the disposition in every sickness; some part recovers, through this healthy disposition (existing in a habitual manner) comes about the turning away from sickness (according to predominant act), to health according to act. Thus, just like evil cannot completely exist without being intermixed with the good, but on the contrary it is good that this happens, so sickness can never exist completely without being intermixed with health, nor similarly the other way round in these mortals. Thus, it is not completely the same regarding good and evil, and health and sickness.

[A Further Objection] However, against this it can be objected regarding that which the medical authorities state that in the body of an old man there is no particle which does not become ill, and thus since illness is sickness, it means that it is intermixed with health. This can be understood in two ways: for if this word "to become ill" means that which "becoming" means, then it is true; if, however, it means "to have become", then it is false.

If someone were to doubt whether old age is a sickness, that can be shown by means of the definition of sickness which can be obtained by reason of opposition through the definition of health: for the one who defines well, indicates the contraries, as is held in the *Topics*.[18] Since, therefore, health is a reciprocal internal proportion of hot, cold, dry and moist things, either in respect of the environment or internally, that is in respect of the internal principle which is nature; "principle", I say, of the activities of the simple organs by means of the bodily constitution; "in respect of the environment", that is with regard to the soul which is the principle

---

17 A habitus is an acquired disposition.
18 Aristotle, *Topica* VI ii, 140a 18–19.

nicorum mediante complexione. Si igitur senectus sit in commensuracione calidorum, frigidorum, siccorum et humidorum, quod patet per id quod dicit auctor *Topicorum* quod senectus est frigida et sicca, non tamen in fine frigiditatis et siccitatis quia, si sic, nichil aliud esset quam mors, sicut innuit Aristotiles consequenter[8] ex quo patet quod senectus est egritudo.

Quod patet iterum per Aristotilem in libro *De Animalibus* dicentem quod rectus sermo est qui dicit quod senectus est egritudo naturalis et quod egritudo est senectus accidentalis. Ex quo patet quod omnis egritudo uia est ad mortem et festinat eius introduccionem; non tamen propter hoc sequitur quod onmia egrotancia secun|dum naturam sunt illa que ⟨sunt⟩ talia ex primis generantibus, sicut patet in hiis que generantur ex leprosis et in aliis egritudinibus hereditariis.

⟨Questio 2⟩

Consequenter dubitatur, cum *iiii sint coniugaciones*, sicut habetur in principio *De Sensu et Sensato*, scilicet *mors et uita, sompnus et uigilia, iuuentus et senectus, respiracio et inspiracio*, propter quod in principio huius libri facit mencionem de sompno et uigilia et non de aliis duobus que sunt coniuga mortis et uite?

Ad quod dicendum quod, sicut habetur in libro *De Animalibus*, sompnus sequetur animal conceptum; et hoc ostendit, quia mutacio que habet fieri ex non esse ad esse simpliciter debet fieri per medium. Vnde inter uiuere et non uiuere medium est sompnus. Et hoc iterum ostendit, quia non potest dici quod dormiens simpliciter sit non uiuens neque potest dici quod sit uiuens, quemadmodum et uigilans: uigilia enim non accidit nisi cum sensu, est ergo uigilia sicut uita manifesta, sompnus autem non est simpliciter uita nec simpliciter mors, set medium participans naturas utriusque; et propter hoc istam conuenienciam sompni et uigilie cum morte et uita facit mencionem de somp-

---

8 Aristotiles consequenter: Aristotiles, consequenter L.

of the activities of the composite organs by means of the bodily constitution.[19] If, therefore, old age is commensurate with hot, cold, dry and humid things, which is clear from what the author of the *Topics* says, that old age is cold and dry, but not the uttermost of coldness and dryness because if that were the case it would be nothing other than death, as Aristotle suggests later on, from which it is clear that old age is sickness.

This is again clear from Aristotle in the book *On Animals*,[20] where he states that the one who says that old age is a natural sickness and that sickness is accidental old age speaks correctly. From this it is clear that all sickness is a way towards death and hastens its introduction. However, it does not follow because of this that all sicknesses which are according to nature are like those which result from the parents, as is clear in those who are born from lepers and in other hereditary illnesses.

Question Two

Next, the question arises, since *there are 4 groups*, as is held in the beginning of *On Sensation and What is Sensed*,[21] namely, *life and death, sleep and waking, youth and old age, respiration and inspiration*, why at the beginning of this book does Aristotle mention sleep and waking and not the other two which are linked with death and life?

[Response] To which it should be answered that, as is held in the book *On Animals*,[22] sleep follows upon the conception of an animal. And Aristotle shows that this is the case since a change, which takes place from non-being to being directly, has to occur through an intermediate, and the intermediate between living and non-living is sleep.[23] And Aristotle demonstrates this once more since it cannot be said that sleeping as such is non-living nor can it be said that it is living in the same way that waking can.[24] For waking can only occur with sensation[25] and so, therefore, waking is like a manifestation of life. Sleep, however, is neither life as such nor death as such but an intermediate that shares in the nature of both. And

---

19 The distinction between simple organs (also called consimilar or homoiomerous) and composite or organic members, goes back to Aristotle in *De partibus animalium* II, i, and was taken up, notably, by Galen. Simple parts of the body are homogenous ("simple") in composition, e.g., flesh, bones, sinews, nerves, veins, etc. Organic parts are heterogeneous ("composite"), being composed of homoiomerous parts and function as instruments (organs), e.g., the brain, heart, eye and hand, etc.

20 Aristotle, *De generatione animalium* V iv, 784b 32–35.

21 Aristotle, *De sensu et sensato* i, 436a 13–15.

22 Aristotle, *De generatione animalium* V i, 778b 27.

23 Ibid., 778b 27–30

24 Ibid., 778b 30.

25 See ibid., 778b 31–32.

no et uigilia ⟨pocius⟩ quam de aliis duabus passionibus. Iuuentus enim et senectus determinantur solum contra uitam et non conueniunt in essencia cum morte; similiter patet de inspiracione et respiracione.

Set contra uerbum Aristotilis obicit aliquis: si sompnus sit medium inter uiuere et non uiuere, sequitur unum duorum inconueniencium, scilicet aut quod plante non uiuunt aut si uiuunt, cum sompnus sit medium inter uiuere et non uiuere, sequitur quod sompnus insit eis.

Et uidetur quod plantis debeat inesse sompnus, quia dicit Aristotiles in principio libri *De Sompno et Vigilia* quod quorumcumque est aliquod corpus secundum naturam, si modum excedant, necesse est ipsa languescere; ad hoc ergo quod non languescant necesse est illa quiescere; cum ergo uirtutis naturalis existentis in plantis sit opus secundum naturam, ad hoc quod non languescant, necesse est quod quiescant. Huiusmodi quies si esset, non esset nisi sompnus. Item, cum in animalibus uirtus animalis operetur mediantibus secundariis qualitatibus que non habent contrarietatem nisi per primas: uirtus autem naturalis que est communis animalibus et plantis operatur mediantibus primis qualitatibus quarum per se est contrarietas; magis ergo deberet fatigari uirtus naturalis in suis operacionibus quam aliis; uirtus enim secundum se non debilitatur, set ei accidit debilitacio propter dissolucionem sui instrumenti. Quod patet per Aristotilem in principio *De Anima* dicentem quod, si senex acciperet oculum iuuenis, adeo uideret ut iuuenis: unde dicit quod non fit senium in substinendo aliquid anima. Et ita, si uirtus naturalis operetur mediantibus qualitatibus que per se habent contrarietatem, magis indigebit quiete quam illa que operatur mediantibus secundariis.

Solucio. Ad primum dicendum quod sompnus est medium inter uiuere et non uiuere, secundum quoddam uiuere simpliciter et manifestum; unde, cum non sit uita in plantis manifesta, non est sompnus medium inter uiuere quod est in plantis et non uiuere, set inter uiuere quod est in animalibus et non uiuere est medium.

Ad hoc quod querebatur, utrum sompnus possit esse quies uirtutis naturalis sicut et animalis, dicendum quod non, quia uirtus naturalis est ad restaurandum id quod continue deperdi-

because of this similarity of sleep and waking with life and death, Aristotle mentions sleep and waking more than the other two attributes. Again, youth and old age are understood only in relation to life and are not similar in their essence with death; the same is clear with regard to inspiration and respiration.

[An Objection] However, someone might object to what Aristotle says: if sleep is an intermediate between living and non-living, one of two inconsistencies must follow, namely, either that plants do not live or if they do, since sleep is an intermediary between living and non-living, it follows that sleep is to be found in them.

[1.] And it seems that there must be sleep in plants because Aristotle says at the beginning of the book *On Sleep and Waking* that if all those parts which belong to a body exceed their natural limits then they must become exhausted.[26] Since, therefore, the natural power existing in plants belongs to a natural activity, in order for them not to become exhausted they must rest, and this kind of rest, if it exists, would be nothing other than sleep.

[2.] Again, since the natural power in animals functions by means of secondary qualities which do not have any opposition except due to the first qualities, the natural power which is common to both plants and animals operates by means of the first qualities between which there is contrariety, therefore the natural power should tire more in its operations that others; but a power in itself is not weakened but weakness happens to it on account of the destruction of its instruments. This is clear from Aristotle at the beginning of *On the Soul* where he says that if an old man could get the eye of a youth, then he would see as as a young man does.[27] Thus, Aristotle says that old age does not come about by the soul enduring something.[28] And so, if the natural power functions by means of qualities which in themselves are opposed, it will require rest more than that which functions by means of secondary qualities.

[Solution] Solution: With regard to the first argument it should be stated that sleep is an intermediary between living and non-living in respect of a certain clear and basic living. Thus, since life in plants is not clear, sleep is not an intermediary between the living, which is in plants, and non-living, but is an intermediary between that living which is in animals and non-living.[29]

[1.] With regard to that which was asked, whether sleep can be the repose of a natural power just as it is of the animal power, it should be stated that it cannot because the function of a natural power is to restore that which is continually lost

---

26 Aristotle, *De somno et vigilia* i, 454a 26–28.
27 Aristotle, *De anima* I iv, 408b 21–22; Averroes, *Commentarium magnum in de anima* I 65, 7.
28 Ibid., 408b 22–23.
29 See Aristotle, *De generatione animalium* V i, 778b 25–32.

88   TEXT AND TRANSLATION – LECTIO 2

94   tur per accionem | caloris naturalis et caloris extranei continentis; similiter uirtus spiritualis in animalibus est ad restaurandum id quod continue deperditur de calore naturali et spiritu uitali; unde, sicut est continua deperdicio, ita necesse est quod sit continua restauracio; et sicut continua debet esse restauracio, ita oportet quod continue sint operaciones mediantibus quibus restauratur calor et humor, que sunt causa continuacionis uite in uiuente, et ita non deberent quiescere uirtus naturalis et spiritualis; nec indigent quiete eo quod per id quod fit mediantibus operacionibus illarum uirtutum confortantur ipse uirtutes et fortificantur in suis operacionibus, eo quod confortantur membra per restauracionem eorum que deperduntur de substancia et complexione. Illud autem non est reperire in uirtute animali, et propter hoc necessaria est quies secundum operacionem uirtutis animalis, cum excedat modum; operaciones autem aliarum uirtutum non possunt excedere modum, sicut ostensum est. Per hoc patet responsio.

Ad id quod querebatur, quod magis indigeret quiete uirtus operans mediantibus qualitatibus primis quam illa que[9] operatur mediantibus secundariis, dicendum quod id esset uerum nisi per operaciones uirtutum operancium mediantibus primis continue restauratur id quod deperditur ex parte duorum instrumentorum de complexione et compositione; set mediante eo quod efficitur operacione uirtutis animalis non restauratur alico modo id quod deperditur de medio uirtutis animalis. Et propter hoc necesse est ipsam languescere, si modum excedat.

---

9 illa que: illa, que L.

through the action of natural heat and the external heat of the environment. Similarly, the function of the spiritual power in animals is to restore that which is continually lost from natural heat and vital spirit.[30] Thus, just as there is a continual loss so also must there be a continual restoration, and just as the restoration has to be continual it follows that the activities by which the heat and the humours which are the causes of the continuation of life in a living thing are restored must also be continual, nor do they need rest because it is by means of those powers that the powers themselves are strengthened and they become strengthened by their own functioning, and because also the bodily organs are strengthened by the restoration of that which was lost from the substance and bodily constitution. This, however, is not to be found in the animal power and because of this rest is necessary with respect to the functioning of the animal power when it exceeds its limits; the other powers cannot exceed their limits through their functioning, as has already been shown. In this way the answer is clear.

[2.] As regards that which was asked, that a power functioning by means of first qualities requires rest more than one which operates by means of secondary qualities, it must be stated that this would be true except that by means of the functions of those powers which operate by means of first qualities, that which is lost from the two instruments of bodily constitution and make up is continually restored. However, by means of that which is carried out through the operation of the natural power, that which is lost of the medium of the animal power is not restored in any way, and for this reason it is necessary for it to become exhausted if it exceeds its limits.

---

30 The origin of vital spirit is in the heart and which is communicated to the rest of the body through the arteries; the origin of the animal spirit is in the brain and is communicated to the rest of the body through the nerves.

⟨Lectio 3⟩

[465a 2] Preter[1] autem et hanc habentia differentiam tota ad tota genera, et que sunt sub una specie, altera ad altera. Dico autem secundum genus differe, [5] ut hominem ad equum (longioris enim uite est hominum genus quam equorum), secundum speciem hominem ad hominem. Sunt enim homines hii quidem breuioris, hii quidem longioris et secundum alios modos conuenientes. Alii enim in calidis locis gentium longioris uite sunt, [10] alii uero in frigidis breuioris, et eundem locum habentium differunt similiter quidem hac que est ad [12] inuicem differentia.

Preter autem et hanc habencia differenciam, et cetera [i, 465a 2]. Hic incipit ultima pars huius proemii, in qua ostendit Aristotiles secundum que attenditur differencia inter longitudinem uite et breuitatem, quia ista differencia in longitudine et breuitate diuersificatur secundum quod diuersificantur uiuencia.

Vnde recipit ista pars multiplicacionem secundum quod diuersificatur diuersum, et diuersum multiplicatur secundum quod diuersificatur idem; idem autem diuersificatur per substanciale et accidentale, et substanciale diuiditur in eodem genere, specie et numero, et similiter recipit diuersam diuisionem. Potest ergo attendi differencia in longitudine et breuitate uite secundum comparacionem generis ad genus, ut planta est longioris uite quam animal, et secundum comparacionem speciei ad speciem, ut ⟨homo⟩ est longioris uite quam equus; aut potest attendi differencia ista secundum quoddam modum, scilicet secundum diuersitatem loci, ut homines manentes in locis calidis et humidis sunt longioris uite quam qui manent in locis frigidis et siccis. Et eciam differencia inuenitur in hominibus existentibus in eodem loco, quia sanguinei sunt longioris uite quam flegmatici, colerici uel melancolici. Ita exponit Auerrois istum locum.

Causas autem propter quas aliqua sunt longioris uite assignat duas, quarum una est dominium qualitatum actiuarum super pas|siuas; quod probat ipse per proporcionem sumptam

---

1 Preter: Sunt L.

Lecture Three

Text (465a 2–12)

In addition, however, there are those having this difference of complete genera to one another, and those which come under one species, one to another. For I say that it differs according to genus, such as a man in respect of a horse (for the life of the genus of human beings is longer than that of the genus of horses), or according to species one man in respect of another. For there are some men of which these are short-lived and these others are long-lived and differ according to other certain ways. For there some people in hot regions which are long-lived whereas others in cold regions are short-lived, and there are those from the same place who differ similarly in respect of some mutual difference.

Besides, however, and those having this difference, etc. Here begins the last part of this prologue in which Aristotle shows according to what things a difference in length and shortness of life depends, because this difference in length and shortness is diversified according as living things are diversified.

Ibn Rushd's Explanation of the Text[1]

Therefore, this part gets multiplied inasmuch as what is diverse is diversified and what is diverse is multiplied inasmuch as what is the same is diversified; what is the same is diversified by what is substantial and accidental, and what is substantial is divided into the same genus, species and number, and similarly gets a diverse division. Therefore one can note a difference in length and shortness of life by comparing one genus to another, for example, a plant has a longer life than an animal; by comparing one species to another, for example a man lives longer than a horse; or one can note this difference in some other way, namely according to a difference of location, for example, people who dwell in warm and humid places live longer than those who dwell in cold and dry places. Again, even a difference can be found between people living in the same place, because those who are sanguine live longer than those who are phlegmatic, choleric or melancholic. This is how Ibn Rushd explains this part of the text.

Ibn Rushd assigns two causes as to why some live longer,[2] of which one is the predominance of the active qualities over the passive which he proves by means of

---

1 See Averroes, *De causis longitudinis et brevitatis vitae*, 130–31.
2 Ibid., 131.

a quarto *Metheororum*, que est ista: Gignunt autem calidum et frigidum uincencia materiam, cum autem non uincunt, molensis et indigestio fit. Dicit ergo quod caliditas commensurata cum frigiditate generat speciem et humiditas commensurata cum siccitate recipit speciem. Vnde dum qualitates actiue comproportionate alicui enti dominantur super passiuas, semper saluatur illud ens, et ⟨si econtrario⟩ tunc de necessitate illud corrumpitur; uerbi gratia dum caliditas naturalis commensuratur cum humore nostri corporis, saluatur esse; set si calor sit remissus, tunc accidit per indigestionem humorem corrumpi; si autem sit nimis intensus, accidit quod humor aduritur, et sic simiiter accidit corrupcio. Quanto ergo proporcio fuerit maior inter qualitates actiuas et passiuas in alico ente, tanto remocior est eius esse a corrupcione, et quanto minor est proporcio, tanto magis appropinquatur corrupcioni. Vnde dicit quod entia in quibus dominatur mixtio ignis et aque super mixtionem aeris et terre, sunt longioris uite et permanencie. Et reddit causam, eo quod in istis duobus elementis sunt qualitates actiue fortiores. Si autem econtrario, erit econtrario.

Et hec est una causa quare secundum diuersitatem specierum et generum diuersificatur longitudo et breuitas existencie et uite. Secunda causa accidit secundum proporcionem qualitatum actiuarum inter se et passiuarum inter se ut cum caliditas dominatur super frigiditatem et humiditas super siccitatem magis in uno ente quam in alio, et hoc secundum diuersitatem in genere uel in specie. Et similiter in numero accidit quod illud ens sit longioris uite quam reliqua. Longitudo ergo et breuitas uite sequetur complexionem proporcionalem actiuarum qualitatum ad passiuas et actiuarum inter se et passiuarum inter se. Vnde cum uirtutes actiue debilitantur, tunc accidit in corpore multiplicari humores crudi et indigesti, et sic sequitur | mortis festinacio preter naturam. Similiter cum humiditas fuerit pauca et caliditas multa, festinatur consumpcio humiditatis, et sic sequitur festinacio mortis secundum naturam. Et ex hoc accidit, sicut dicit Commentator, quod homines magni et habentes uirtutes fortes aliquando cicius moriuntur quam homines habentes debiles uirtutes, quamuis regantur ex toto eodem regimine.

an analogy taken from the fourth book of the *Meteorologica*[3] which is this: "Heat and coldness generate by overcoming matter, when they do not overcome it what results is half-cooked and undigested". Therefore, Ibn Rushd says[4] that heat equally proportioned with coldness produces the species and humidity equally proportioned with dryness receives the species. Thus, while the mutually proportioned active qualities in any being predominate over the passive qualities, that being continues to be preserved, but if the opposite happens then that being of necessity will decay. For example, as long as natural heat is equally proportioned with a humor of our body, its being is preserved; but if the heat becomes lessened, then it happens that the humor is corrupted through indigestion; if, however, the heat is too intense, it happens that the humor is hardened, and thus, similarly, decay occurs. Therefore, the more the proportion is greater between the active and passive qualities in any being, the more remote is its being from corruption, and to the extent that the proportion is less, so much more does it come closer to destruction. Thus Averroës says that those beings in which a mixture of fire and water predominate over a mixture of air and earth are longer-lived and enduring. And he gives the reason, because stronger active qualities are in these two elements [fire and water]; if, however, the other way around, then it will be the opposite.

And this is one cause why length and shortness of existence and life is diversified according to the diversity of species and genera. The second cause[5] is due to the proportion of the active qualities to each other and the passive qualities to each other, such as when heat predominates over cold and humidity over dryness more in one being than in another and this according to a diversity in genus or in species. And similarly it happens according to number that that being is longer-lived than the rest. Therefore, length and shortness of life follow the constitutional proportion of the active qualities to the passive, and of the active qualities to each other and of the passive qualities to each other. Thus, when the active powers are weakened, then it happens that raw and undigested humors are multiplied in the body, and in this way death is unnaturally hastened. Similarly, when the amount of humidity is small and that of heat is great, the consumption of humidity is increased, and in this way the hastening of death according to nature follows. And from this it happens, as the Commentator says,[6] that people who are large and who have strong powers sometimes die more quickly than people who have weak powers, even though they are both governed by the same routine.

---

3 Aristotle, *Meteorologica* IV i, 379a 1–2.
4 Averroes, *De causis longitudinis et brevitatis vitae*, 131–32.
5 Ibid., 134–38.
6 Ibid., 137–38.

⟨Questiones⟩
⟨1⟩

Hiis uisis, queritur propter quid Aristotiles ponit differenciam in longitudine et breuitate uite secundum comparacionem uiuencium ad loca et non per comparacionem ad tempus, cum tempus per se sit causa corrupcionis et ita breuitatis uite? Quod attestatur Aristotiles in 18 *De Animalibus*, dicens: recte, sunt spatia inpregnacionis et uite omnium generum animalium determinata et distincta secundum reuoluciones; et est dicere reuoluciones: diem, noctem, mensem, annum et tempora alia numerata secundum ista.

Ad quod dicendum quod, sicut dicit Aristotiles in principio huius libri [Cf. i, 464b 20–21] quod non intendit nisi de tota longitudine uite que debetur animali secundum naturam, unde cum tota longitudo uite uiuencium[2] diuersificetur secundum diuersitatem loci, necessarium fuit ut ipse assignaret differenciam longitudinis et breuitatis uite secundum comparacionem ad loca. Locus enim unus potest se commensurare toti longitudini uite; tempus autem, cum sit successiuum unum, non potest sic commensurare toti longitudini, ne⟨c⟩ similiter se habet ad quamlibet partem sui ad totam longitudinem, quemadmodum potest et locus. Si enim aliquid sit uiuens cuius peryodus sit annus, secundum quadras anni oportet quod diuersificetur disposicio uite; unde si bene se habet in yeme, non est necesse quod bene se habeat in estate, et similiter de aliis quadris. Vnde non est differencia secundum longitudinem et | breuitatem uite respiciendo ad totum peryodum quo mensuratur[3] aliquid uiuens in comparacionem ⟨ad⟩ aliud uiuens. Et hec et causa quare non tangit tempus.

⟨Questio 2⟩

Consequenter queritur de hoc quod dicit quod *homo est longioris uite quam equus* [Cf. i, 465a 5–6].

Istud uidetur esse falsum, cum uita stet per calidum et humidum; ergo ubi magis est de calido et humido, longior debet esse uita; set constat quod in equo magis est de calido et humido, cuius signum est quod cibaria digerit que non digerit calor hominis.

Et ad illud dicendum quod, etsi in equo sit plus de calido et humido quam in homine, tamen non est plus de humido quod

---

2 uiuencium] + animalium L.
3 mensuratur: mensurantur L.

Question One

Having seen the above, it might be asked on account of what does Aristotle posit a difference in length and shortness of life by comparing living things to regions and not by comparison to time, since time in itself is the cause of the destruction and so of the shortness of life. This is what Aristotle states in book 18 of *On Animals*,[7] where he says: rightly, the length of time of impregnation and of the life of all kinds of animals is determined and distinguished according to cycles; and these cycles are named day, night, month, year and other lengths of time measured according to these.

[Solution] With regard to this, it must be stated, just like Aristotle says at the beginning of this book,[8] that his aim is to investigate the complete length of life which an animal should have according to nature and so since the complete length of life of animals is diversified according to different regions, it was necessary for him to assign a difference in length and shortness of life by comparison with regions. For one region can in itself be commensurate with complete length of life; time, on the other hand, since it is one in succession, cannot be commensurate with complete length of life in this way, nor similarly is time constituted in respect of its own parts with regard to complete length in the same way that a region can. For if anything is alive for a period of one year, it would be necessary that the disposition of its life would be diversified according to the seasons of the year; thus, if it lives well in winter, it is not necessary that it will live well in summer, and the same is true of the other seasons. Thus, there is no difference according to length and shortness of life with regard to the total period in which any living thing is measured in comparison with another living thing, and this is the reason why Aristotle does not refer to time.

Question Two

Following this, a question might arise concerning what Aristotle says, that "a man is longer-lived than a horse".

This seems to be false since life relies upon the hot and the moist; therefore, where there is more of the hot and the moist, life should be longer; but it is clear that there is more of the hot and the moist in a horse, a sign of which is that it digests fodder which the heat of a human being cannot.

[Solution] Again, with regard to this it must be stated that, even if there is more heat and moisture in a horse than in a man, yet it is not more moisture that

---

7 Aristoteles, *De generatione animalium* IV x, 777b 16–20.
8 See i, 464b 20–21.

facit ad conseruacionem uite, immo ibi est plus de humido aquoso et minus de humido aereo; humidum autem aquosum de facili dissoluitur a calido et coagolatur a frigido. Quod testatur Galenus in libro *De Simplici Medicina*, dicens quod si misceatur aqua oleo cicius a calido euaporat aqua quam oleum; istud uidemus in omnibus habentibus istam duplicem humiditatem, sicut in uino cicius uaporat humiditas aquosa quam humiditas aerea. Istud similiter attestatur Aristotiles in libro hoc quod humidum pingue non de facili est desiccabile eo quod aereum [Cf. v, 466a 22–24]. Quia ergo humidum quod est in equo est aquosum magis quam aereum, de facili desiccatur et resoluitur a calido et coagolatur a frigido. Quod attestatur Aristotiles in 4 *Metheororum*, dicens quod quecumque coagolantur a frigido sunt aque uel aque species; et iterum humidum aquosum contrarietatem habet cum calore naturali et propter hoc ipsum extinguit. In homine autem multum est de humido aereo, quod de facili non desiccatur a sicco consummente nec de facii dissoluitur a calido, nec de facili coagolatur a frigido.

Ex hiis patet [quod] quare sanguinei sunt longioris uite quam alii, quia plus habent de humiditate aerea et unctuosa. Item patet quare in locis frigidis et siccis uiuencia sunt breuioris uite, eo quod frigiditatis est congelare ⟨et⟩ ingrossare spiritum et calorem innatum, et sic|citatis consumere humiditatem; continens enim inmutat contentum ut ad propriam crasim. Et propter hoc dicit Aristotiles, in ultimo capitulo libri *De Vegetabilibus*, quod in locis remotis a sole non est multa[4] multitudo plantarum; et hoc est propter dominium frigiditatis coagolantis ⟨humiditatem et⟩ extinguentis calorem, cuius est uiuificare.

---

4 multa: [multis] L.

preserves life but rather there is more watery humidity there [in a horse] and less airy humidity; for watery humidity is easily dissolved by heat and solidified by cold. This is what Galen states in the book *On Simple Medicines*,[9] saying that if water is mixed with oil, the water evaporates more quickly from the heat than does the oil; we can observe this in all of those which have this twofold humidity, just as the aqueous moisture in wine evaporates more quickly than the airy moisture. Aristotle similarly attests this in this same book, that watery fat does not dry up easily because it is airy. Therefore, because the humidity which is in a horse is more watery than airy, it is more easily dried up and dissolved by heat and solidified by cold. This is attested by Aristotle in the fourth book of the *Meteorologica*,[10] saying that whatever is solidified by cold is either water or is watery in kind; and again, watery humidity is in opposition to natural heat and because of that it extinguishes it. However, in human beings there is a lot of airy moisture which is not easily dried up by the consuming dryness, nor is it easily dissolved by heat nor easily solidified by the cold.

From these it is clear why sanguineous animals are longer-lived than others, because they have a greater amount of greasy and airy moisture. Again, it is clear why living things are short-lived in cold and dry regions because it is of the nature of cold to congeal and thicken the spirits and the innate heat, and it is of the nature of the dry to consume the humidity; for the environment changes that which it contains into its own temperament. And because of this, Aristotle says in the final chapter of the book *On Plants*,[11] that in regions far from the sun there is not a great quantity of plants; and this is because of the predominance of coldness which solidifies the humidity and extinguishes the heat which gives rise to life.

---

9 Galenus (1490), *De simplici medicina* not found. There is a passage which resembles this in Book IX but it seems that only the first five books were translated by Gerard of Cremona from Arabic in the mid twelfth century with the remaining books being translated from Greek by Nicholas of Reggio in the mid-fourteenth century. See Arnald of Villanova II, 'The Development of Medieval Pharmaceutical Theory', 4–5.

10 See Aristotle, *Meterorologica* IV vi, 383a 6–13.

11 Nicholaus Damacenus (Ps. Aristotle), *De plantis* II vi.

⟨Lectio 4⟩

2. [465a 13] Oportet autem accipere quid sit corruptibile in hiis que natura subsistunt et quid incorruptibile. Ignis autem et aqua et [15] hiis proxima non habent eandem[1] potentiam, generationis et corruptionis contingunt causas esse aliorum. Vnde et aliorum unumquodque fit ex hiis et sic constantia participare horum naturam rationabile est. Quecumque uero composita ex aliis sunt, ut domus. Et de aliis altera ratio est.

Insunt autem [20] proprie corruptiones multis eorum que sunt, ut scientia, sanitas, egritudo. Hec enim corrumpuntur et non corruptis susceptiuis, sed saluantibus,[2] ut ignorantie quidem corruptio reminiscibilitas et docibilitas est; scientie, obliuio et deceptio. Secundum accidens autem consequuntur ad physica aliorum [25] corruptiones. Corruptis enim animalibus corrumpuntur et doctrina et sanitas que in animalibus est. Vnde de anima rationabitur aliquis ut de hiis. Si autem non natura sed, sicut in anima scientia, in corpore anima est, sic utique est alia eius corruptio preter corruptionem qua corrumpitur [30] corrupto corpore; quare, quoniam non uidetur huiusmodi esse, aliter utique se habebit ad corporis [32] corrupcionem.[3]

3. [465b 1] Fortassis utique dubitabit aliquis rationabiliter: ergo non est eius cuius esse est incorruptibile, corruptibile? Non utique nisi aliquod contrarium est. Corrumpuntur enim alia quidem, quoniam subsunt contrariis [4] secundum accidens ex eo quod est et illa corrumpi.

Oportet autem accipere quid sit corruptibile in hiis que natura subsistunt, et cetera [ii, 465a 13]. Hic accedit auctor ad principale propositum.

Sciendum ergo quod in hoc capitulo primo tractatus intendit duo determinare, et secundum hoc diuiditur capitulum in duas partes, in quarum prima determinat quot modis aliquid corrumpitur per se siue per accidens; in secunda parte ostendit quod omne quod corrumpitur per se corrumpitur a suo con-

---

1 eandem: eamdem L.
2 saluantibus: sanatibus L.
3 corrupcionem: communionem L.

Fourth Lecture

Text (465a 13–465b 4)

It is necessary, however, to grasp what is corruptible in those things which underlie nature and what is incorruptible. For fire and water and those which are close to them do not have the same power, it must be that they are the causes of the generation and corruption of the others. Whence it is reasonable that of those whatever arises from these elements will also thus share in the nature of these elements. Not, however, those which are composed from others, such as a house. Therefore, with regard to other things it is a different matter.

Moreover, in many of those things which are, they have their own particular kinds of corruption, such as knowledge, health and sickness. For these are destroyed without the destruction of what receives them but they are preserved, for instance, learning and recollection are indeed a destruction of ignorance; forgetfulness and error are a destruction of knowledge. However, in an accidental manner the destruction of others follows upon the destruction of natural objects. For when animals are destroyed then so also is the knowledge and health which is in the animals. Thus, in the same way as these someone might argue about the soul. For if the soul is not by nature in the body but in the way that knowledge is in the soul, so of course there might be entirely another destruction of it besides the destruction by which a corrupted body is destroyed; and so since the likes of this does not seem to be, the soul is associated with the body in quite a different way.

Perhaps someone might indeed reasonably wonder is there not, therefore, something corruptible of that whose being is incorruptible? Not indeed unless there is something contrary. For those are indeed destroyed because there are contraries underlying them and because of these those others are destroyed in an accidental manner.

It is necessary, however, to grasp what is corruptible in those things which underlie nature, etc. This is where the author arrives at the central point.

Division of the Text

It should, therefore, be known that in this first chapter of the treatise Aristotle wishes to resolve two issues, and because of this the chapter is divided into two parts, in the first part of which he shows the number of ways in which something is corrupted in itself or accidentally; in the second part he shows that everything which is corrupted in itself is corrupted by its contrary. Again, the mutual arrange-

trario. Et patet ordo istarum parcium ad inuicem: prius enim diuidere quam sit determinare de diuidentibus | uel de alico diuidencium. Et terminatur prima pars ibi: *Auferuntur enim contraria ab alterutris*, et cetera [iii, 465b 4]. Prius enim oportet quod corrumpantur quedam per accidens quam ostendatur quomodo corrumpuntur illa que corrumpuntur per se.

Quantum ad primam partem procedit hoc modo. Primo ostendit que sunt cause prime corrupcionis; et quia omnis causa per accidens reducitur ad causam per se, propter hoc in secunda parte ostendit quomodo omne quod corrumpitur per accidens reducitur ad corrupcionem eius quod per se corrumpitur; et cum hoc sint due partes in prima parte huius capituli. Et quia omne quod est per se antecedit illud quod est per accidens respectu ipsius, propter hoc prima pars antecedit secundam. Et terminatur prima pars prime partis huius capituli ibi: *Secundum autem accidens sequuntur ad physicam*, et cetera [ii, 465a 23–24].

Quantum ad primam partem procedit hoc modo. Dicit enim quod *ignis et aqua et hiis proxima non habentes eandem potenciam sunt cause generacionis et corrupcionis aliorum* [Cf. ii, 465a 1416]. Et bene tangit ignem et aquam magis quam alia elementa, quia in hiis dominantur magis qualitates actiue et in aliis passiue; ab actiuis autem per se est generacio et corrupcio eo quod per se accio et passio. Per hoc quod dico "proxima" supponuntur alia duo elementa. Et bene dixit: *"non habentes eandem potenciam"*, eo quod maior est potencia ignis quam aque, eo quod non solum corrumpit suum contrarium, set separat quod est secundum speciem ab eo quod est secundum materiam, et quod est subtile a grosso, et consumit humiditatem que est causa commoracionis parcium. Vnde, ubi ignis est causa motus, frigiditas semper est causa quietis. Vnde dicit Auicenna quod caliditas est unita omnibus operacionibus naturalibus; et alibi dicit quod frigiditas non ingreditur opus alicuius uirtutis posita proporcione, in qua supponit quod ista elementa sunt causa generacionis et corrupcionis aliorum. Subiungit uerificacionem eius, ibi: *Vnde et aliorum unumquodque fit*, et cetera [ii, 465a 16–17]; *unde*, id est ex quibus, *unumquodque* aliorum *fit*; quare et *racionabile est alica constancia ex hiis participare horum naturam* [cf. ii, 465a 17–18]. Demonstracio sua debet esse talis: quia alia compo|nuntur ex istis; omne autem compositum habet esse per sua componencia et destrui-

ment of each part is clear since first of all one should divide before resolving the issue with regard to either those which are to be divided or with regard to some aspect of those to be divided. And the first part ends here: *For contraries are removed by other contraries*, etc. For first of all one should show that some things are corrupted by accident rather than showing how those things that are corrupted in themselves are corrupted.

With regard to the first part, Aristotle proceeds in the following way. First of all he shows what are the first causes of corruption; and since every accidental cause can be led back to a cause in itself, for this reason, in the second part he shows how everything which is corrupted by accident can be led back to the corruption of that which is corrupted in itself; and since this is the case there are two parts in the first part of this chapter. And since everything, which is in itself, comes before that which is accidental in its regard, for this reason the first part comes before the second. And the first part of the first part of this chapter finishes here: *In an accidental manner the destruction of others follows upon the destruction of natural objects.*

Literal Explanation of the Text

With regard to the first part Aristotle proceeds in the following manner. For he says that *fire, water and those which are close to them do not have the same power, it must be that they are the causes of the generation and corruption of the others.* And he does well to mention fire and water rather than the other elements because the more active qualities predominate in these and the more passive qualities in the others; for from the active qualities as such is generation and corruption inasmuch as in itself there is action and passion. By that which I say "close to them" [I mean that] the other two elements are presupposed. And well he says: *not having the same power*, since the power of fire is greater than that of water, inasmuch as it does not only destroy its contrary but it separates what is according to species from that which is according to matter, and what is fine from what is thick, and it destroys the humidity which is the cause of the staying together of the parts. Thus, where fire is the cause of movement, coldness is always the cause of rest. Thus, Ibn Sīna says[1] that heat is united to all natural activities; and elsewhere he says that coldness does not enter into the operation of any power once the proportion has been established, in which he presupposes that these elements are the cause of the generation and corruption of the others. Aristotle adds his proof there: *Whence ... whatever of those arises from these elements*, etc.; *whence*, that is from which, *of those whatever others arises; so it is reasonable that of those arising from these elements will also share in the nature of these elements.* Aristotle's proof should be like this: because others are composed from these; every composed thing, however, has existence through its components and is destroyed through the destruction of

---

1 See Avicenna, *Liber de anima* II i, 110.

tur per destructionem ipsorum componencium, cum igitur ista sese semper destruant, quia sunt contraria; et istud subponit quia consequenter demonstrabit. Necesse est ergo destructionem compositorum ex hiis sequi ad destructionem horum.

Et quia quedam componuntur ex primis, et hoc naturaliter, quedam autem ex hiis que componuntur ex primis, et hoc artificialiter, propter hoc tangit illam secundam compositionem ibi, scilicet: *que uero ex aliis compositione sunt, ut domus*, et cetera [ii, 465a 18–19]; per hoc tangit ipse quod quedam fiunt a natura et quedam per se ab arte. Et quia pluribus modis potest aliquid fieri per artem quam compositione, subiungit: *De aliis igitur*, et cetera [ii, 465a 19]; quedam enim fiunt addicione, sicut ea que augmentantur; quedam enim subtractione, sicut mercurius fit ex lapide; quedam transfiguracione, ut ex ere statua; quedam compositione, de quo facit hic mencionem; quedam autem conuersione, et istud fieri proprie est in naturalibus, sicut conuertitur ignis in aqua uel econtrario.

Istis diuersitatibus suppositis ei quod est fieri per se, determinat diuersitates corrupcionis, ibi: *Insunt enim et proprie corrupciones*, et cetera [ii, 465a 19–20]. Et dicit quod quorumdam sunt proprie corrupciones et sunt proprie corrupciones [illorum] illorum que corrumpuntur non corruptis hiis in quibus sunt, quomodo corrumpitur sciencia, sanitas et egritudo. *Hec enim corrumpuntur ⟨et⟩ non corruptis susceptiuis* [ii, 465a 21–22], saluantibus alia, et quibus saluantur alia que sunt in ipsis, *ut ignorancie quidem corrupcio reminiscibilitas et docibilitas* [ii, 465a 22–23]. Et dicitur reminiscibilitas accepcio sciencie a se siue a uirtute quam habet in se, et docibilitas est accepcio sciencie ab alio. Et istis duobus modis corrumpitur ignorancia. Eodem modo corrupcio *sciencie* dicitur *obliuio et decepcio* [ii, 465a 23]; et est obliuio corrupcio sciencie in se; decepcio autem corrupcio eius orta ab alio.

Secundum autem accidens consequenter [ii, 465a 23–24]. Determinatis corrupcionibus per se determinat corrupciones que fiunt per accidens. Et dicit quod *secundum accidens consequuntur corrupciones aliorum ad physica*[4] [ii, 465a 23–25], supple corrupciones. Et hoc ostendit: *corruptis animalibus corrumpitur doctrina et sanitas in animalibus* [ii, 465a 25–26]. Vnde dicit quod *de ⟨anima⟩ rationabitur aliquis idem* [ii, 465a 26–27]. Et sciendum quod in hoc loco intendit Aristotiles remouere dubitacionem que posset incidere ex hiis que dicta sunt, quia uidetur quod anima sit in corpore, sicut sciencia in anima, et ita

---

4 physica: physicam L.

these components, as therefore these always destroy each other because they are contraries; and here Aristotle presupposes this because later he will prove this. Therefore, it is necessary that the destruction of things composed out of these will follow upon the destruction of the same.

Again, because some things are made up of the first things, and this naturally, some, however, from these things which are made up of the first things, and this artificially, for this reason Aristotle mentions that second composition there, namely: *Not, however, those which are composed from others, such as a house*, etc.; by which he points out that some things arise from nature and some in themselves by art. And since something can arise in many ways through art as well as through composition, Aristotle adds: *Therefore, with regard to others*, etc. For some arise through addition, such as those who increase; again, some through subtraction, such as mercury which arises out of stone; some by transfiguration, such as a statue from bronze; some by composition, of which Aristotle makes mention here; some, however, by conversion, and this becoming is properly speaking in natural things, such as fire being converted into water, or vice versa.[2]

Taking into account these various things in what is becoming as such, Aristotle identifies the various kinds of corruption, at that place in the text: *Moreover ... they have their own particular kinds of corruption*, etc. And Aristotle says that there are corruptions proper to some things and there are corruptions proper to those things which are corrupted without those in which they are being corrupted, in the way that knowledge, health and sickness are corrupted. *For these are destroyed without the destruction of what receives them*, while others are *preserved*, and by which others which are in them are preserved, *for instance, learning and recollection are indeed a destruction of ignorance*. Again, the ability to reminisce is said to be the receipt of knowledge from oneself or from some power which one has in oneself, and the aptitude to be taught is the receipt of knowledge from another. And ignorance is destroyed in these two ways. In the same way the destruction of knowledge is called *forgetfulness and error*; and forgetfulness is the destruction of knowledge in itself whereas deception [is the destruction] of science which has its origin in someone or something else.

However, in an accidental manner ... follows. Having identified corruptions in themselves, Aristotle identifies the corruptions which happen by accident. And he says that *in an accidental manner the destruction of others follows upon* (add: "the destruction of") *natural objects*. And he shows this: *for when animals are destroyed then so also is the knowledge and health which is in the animals*. And so he says that *in the same way ... someone might argue about the soul*. Again, it should be known that in this part of the text Aristotle wishes to remove any doubt which might arise from what has been said since it seems that the soul is in the body in the same way as knowledge is in the soul. And thus just as knowledge is destroyed in itself by its

---

2 See Aristotle, *Physica* I vii, 190b 5–9.

sicut sciencia destruitur per se a suo contrario et per accidens, scilicet per destructionem sui subiecti, ita crederet aliquis de anima. Et hoc tangit ibi: *Set sicut in anima ⟨sciencia⟩, sic* dici *anima in corpore est* [ii, 465a 27–28]. Set hoc supposito sequitur inconueniens, quod ostendit per hoc quod dicit: *sic utique ipsius*, id est anime, *et altera corrupcio preter corrupcionem qua corrumpitur corrupto corpore* [ii, 465a 28–30]. Id est sequitur quod anima haberet aliam corrupcionem per se preter illam corrupcionem qua corrumpitur per corrupcionem sui subiecti. Hoc autem non est uerum, quia non habet contrarium a quo corrumpitur per se, quemadmodum sciencia habet contrarium ignorancia. Et hoc intendit dicere ibi: *Quare ⟨quoniam⟩ non uidetur huiusmodi esse* [ii, 465a 30–31], id est quod eodem modo corrumpitur anima sicut et sciencia, propter hoc dicit: *aliter utique* est *se* [ii, 465a 31], id est anima, *habere ⟨ad⟩ corrupcionem corporis* [ii, 465a 31–32], aliter, supple quam contingat scienciam habere se.

Et illud dubitaret aliquis. Et hoc dicit ibi: *Fortasse autem aliquis dubitabit* [iii, 465b 1].

Et ostendit ibi: *Rationabiliter* [iii, 465b 1], quod non corrumpitur anima per se, eo quod non habet contrarium. Et propter hoc corrumpuntur alia per accidens cum subsunt contrariis quibus corruptis corrumpuntur alia. Et id innuit per litteram istam: *Corrumpuntur enim alia secundum accidens quoniam subsunt contrariis, ex eo quod est illa* contraria *corrumpi* [iii, 465b 3–4].

Numerus modorum corrumpendi potest haberi hoc modo: Omne quod corrumpitur aut corrumpitur per se aut non per se aut utroque modo. Si non per se, hoc contingit dupliciter: aut naturaliter aut non | naturaliter; si naturaliter, hoc iterum contingit dupliciter, aut per corrupcionem subiecti in quo est, sicut corrumpitur sanitas corrupto corpore; aut per corrupcionem alicuius quod est in corpore quod est causa illius quod consequenter corrumpatur, sicut corrupcio raritatis in aere per corrupcionem caliditatis, et densitatis in aqua per corrupcionem frigiditatis; et secundum hanc uiam corrumpitur uita in uiuente, per corrupcionem calidi scilicet et humidi, que per se corrumpitur a suis contrariis. Et hoc intendit hic Aristotiles ostendere. — Si per se, hoc solum contingit cum corrumpitur aliquid a suo contrario, quod ostendit Aristotiles in proxima leccione. — Vtroque modo potest corrumpi, sicut sciencia et sanitas et egritudo, que tangit Aristotiles in littera. Ista enim per se possunt corrumpi a suis contrariis et per accidens corrumpuntur per corrupcionem eorum in quibus sunt; anima ergo et

contrary, and also in an accidental manner, namely, by the destruction of its subject, so someone might think the same about the soul. And Aristotle touches upon this here: *For in the way that knowledge is in the soul so* it might be said that *the soul is in the body*. However, if this is assumed, an error in the argument follows, which Aristotle points out in what he says: *so of course there might be entirely another destruction of it*, that is "of the soul", *besides the destruction by which a corrupted body is destroyed*. That is, it would follow that the soul would have another corruption in itself besides that corruption by which it is corrupted through the corruption of its subject. However, this is not true because it does not have a contrary by which it would be corrupted in itself, such as the way knowledge has a contrary in ignorance. And that is what Aristotle wishes to say here: *And so, since the like of this does not seem to be*, that is that the soul is corrupted in the same way as knowledge, because of this he says: *in quite a different way*, that is the soul, *is it associated with the corruption of the body*, in a different way than that regarding what applies to knowledge.

And somebody might question this. And that is what Aristotle says here: *Perhaps someone might indeed wonder.*

And he answers that here: *Reasonably*, that the soul is not corrupted in itself because it does not have a contrary. And for this reason other things are destroyed in an accidental manner since they lie under the contraries which, having been destroyed, then others are destroyed. And Aristotle points to this in this part of the text: *For those others are destroyed in an accidental manner because there are contraries underlying them, and because of these those* contraries *are destroyed.*

The number of ways of being corrupted can be had in the following way: Everything which is corrupted is either corrupted in itself or not in itself, or in both ways. If not in itself, then this happens in two ways: either naturally or not naturally. If naturally, this again happens in two ways: either through the destruction of the subject in which it is, just as health is destroyed when the body is destroyed; or through the destruction of something which is in the body which is the cause of that which is subsequently destroyed, just as the corruption of the rarity in the air through the destruction of heat, and the density in water through the destruction of coldness. And according to the latter way, life in a living thing is destroyed, namely through the destruction of heat and humidity, which are corrupted in themselves by their contraries. And this is what Aristotle wishes to show at this point in the text. If in itself, this can only happen when something is destroyed by its contrary, which Aristotle shows in the next lecture. Something can be destroyed in both ways, just like knowledge and health and sickness, which Aristotle mentions in the text. For these can be destroyed in themselves by their contraries and they are also destroyed in an accidental manner by the destruction of those in which they are; therefore, the soul and life are not destroyed except in

uita non corrumpuntur nisi secundum accidens, nec aliqua substancialis forma, cum nullum habeat contrarium in corrupcione formarum substancialium corporum simplicium. Illud patet quia inpossibile est quod igneitas corrumpatur in igne nisi frigidum prius agat in materiam ignis contrahendo dimensiones ignis, quia frigiditatis est facere motum parcium circumferencialium ad centrum; et cum tarda sit contraccio dimensionum quanta debetur materie ad recipiendum speciem aque, tunc de necessitate soluitur species ignis et introducitur species contrarii: appropriate enim sunt dimensiones in materia ad recipiendum speciem aque, et alie dimensiones sunt appropriate in ipsa ad recipiendum alias species. Et econtrario si calidum ignis agat in materiam aque, distendendo ipsam ultima distencione soluitur species eius. Et datur species a datore formarum, que nata est inesse materie mediantibus illis dimensionibus, et materia facto opere caliditatis sub talibus dimensionibus dicitur necessitas ab Aristotile; et ipse dimensiones appropriantes ipsam cum caliditate agente dicuntur species secundum materiam et ipsa igneitas que est forma substancialis dicitur species secundum racionem, de quibus facit Aristotiles mencionem in primo *De Generacione* dicens | quod in subiecto duo sunt, hoc quidem secundum materiam, hoc quidem secundum racionem.

Similiter patet ⟨quod⟩ per naturam istarum qualitatum corrumpuntur composita, uidelicet aut per calorerm dissoluentem humiditatem facientem commoracionem parcium et extrahentem calorem innatum; et hoc per uiam putrefactionis, secundum quod diffinitur putredo in principio quarti *Metheororum* sic: putrefaccio est corrupcio in unoquoque humido proprie et secundum naturam caliditatis a caliditate extranea. — Aut eciam fit corrupcio a frigiditate congelante, et hoc contingit dupliciter: uno modo per uiam accidentis, sicut habetur in 4 *Metheororum* quod frigidum circumstando calefacit, et hoc quia nata sunt contraria mouere sese motu elongacionis; et propter hoc in yeme frigidissima contingit calorem naturalem in tantum congregari interius quod in quibusdam uiuentibus habentibus parum de humiditate, que est pabulum caloris, quod statim finitur ipsa humiditas, et sic fit corrupcio.

Item, per aliam uiam fit corrupcio a frigido per expulsionem calidi: frigidum enim comprimens aliquid per consequens

an accidental manner, nor is any substantial form since there is no contrary to be had in the destruction of the substantial forms of simple bodies. This is clear, because it is impossible that fieriness in fire is destroyed unless cold first acts on the matter of the fire by constricting its dimensions, because it is of the nature of cold to make the parts at the circumference move to the centre; and since the contraction of the dimensions is slow to the extent of what is due to the matter in receiving the form of water, then of necessity the form of fire is destroyed and its contrary form is introduced; for the dimensions in matter are appropriate to receive the form of water, and other dimensions in it are appropriate to receive other forms. And vice versa if the heat of fire acts on the matter of water, stretching it to the furthest it can be distended, then its form will be destroyed. And the species is given by the Giver of Forms and is produced in such a way to exist in matter by means of those dimensions, and the matter, having been acted on by heat under these dimensions is said to be a "necessity" by Aristotle. And these dimensions making the matter appropriate, together with the action of heat, are called the species according to matter, and this fieriness which is the substantial form is said to be the species by definition. Aristotle makes reference to this in the first book of *On Generation and Corruption*,[3] saying that in a subject there are two factors, one indeed according to matter and the other according to how it is grasped.

Similarly, it is clear that through the nature of these qualities composed bodies are destroyed, namely: either through heat dissolving the humidity which makes the parts stay together, and drawing out innate heat. (And this is by way of putrefaction, according to how putrefaction is so defined at the beginning of the fourth book of the *Meteorologica*:[4] putrefaction is corruption in any humid thing of its own proper heat according to nature by heat external to it.) Or again destruction occurs through congealing by coldness, and this happens in two ways: one way in an accidental manner, as is held in the fourth book of the *Meteorologica*,[5] that cold at times heats, and this because contraries are made to move themselves in a separating movement; and because of this in a very cold winter it happens that insofar as the natural heat withdraws internally that in those living things which have only a little humidity, which is the fuel of the heat, that the humidity is used up immediately, and so destruction occurs.

Again, another way that corruption occurs from cold is through the expulsion of heat; for when cold compresses something as a result it expresses what is thin-

---

3 Aristotle, *De generatione et corruptione* I ii, 317a 24–25.
4 Aristotle, *Meteorologica* IV i, 379a 16–18.
5 Ibid., 382b 8–10.

exprimit quod subtile est in ipso, et secundum hanc uiam fit glacies ex aqua et cristallus. Et similiter secundum hanc uiam accidit homines frequenter incurrere reuma, ex quo generantur multe egritudines mortales; frigiditas enim comprimens cerebrum exprimit per consequens illud quod in ipso continetur fluidum, et sic fit fluxus humorum.

Item patet quomodo humiditas et siccitas sunt causa corrupcionis; omnis igitur corrupcio naturalis debetur primis qualitatibus et nullo modo secundariis, nisi secundum accidens, sicut dicit Commentator super istum locum.

Et si obiciat aliquis quomodo corrumpuntur tunc alia que non sunt physica, ad hoc respondet Aristotiles in littera [Cf. ii, 465a 24–26] | dicens quod corrupciones aliorum que non sunt physica, "consequuntur ad physicam" sicut ad corrupcionem aliquorum in animalibus sequitur corrupcio doctrine, et similiter sanitatis et anime.

⟨Questiones⟩
⟨1⟩

Set dubitabit aliquis de littera: dicit enim quod ignis et aqua non habent eandem potenciam [Cf. ii, 465a 14–15].

Illud uidetur esse falsum, cum sint contraria, et contraria debent esse maxime distancia. Vnde quantum unum eleuatur in suo genere, tantum alterum debet eleuari; nam si magis eleuaretur unum quam reliquum, ut ignis in caliditate magis quam aqua in frigiditate, tunc esset possibile addicio frigiditati aque, et tunc istud magis esset contrarium quam primum cui facta fuit addicio, et sic sequeretur duo esse contraria uni et maxima distancia esset maior distancia, quorum utrumque est inpossibile. Necessarium est ergo ponere quod contraria equaliter sunt eleuata in suis speciebus, et si hee, tunc equales erunt potencie eorum in producendo suos effectus.

Ad hoc dicendum quod contraria equaliter debent esse eleuata secundum quod talia, non tamen ignis et aqua sunt equales potestate et causa huius est quod ignis non est in proprio suo ubi, quemadmodum aqua, ut constituunt mistum, et unumquodque quod est extra suum ubi proprium naturaliter mouetur ad ipsum. Et propter hoc ignis in locis contra medium magis natus est moueri quam aqua, cum locus contra medium sit appropriatus aque; set ignis et aqua in suis propriis ubi equa-

ner in it, and it is in this way that ice and crystal occur out of water.[6] And similarly, it is in this way that it happens to people to incur phlegm, from which many mortal sicknesses are produced. For when coldness compresses the brain, as a result it expels the fluid that is contained in the brain, and so a fluctuation in the humors occurs.

Again, it is clear in what way humidity and dryness are a cause of destruction; since all natural destruction is due to primary qualities and in no way to secondary qualities, except in an accidental manner, as the Commentator says regarding this part of the text.[7]

And if someone objects as to how then are those things destroyed which are not natural bodies, Aristotle replies to this in the text, saying that the destruction of those other things which are not physical, "follows upon natural bodies" just as in how the destruction of some things in animals follows the destruction of knowledge, and similarly of health and the soul.

Question One

However, someone may doubt what is said in the text: for Aristotle says "fire and water do not have the same power".

This seems to be false, since they are contraries, and contraries should be at the greatest distance. Thus, to the extent that one is increased in its kind, so also the other should be increased to the same extent. For if one were increased more than the other, for example, fire more in heat than water in coldness, then it would be possible for an addition of coldness to water, and then this would be more contrary than before the addition was made to it, and thus it would follow that two would be contrary to one and that the greatest distance would be a greater distance, of which both are impossible. Therefore, it is necessary to state that contraries are equally increased in their kinds, and if this is so, then their powers will be equal in producing their effects.

[Solution] To which it should be said that contraries should be equally increased inasmuch as they are such, yet fire and water are not equal in power and the reason for this is that fire is not in its own natural place in the same way as water is, so that they make up a mixed body, and whatever is outside of its own natural place naturally moves towards it. And because of this, fire that is placed near the middle region is more likely to move than water since the place that is the middle region is more appropriate to water; but fire and water in their own natural

---

6 Ibid., IV vii, 384a 10. See also, Alfred of Sarashel, *Commentary on the Metheora*, 68.

7 Averroes, *De causis longitudinis et brevitatis vitae*, 129–30.

liter nata sunt producere suos effectus. Vnde quantum potest ignis rarefaciendo et faciendo motum suum a centro, tantum potest aqua econtrario.

Set sciendum, sicut uult Aristotiles, quod non [est] equaliter participant speciem elementa, set secundum magis et minus. Ignis enim plus habet de specie quam aer et aer quam aqua. Vnde dicitur in 3 *De Anima* quod ignis est species elementorum; ignis enim est esse in termino, et hoc est proprium speciei. Vbi ergo est plus de specie, ibi est plus de potencia ad agendum. Et propter hoc dicit Aris|totiles quod non sunt equales potestate ignis et aqua, quia potencia non solum attribuitur speciei contrarietatis, set speciei uniuersali.

Et si quis querat que est ista species uniuersalis que participatur ab elementis secundum magis et minus, dico quod est lux.

Dico ergo quod ignis et aqua equales sunt in potencia, respiciendo contrarietatis species; set quia aliquid est in igne quod eius effectum magis promouet, quantum ad hoc est inequalitas in potenciis.

⟨Questio 2⟩

Consequenter queritur de hoc quod dicit quod quorumdam sunt proprie corrupciones; et ponit exemplum de sanitate et egritudine.

Id uidetur esse falsum, per id quod dicit in se⟨ptimo⟩ *Physicorum* quod quale in eo quod sensibile alteratur; et alibi: omnia que alterantur, alterantur a sensibilibus; ergo secundum scienciam non debet esse alteracio, cum non sit qualitas sensibilis.

Item, dicit quod in sedendo et quiescendo fit omnis anima sciens, secundum ergo scienciam non contingit alteracionem, scilicet corrupcioni, fieri.

Item, ibidem dicit quod sciencia et sanitas sunt ad aliquid et ad aliquid autem non est motus; ergo non contingit corrupcionem proprie esse horum; et ipse dicit quod horum su⟨n⟩t proprie corrupciones.

places are equally apt to produce their effects. Thus, to the extent that fire can do so by rarefaction and making centrifugal motion, so also can water do the opposite.

However, it should be known, as Aristotle says, that the elements do not equally participate in form but do so to a greater or lesser extent. For fire has more of species than air, and air has more than water. For this reason, it is said in the third book of *On the Soul*[8] that fire is the form of the elements; for fire is completed being, and this is proper to form. Therefore, where there is more of species, there is more of potency to act. And because of this Aristotle says that fire and water are not equal in power, because potency is not only attributed to the species of contrariety but to the universal species.

And if someone were to ask what is that universal form which all elements share in to a greater or lesser extent, I say that it is light.[9]

Therefore, I say that fire and water are equal in power with respect to the contrariety of species; but because there is something in fire which furthers its effect more, in this regard there is an inequality in powers.

Question Two

Next a question is raised about that which Aristotle says, that some have "their own particular kinds of corruption"; and he gives the example of health and sickness.

[1.] This seems to be false, according to what Aristotle says in the seventh book of the *Physics*,[10] that insofar as something is sensible it is changed; and elsewhere: everything which is changed is changed by sensible things.[11] Therefore, there should not be change in regard to knowledge since it is not a sensible quality.

[2.] Again, Aristotle says[12] that in sitting and becoming quiet each soul becomes knowledgeable, therefore there should be no change, namely, to become corrupted, in respect of knowledge.

[3.] Again, Aristotle says[13] elsewhere that knowledge and health are in respect of another but there is no movement in respect of another; therefore, it should not happen that there is a corruption proper to these; yet Aristotle says that there are corruptions proper to these.

---

8 Aristotle, *De anima* III not found, but see *De generatione et corruptione* II viii, 335a 18–20. Here it seems to be used as an adagium.

9 See Adam de Belle Femme, *De intelligentiis*, 8.

10 Aristotle, *Physica* VII ii, 244a 27–28.

11 Ibid., VII iii, 245b 19–21.

12 Ibid., VII iii, 247b 23–24.

13 Ibid., VII iii, 247a 29.

Et ad hoc dicendum quod non intelligit hic quod ista corrumpuntur per se et proprie a se inuicem; set intelligit quod ista habent proprias causas simillime corrupcionis; cause enim que inducunt sanita|tem in ali⟨qu⟩o subiecto destruunt egritudinem in eodem et econtrario; similiter cause que inducunt scienciam in ali⟨qu⟩o, ille eedem destruunt ignoranciam in eodem, preter corrupcionem qua corrumpuntur subiectis corruptis. Et propter hoc dicuntur esse proprie corrupciones horum, ad differenciam corrupcionum que sunt communes ipsis et suis subiectis. Et hoc tangit per hoc quod dicit: *hec enim corrumpuntur non corruptis subsceptiuis*, et cetera [ii, 465a 21–22], quasi diceret: ista corrumpuntur propria corrupcione, ⟨preter corrupcionem⟩ qua corrumpuntur per corrupcionem subiectorum.

Ex hoc patet solucio ad omnia que obiecta fuerunt.

Concedendum enim est quod secundum ista primo et per se non attenditur alteracio neque corrumpuntur nisi secundum accidens.

⟨Questio 3⟩

Consequenter dubitabit aliquis quomodo reducitur corrupcio ignorancie que fit a reminiscibilitate et docilitate ad corrupcionem que attenditur secundum qualitates primas. Additur enim communiter quod corrupciones aliorum secundum accidens reducuntur ad corrupcionem physicam.

Ad quod dicendum quod in ueritate necessarium est corrupcionem horum sequi ad corrupcionem physicam, id est ad corrupcionem primarum qualitatum.

Ad euidenciam huius sciendum, sicut dixit Aueroys, quod tres sunt uirtutes que habent affinitatem: rememoracio, inuestigacio per rememoracionem, et conseruacio. Rememoracio est reuersio eiusdem in presenti intencionis que prius erat post obliuionem; inuestigacio per rememoracionem est inquisicio intencionis prius habite per uoluntatem et facere eam perscrutari post absenciam. Et ideo uisum est aliquibus quod inuestigacio per rememoracionem est uirtus approximata soli ⟨homini⟩, rememoracio autem et conseruacio sunt communes omnibus habentibus imaginacionem, et non differunt conseruacio et ⟨re⟩memoracio nisi secundum modum, quia conseruacio est rememoracio continua et rememoracio est conseruacio | intercisa. Fortitudo autem et debilitas istarum uirtutum sequuntur

[Solution] And with regard to this it should be said that Aristotle does not mean here that these are destroyed in themselves and properly by each other; but he means that they have their own causes which are most similar to corruption; for the causes which induce health in any subject destroy the sickness in the same subject, and vice versa. Similarly, the causes which induce knowledge in something, those very same causes destroy ignorance in the same subject, besides the corruption by which corrupt subjects are destroyed. And for this reason it is said that there are corruptions proper to these, as distinct from the corruptions that are common to both these and to their subjects. And Aristotle touches on this in what he says: *For these are destroyed without the destruction of what receives them*, etc., as if to say: these are destroyed by their own corruption, besides the corruption by which they are corrupted through the corruption of the subjects.

And from this the solution is clear to everything that was objected.

For it should be conceded that according to these, firstly and in themselves, no change results nor are they corrupted except by accident.

Question Three

Next someone might have a doubt as to how the destruction of ignorance that occurs through remembrance and openness to learning can be led back to the corruption that arises with regard to the first qualities. It is also commonly added that the corruptions of others by accident are led back to physical corruption.

To which it should be stated that in truth it is necessary for the corruption of these to follow on from physical corruption, that is, from the corruption of primary qualities.

As proof of this, it should be known, as Ibn Rushd says,[14] that there are three powers which have an affinity: remembering, investigation through remembering, and preservation of memory. Remembering is the return after forgetting into a present intention of the same as that which was there before; investigation through remembering is the examination of an already held intention by means of the will and to bring it about that the intention is examined after its absence. And therefore it seemed to some people that investigation through remembering is a power which is something familiar only to man, remembering and the preservation of memory is to be found common to all who have imagination, and preservation and memory do not differ except in a modal fashion, because preservation is a continual remembering and remembering is an interrupted preservation. However, the strength and weakness of these powers depends on the composition of the

14 Averroes, *De memoria et reminiscentia*, 48–49.

complexionem posterius cellule cerebri, que si fuerit sicca, fit bona rememoracio, set mala conseruacio. Et appellat Auerroes conseruacionem hic recepcionem speciei. Si autem sit posterior cellula humida, accidit tunc bonam esse conseruacionem, set non bonam esse rememoracionem. Et hoc est quia in humido non figuntur species, etsi recipiantur; econtrario autem in sicco. Et propter hoc pueri et senes sunt male rememoracionis, propter tamen diuersas causas; pueri propter naturalem complexionem, quia naturaliter habundantur eciam humiditates, senes quia in ipsis accidentaliter multiplicatur humiditas propter indigestionem; set, cum ista complexio accidentaliter remittitur in quibusdam senibus, accidit tales habere bonas memoraciones. Iuuenes ergo propter temperamentum sue complexionis, quantum est de natura etatis, sunt bone conseruacionis et bone rememoracionis. Docibilitas autem cum dicat facilitatem recipiendi in discipulo, cum facilitas recipiendi sit ab humido, patet quod docibilitas sequitur complexionem humidam. Et sic patet quomodo ista corrupcio ignorancie per docibilitatem et reminiscibilitatem reducitur ad corrupcionem primarum qualitatum.

Et sciendum quod docibilitas et reminiscibilitas differunt in hoc quia docibilitas dicit magis motum ad animam, reminiscibilitas econtrario. Similiter fortificantur isti motus secundum quantitatem subtilitatis et claritatis spirituum animalium, et remittuntur secundum disposiciones opposita, et eciam per disposicionem uiarum per quas discurrunt spiritus, si sint oppilate uel non. Et inpeditur reminiscibilitas per hoc quod de facili non potest eleuari corpus uermi simile quod claudit foramen per quod ingreditur spiritus a media cellula in | posteriorem ⟨cerebri⟩, sicut habetur in libro *De Differencia Spiritus et Anime*.

⟨Questio 4⟩

Hiis uisis, dubitabit aliquis utrum anima corrumpatur corrupto corpore, non dico solum in quantum est anima, set in sui essencia; anima enim id quod dicit ad aliquid dicit.

Et ad hoc probandum quod non corrumpitur, sufficiunt raciones Auicenne. Omne enim quod corrumpitur corrupto alio necesse est quod ali⟨c⟩o modo dependeat secundum esse ex illo; omne autem quod dependet ab alio secundum esse,

posterior ventricle of the brain,[15] which if it is dry, then good remembering occurs, but bad preservation. And Ibn Rushd here[16] calls preservation the reception of the species. If, however, the posterior ventricle is humid, then it happens that the preservation is good but that remembering is not good. And this is because the species do not stick in the humid even if they are received; the opposite, however, in the dry. And because of this, the young and the old are bad at remembering on account of various causes; youths because of their natural constitution since they indeed abound in humidity, old people because humidity naturally increases in them because of indigestion. However, since this constitution is abated in some old people, it happens that these have a good memory. Young people, therefore, because of the balance of their constitution, inasmuch as this is due to the nature of age, are good in preserving and remembering. Since the ability to learn indicates an ability to receive in a student, and because the ability to receive is from the humid, it is clear that this ability to learn follows from a humid constitution. And thus it is clear how this corruption of ignorance through the ability to learn and through remembering can be led back to the corruption of the first qualities.

And it should be known that the ability to learn and remember differ in this inasmuch as the ability to learn indicates more a movement towards the soul, and remembering the opposite. Similarly, these movements are strengthened according to the quantity of fine and clear animal spirits,[17] and they are reduced by opposite conditions, and also by the condition of the ways through which the spirits run, whether these are blocked or not. And remembering is impeded inasmuch as the wormlike body cannot be easily elevated so that the opening through which the spirit enters from the middle ventricle to the posterior ventricle is closed, as is held in the book, *On the Difference Between Spirit and Soul.*[18]

Question Four

Having seen the above, someone might wonder if the soul is destroyed through the destruction of the body, I mean not only inasmuch as it is a soul, but in its essence; for the soul indicates that which "in respect of another" does.

And to show that it is not destroyed, the arguments offered by Ibn Sīna are sufficient.[19] For it is necessary that everything which is destroyed through the destruction of another is in some way dependent in respect of its being on the

---

15 Averroes, ibid., 69.
16 Averroes, ibid., 70.
17 Costa ben Lucca, *De differentia spiritus et animae* II, 127.
18 Ibid., II, 125.
19 Avicenna (1968–1972), *Liber de anima* V iv, 113 ff.

necesse est quod sit natura et non tempore prius illo, uel posterius illo uel simul cum ipso; si dicam quod anima dependet sic ex corpore sicut aliquid quod est simul cum alio, hoc contingit dupliciter: aut quod ista dependencia sit essencialis, id est quod attendatur secundum essenciale aliquod existens in ipsis, aut secundum accidens. Si ista dependencia attendetur secundum similitatem essencie, tu⟨n⟩c substancia esset ad aliquid, quod est inpossibile; si secundum accidens, tunc destructo illo accidente, posset utrumque manere. Si ergo propter istam dependenciam, destructo corpore, non destrueretur anima. Si propter hoc dicam quod dependet a corpore tamquam a priori, tunc oportet quod corpus sit sicut causa respectu illius, uidelicet sicut efficiens uel sicut materialis uel formalis uel finalis. Non potest dici quod sit sicut efficiens, quia corpus in eo quod corpus nichil agit, quia si corpus in eo quod corpus ageret aliquid, omne corpus ageret illud; si ergo corpus est causa efficiens, hoc non est nisi per uirtutes quas habet a formis existentibus in ipso; set inpossibile est quod forme accidentales uel materiales dent esse essencie existenti per se | et inmateriali; non ergo aliquo⁵ modo corpus est causa efficiens anime per modum composicionis, sicut elementa per modum composicionis recipiunt corporeitatem, uel per modum simplicitatis, quemadmodum es se habet respectu statue. Constat quod primo modo non potest esse corpus causa materialis anime, nec secundo modo, quia non potest esse anima sicut forma inpressa in corpore, quod ostendit ipse alibi, nec potest esse corpus sicut forma uel finis, quod est idem quod perfeccio, quod non indiget probacione. Corpus ergo non est causa essencialis ipsius anime respectu anime. Vnde si est causa, est accidentalis, quia ex corpore solum derelinquitur debitum ore causacionis ipsius. Cum enim corpus sit organicum et complexionatum ut materiatum est instrumentum et organum anime, tunc est hora debita eius creacionis; tamen eius esse non procedit a corpore, set a causis existentibus per se, separatis a mensura et tempore. Et sic patet quod corpus nullo modo est causa essencialis ipsius anime, et sic non dependet anima ab ipso tanquam a priori.

Si propter hoc dicatur quod dependet ab ipso tanquam a posteriori: — itaque, si anima corrumpatur corrupto corpore, hoc non potest esse ali⟨qu⟩o modo, si anima sit prius in tempore ipso, quia destructo posteriori, non propter hoc destruitur prius tempore. Sic ergo anima dependet a corpore sicut id quod

---

5 aliquo: alio L.

other; but it is necessary that everything which depends upon another in respect of its being must be prior in nature and not in time to it, or coming after it, or simultaneous with it. If I were to say that the soul depends in the same way upon the body as something which is simultaneous with it, this would happen in two ways: either that this dependence would be essential, that is, that it would arise in accordance with something essential existing in them, or in an accidental manner. If this dependence arises in respect of a similarity in essence, then substance would be in respect of another, which is impossible; if in an accidental manner then when the accident is destroyed, both can remain. If, therefore, on account of this dependence the body is destroyed, the soul is not destroyed. If because of this I were to say that the soul depends upon the body in a prior manner as it were, then it would have to be that the body was like a cause in its regard, namely like either an efficient, or material, or formal, or final cause. One cannot say that the body is like an efficient cause because the body as body does nothing, because if the body as such were to do something, then every body would do it. Therefore, if the body is an efficient cause this is only because of the powers that it has from the forms existing in it. However, it is impossible that the accidental or material forms would give being to an essence which exists in itself and in an immaterial way. Therefore, the body is not an efficient cause of the soul in any way: not through the mode of composition, in the way that the elements receive corporeity through the mode of composition, nor through the mode of simplicity, in the way that bronze is constituted in respect of the statue. It is clear that in the first way the body cannot be the material cause of the soul, nor in the second way because the soul cannot be like an impressed form in the body, which Ibn Sīna shows elsewhere,[20] nor can the body be like a form or an end, which is the same as a perfection, and which does not need proof. Therefore, the body is not the essential cause of the soul itself with respect to the soul. Thus, if it is a cause, it is an accidental cause, because from the body only remains the due time of its causation. Since then the body is structured and constituted so that it is structured as an instrument and organ of the soul, then is the due time of its creation; but its being does not proceed from the body but from causes which exist in themselves, separated from time and space. And thus it is clear that the body in no way is the essential cause of the soul itself, and thus the soul does not depend upon the body in a prior manner.

If, because of this, it were said that the soul depends upon the body in the way in which something comes afterwards, then if the soul were to be destroyed when the body is destroyed, this could not be at all, for if the soul were prior in time to the body, if what comes after is destroyed, it does not follow that because of this what is prior in time is destroyed. Therefore, it is the case that the soul depends

---

20 Ibid., 115; VI ii, 81 ff.

est prius natura alio. Set quando ita est, inpossibile est quod id quod est posterius non destruatur per causam aliquam destructionis que sit in se. Set si destruitur, oportet quod prius causa destruccionis insit ei quod est prius natura, cum per eius destruccionem destruatur posterius, sicut inpossibile quod risibili accidat destructio per causam que sit in se, immo si destruatur, hoc erit per causam destructionis que fit in homine. — Set oppositum uidemus in corpore. Hic enim est causa destruccionis in se, uidelicet contrarietatem; nullam ergo dependenciam contingit reperiri inter animam et corpus per quam destructo corpore destruatur anima.

Aliam demonstracionem ponit ipse: Quicquid corrumpitur per aliquam causam que sit in ipso, in illo est potencia corrumpendi in contrario, et ante corrupcionem est effectus permanendi; aptitudo | autem corrupcionis non est in ipso ex ipso effectu permanendi. Intencio enim potencie alia est omnino ab intencione effectus et relacio potencie alia est a relacione effectus, et aptitudo alia ab aptitudine; aptitudo enim potencie est ad destruendum, et effectus ad permanendum. Si ergo ista duo reperiantur in ali⟨qu⟩o, necesse est quod reperiantur in ipso secundum diuersa, ita quod ab uno sit potencia ad corrumpendum et ab alio effectus permanendi; ⟨in ipso effectu permanendi⟩ non est potencia ad corrumpendum, immo in eo quod suscipit effectum permanendi est potencia ad corrumpendum. Illud autem quod suscipit effectum est materia; effectus autem permanendi non est ab eodem; necesse est ergo quod a forma. Si igitur aliquid sit simplex in essencia, et sit in eo reperire effectum permanendi, inpossibile est in eodem esse potenciam ad corrumpendum; et si in ali⟨qu⟩o simplici est reperire potenciam ad corrumpendum, inpossibile est quod sit in ipso effectus permanendi; et sic non corrumpitur in se. Cum igitur anima sit essencia simplex inmaterialis, non erit in ipsa potencia ad destruendum, cum sit ipsa effectus permanendi. Et sic non corrumpitur in se, nec per corrupcionem corporis.

upon the body in the way of that which is prior in nature to another. However, when this is so, it is impossible that what comes afterwards is not destroyed by some cause of destruction which is in itself. However, if it is destroyed, it is necessary that the cause of destruction was previously in that which is prior in nature, since through its destruction what comes afterwards is destroyed, just as it is impossible for destruction to happen to man, the animal that can laugh, through a cause which is in itself, rather if it is destroyed this will be by means of a cause of destruction which arises in man. Yet we see the opposite in the body, for here there is a cause of destruction in itself, namely contrariety; therefore, it does not happen that a dependency is found between the soul and the body by means of which were the body to be destroyed the soul would also be destroyed.

Ibn Sīna puts forward another proof:[21] whatever is destroyed through another cause which is in it, in that there is a potential of corrupting into the contrary, and before corruption there is an effect of permanence; the tendency, however, to corruption is not in this from that effect of permanence. The aim of the potency is completely different from the aim of the effect and the relation of the potency is other than the relation of the effect, and the tendency of one is other than the tendency of the other. For the tendency of the potency is towards destruction, and of the effect is towards permanence. If, therefore, these two are to be found in something, it is necessary that they are found in it according to different ways, such that from one there is the potential towards destruction and from the other is the effect of permanence; in this effect of permanence there is no potential towards destruction, on the contrary it is in that which receives the effect of permanence where there is a potential towards destruction. However, that which receives the effect is matter but the effect of permanence is not from the same; therefore, it is necessary that it comes from the form. If, therefore, there is something which is simple in its essence, and the effect of permanence is to be found in it, it is impossible for the potential towards destruction to be found in the same. And if there is any potential towards destruction to be found in anything which is simple, it is impossible that there is an effect of permanence in it and thus it is not corrupted in itself. Since, therefore, the soul is an immaterial simple essence, there will not be in it a potential towards destruction, since it is that effect of permanence. And thus is it not corrupted in itself, nor through the corruption of the body.

---

21 Ibid., V iv, 120 ff.

⟨Lectio 5⟩

[465b 4] Auferuntur enim [5] contraria sub alterutris. Secundum autem accidens nichil que sunt in substantiis contrariorum corrumpuntur propter id quod de nullo subiecto est predicari substantiam. Quare si non est contrarium et ubicumque non est, inpossibile erit corrumpi. Aliquid enim est corrumpens. Si uero a contrario contingit corrumpi solum, [10] hoc autem non est aut omnino aut hic, aut hoc sic quidem uerum, sic autem non. Inpossibile enim est materiam habenti non inesse contrarium. Mox enim cum potentia inest contrarium passibili materie. Vndique quidem inesse calidum aut rectum contingit, ⟨...⟩ Si uere passiones non sint separabiles. Si igitur [15] quodcumque sit actiuum et passiuum, hoc quidem semper facit, illud autem patitur, inpossibile est non mutari. Amplius, si necesse est superfluum facere, superfluum autem contrarium; ex contrario enim semper mutatio, superfluum autem ab acceptione prioris, si autem omne consumitur quod actui contrarium est, et si [20] hoc corruptibile utique; si autem non, sed a contingente corrumpitur. Si igitur sufficiens, ex dictis est; si autem non, subicere oportet quod aliud est contrarium, et superfluum fit. Vnde minor flamma comburitur a multa secundum accidens, quoniam alimentum quod est in illa, in multo tempore [25] consumit fumum, hunc multa uelociter. Vnde omnia in motu semper sunt et fiunt aut corrumpuntur. Continens autem aut simul agit aut e contrario agit. Et propter hoc transplantata pluris temporis fiunt et minoris temporis natura quidem fiunt. Facultas autem nequaquam est, quibuscumque contraria insunt; mox [30] enim materia contrarium habet. Quare siquidem, quod est alicubi, mutabitur; si uero est quantitatis, secundum augmentum et decrementum; si [32] autem passibile, alterans aliquod est.

4. [466a 1] Est autem, nec maxime incorruptibiliora esse (equus enim homine breuioris uite est) neque parua (citra enim annum incisorum multa sunt) nec plante omnino animalibus (intra enim annum plante quedam sunt), nec sanguinem habentia (apes enim [5] longioris uite sunt quibusdam sanguinem habentibus) nec que sine sanguine sunt (debila enim quedam infra annum sunt sine sanguine) nec que sunt in terra (et plante infra annum sunt et animalia pedibus gressibilia) neque

Fifth Lecture

Text (465b 4–466a 17)

For contraries are destroyed by each other. In an accidental manner nothing that is in the substances of contraries is corrupted because substance is that which is not predicated of any subject. For which reason if there is no contrary, and wherever there is none, it is impossible for destruction to occur. For what is destroying if indeed it happens that to be corrupted is only from a contrary; this, however, is not at all, or is not here; this is in a way true, in another way not. For it is impossible for there not to be a contrary in something which has matter. For when it is posited, soon a contrary inheres in possible matter. Heat and straightness can be present everywhere [in a thing] if, however, attributes cannot have a separate existence. If, therefore, something is active and passive, this one always acts and that one is always acted upon, it is impossible for this not to be changed. Moreover, if then it is necessary for a waste product to be made, and a waste product is a contrary; for change is always from a contrary, and a waste product is from a previous situation. If then everything were consumed which is a contrary in act and if this is corruptible, could it then not be so? No, it is destroyed by the environment. If therefore this is sufficient from what has been said [to account for the change] but if it is not, it is necessary to assume that there is another contrary and a waste product is produced. Thus, the lesser flame is destroyed by the greater in an accidental way, because the food that is in the first consumes the smoke in a long time, the latter very quickly. Thus, all things are always in motion and become and are corrupted. For the environment either works together with it or works against it. And for this reason, things that are moved from one place to another arise in a longer or lesser time than they would have by their nature. The ability, however, is in no way there in those in which there are contraries; for as soon as there is matter there is a contrary. That is why that which is anywhere is changed; if it is a matter of quantity, according to increase and decrease; if however it is possible, the thing that alters is another.

However, it is so that incorruptibility is not a matter of the greatest animals (for the horse is shorter-lived than a man), nor the small (for many insects live for around a year), nor plants in every way more than animals (for some plants live less than a year), nor sanguineous (for bees live longer than some animals which have blood), nor those who do not have blood (for mollusks live for less than a year and do not have blood), nor those which are in the earth (both plants live for less than a year and animals who move around on their feet) nor those who are in

114 que | sunt in mari (ibi enim breuioris uite sunt, ut ostraca et debilia). Omnino autem nec longioris uite sunt et in plantis [10] et si in sanguinem habentibus magis quam in non habentibus et pede gressibilibus, ⟨…⟩ tamen longioris uite animalium sunt homo et elephas et sic maiora sunt frequentius est dicere minoribus longioris uite sunt [15] et in aliis. Accidit enim longe uite uiuentibus [16] magnitudo, sicut in predictis est.

5. [466a 17] Causam autem de hiis omnibus abhinc utique aliquis considerabit.

Auferuntur enim contraria ab alterutris, et cetera [iii, 465b 4–5]. Hic incipit secunda pars huius partialis capituli, in qua intendit ostendere quod omne quod corrumpitur, a suo contrario corrumpitur.

Et est prima racio talis: Quorumcumque est ablatio per se, per se est corrupcio; set contrariorum per se est ablatio; ergo contrariorum per se est corrupcio. — Et istam demonstracionem innuit per hoc quod dicit: *Auferuntur enim contraria ab alterutris.* Et quia contraria sunt in subiectis, ex hoc uidetur quod substancia non posset corrumpi. Ad hoc ponit racionem quam soluit consequenter. Et est racio talis: Omne quod per se corrumpitur, de substancia dicitur, et accipiatur subiectum, sicut dicitur in 5 *Physicorum,* secundum quod dicitur subiectum affirmacione monstratum, uel secundum quod dicitur subiectum aliquod constitutum in sua specialitate occasio aliorum existencium in ipso. Ex quo sequitur quod substancia non sit corruptibilis cum sit subiecta omni corrupcioni. — Maior patet per hoc quod corrupcio per se non debetur nisi contrario; contrarium autem per se dicitur de subiecto esse quia est in subiecto. Minor patet, quia nulla substancia est in subiecto, secundum quod diffinitur esse in *Predicamentis* et tamen in hic de quantum in ibi. Et id innuit actor per hanc litteram: *Secundum autem accidens nichil que sub hiis substanciis,* et cetera [iii, 465b 5–6]. Et reddit causam: *propter id quod de nullo subiecto est predicari*

115 *substanciam,* et cetera [iii, 465b | 6–7]. Vnde subiungit: *Quare si non est contrarium* substancie *et ubique non est,* supple contrarium, *inpossibile utique corrumpi* [iii, 465b 7–8]. Et reddit causam, quia ad hoc ut aliquid corrumpatur, oportet quod sit contrarium corrumpens.

Si a contrario corrumpi contingit solum, hoc autem non est, omnino, et cetera [iii, 465b 9–10]. Hic incipit respondere ad

the sea (for there they are short-lived, such as crustaceans and mollusks). For it is not at all the case that both plants and those who are sanguineous are shorter-lived than those which are not sanguineous and which move around on their feet, for the longest-lived of animals is man and the elephant and thus the larger seem to be often said to be longer-lived than the smaller and compared to others. For it happens that greatness of size contributes to length of life in living things, as is clear in the above.

The cause, however, of all of these things should now be considered.

For contraries are destroyed by each other, etc. Here begins the second part of this divided chapter, in which Aristotle intends to show that everything which is corrupted is corrupted by its contrary.

Literal Explanation of the Text

And the first argument is such: Of those of whom there is destruction in itself, there is corruption in itself; but of contraries in themselves there is destruction; therefore of contraries in themselves there is corruption. And Aristotle indicates this proof by that which he says: *For contraries are destroyed by each other*. And since contraries are in subjects, it seems from this that substance cannot be corrupted. In this regard Aristotle puts forward an argument which he solves later on. And the argument is of this kind: Everything which is corrupted in itself is said of substance, and understood to be a subject, as is said in the fifth book of the *Physics*,[1] according to which subject is said to be shown through affirmation, or according to which subject is said to be something constituted in its specificity to be the opportunity for others to exist in it. From which it follows that substance cannot be corruptible since it is the subject of all corruption. The major premise is clear inasmuch as corruption in itself is due only to a contrary; a contrary, however, in itself is said to be of a subject because it is in a subject. The minor premise is clear because no substance is in a subject according to how "to be in" is defined in the *Categories*[2] and so "in" here in the same way as "in" there. And this is what the author refers to by these words: *In an accidental manner nothing which is in the substances of contraries*, etc. And he gives the reason: *because substance is that which is not predicated of any subject*, etc. And so he adds: *For which reason if there is no contrary*, of substance *and wherever there is none*, add "contrary", *it is impossible for destruction to occur*. And he gives the cause, because for something to be corrupted, it is necessary for there to be a contrary that corrupts.

If indeed it happens that to be corrupted is only from a contrary, this, however, is not at all, etc. Here Aristotle begins to reply to that objection saying that this however

---

1 Aristotle, *Physica* V i, 225a 6–7.
2 Aristotle, *Praedicamenta* v, 2a 11–12.

illam obiec⟨c⟩ionem, dicens quod hoc non est omnino uerum, scilicet quod non contingat substanciam corrumpi, nec est omnino uerum quod substancia non habet contrarium. Et hoc uult dicere per istam litteram: *hoc autem non est omnino*, et cetera. Et distinguit quomodo potest esse uerum ibi: *Sic quidem uerum est, sic autem non* [iii, 465b 10–11]. Et quia per se uerum est, secundum accidens autem non, et hoc ostendit ibi: *Inpossibile enim est materiam habenti non esse contrarium*, et cetera [iii, 465b 11–12]. Demonstracio talis est: Omne contrarium aptum natum est corrumpi a suo contrario, et similiter omne habens contrarium; set omnis substancia physica habet in se contrarium, ergo et cetera. Assumpcionem probat in littera ibi: *Inpossibile materiam habenti non esse contrarium*. Demonstracio talis est: Inpossibile est habenti materiam non esse contrarium; omne corpus physicum est habens materiam; ergo inpossibile est corpori physico non esse contrarium. — Probacionem maioris probat ibi: *Mox enim cum posito*, et cetera [iii, 465b 13 *add.*]. Et faciendum est uim in hoc uerbo "positum": posicio enim dicit situm et ordinacionem. Vnde quam cito materia est ordinata et est habens situm secundum locum et partem, inpossibile est tunc quod sit sine specie contrarietatis; posicio enim non potest esse ex toto infinite, sic nec ordinacio.

Quidam autem libri habent aliam litteram: *Mox enim cum ponitur inest*, et cetera. Et reddit causam huius ibi: *Si uero passiones non sunt separabiles*, et cetera [iii, 465b 14]. Racio talis est: passiones non sunt separate ab hiis quorum sunt passiones; set calidum, frigidum et cetera, sunt passiones passibiles materie; ergo uniuersaliter non possunt separari a passibili materia, sicut nec rectum nec curuum ex toto a linea.

Et hoc est quod determinat usque ad ilium locum: *Si igitur quodcumque sit actiuum*, et cetera [iii, 465b 14–15] in quo ponit aliud | argumentum ad ostendendum quod omne contrarium corrumpitur per se et quod omnis corrupcio per se est a contrario. Et est racio talis: Quorumcumque per se est accio et passio, horum per se est corrupcio; set contrariorum per se est accio et passio; ergo contrariorum per se est corrupcio. Et hoc est quod dicit ibi: *Si igitur quodcumque sit actiuum et passiuum, hoc quidam facit semper, illud autem patitur, inpossibile est* tale *non mutari* [iii, 465b 13–14]. Et potest istud legi melius de uno et eodem, et tunc debet continuari ad precedens: si omne habens in se materiam passibilem habet contrarium, et in quantum habet in se materiam passibilem natum est semper pati, et in quantum habet contrarium, natum est semper agere, inpossibile est quod sic se habet non mutari. Et secundum hoc fiet sic

is not at all true, namely, that it does not happen that substance is corrupted, nor is it at all true that a substance does not have a contrary. And this is what he wishes to say with these words: *this, however, is not at all*, etc. And Aristotle distinguishes how this can be true: *this is in a way true, in another way not*. Again, since it is true in itself, in an accidental manner not, and he shows this there: *For it is impossible for there not to be a contrary in something which has matter*, etc. The proof of such is: Every contrary is so constituted as to be corrupted by its contrary, and similarly everything that has a contrary; but every physical substance has a contrary in it, therefore, and so on. Aristotle proves the minor premise there in the text: *it is impossible for there not to be a contrary in something which has matter*. The proof is such: It is impossible for there not to be a contrary in something which has matter; every physical body has matter; therefore, it is impossible for there not to be a contrary in a physical body. Aristotle demonstrates proof of the major premise there: *For soon with being posited*, etc. And the emphasis is to be placed on that word "posited": for position refers to situation and organisation. Thus, as soon as matter is organised and has a situation with regard to place and part, it is then impossible for it to be without some kind of contrariety; for position cannot be at all infinite, nor can arrangement.

However, some other books have a different text: *For as soon as it is posited, a contrary inheres*, etc. And Aristotle gives the cause of this here: *If, however, attributes cannot have a separate existence*, etc. The argument is such: Attributes are not separable from those of which they are attributes; but the hot, the cold, etc. are attributes of passible matter; therefore, absolutely, they cannot be separated from passible matter, just as neither the straight nor the curved cannot be separated at all from a line.

And this is what Aristotle determines as far as this place in the text: *If, therefore, something is active*, etc., in which he puts forward another argument in order to show that every contrary is corrupted in itself and that all corruption in itself is from a contrary. And the argument is such: Of any of those of which there is act and passion in itself, there is corruption in itself of these; but there is act and passion of contraries in themselves; therefore there is corruption of contraries in themselves. And that is what Aristotle says there: *If, therefore, something is active and passive, this one always acts and that one is always acted upon, it is impossible for* something like this *not to be changed*. And this could be better read with regard to one and the same, and then it should be continued from the preceding: if everything which has in itself passible matter has a contrary, and to the extent to which it has passible matter in itself has the tendency to always be acted upon, and to the extent that it has a contrary it has the tendency to act, it is impossible that it would be constituted in such a way as not to change. And in this regard, the proof can be

demonstracio: Omne quod secundum quoddam sui semper facit et secundum quoddam semper patitur, de necessitate corrumpitur et mutatur; set omne habens passibilem materiam, illi de necessitate inest contrarium, habet quoddam secundum quod natum est semper facere, et aliud secundum quod natum est semper pati, ergo omne tale de necessitate mutatur et corrumpitur.

Amplius autem si necesse est superfluum facere, et cetera [iii, 465b 16–17]. Hic ponit aliam racionem ad idem. Que talis est: Omne contrarium natum est mutare et corrumpere; omne superfluum est contrarium; ergo omne superfluum natum est corrumpere. Maiorem innuit ibi: *E⟨x⟩ contrario enim mutacio est* [iii, 465b 17–18]; assumpcionem ibi: *Superfluum autem contrarium est* [iii, 465b 17]. Subiungit igitur: si omne quod est actiuum quia contrarium, et intelligendum de accione naturali, tunc sequitur quod omne sit corruptibile. Et hoc innuit ibi: *Et si hoc corruptibile, si autem non* [iii, 465b 19–21]. Si non omne quod est actiuum est contrarium, set corrumpitur aliquid a contingente et hoc non per uiam contrarietatis et per se, set per uiam accidentis et quia superfluum, propter hoc subiungit quomodo aliquid corrumpitur a superfluo, et hoc per accionem magis actiui in passibile quam actiui in contrarium.

Est enim duplex accio, sicut dicit Auerroys in commento super librum *De Anima*: actiui in contrarium et actiui in passibile; | et propter hoc dicit Aristotiles hic: *minor flamma destruitur a multa* et hoc *secundum accidens* [iii, 465b 23–24]. Et concludit ex hiis quod *omnia semper in motu sunt, et fiunt et corrumpuntur* [iii, 465b 25–26] uel a continente uel propter contrarietatem in⟨h⟩erentem. Continens enim aliquando simul agit cum ipsa natura, aliquando autem econtrario; unde aliquando iuuat continens naturam in suis operacionibus aliquando autem contra operatur. Et hoc est quod dicit, ibi: *Continens autem simul agit,* et cetera [iii, 465b 26–27]. Relica autem que continentur in littera plana sunt usque ad ilium locum: *Oportet enim accipere quod animal ⟨natura⟩ calidum,* et cetera [v, 466a 18].

Et sumuntur iste 4 raciones sic quod prima sumitur ab essenciis contrariorum, secunda a materia subiecta, tercia ab effectu, quarta ab accione promouente effectum. Quod actu est, superfluitas non est, contrarium destruit, nisi quia est potens supra passibile, et non est potens nisi quia superfluum.

made as follows: Everything which according to something of itself always acts and according to something is always acted upon, of necessity is corrupted and changed; but everything which has passible matter, of necessity there is a contrary in it, it has something according to which it has a tendency always to act, and another according to which it has a tendency always to be acted upon; therefore, everything of this kind of necessity is changed and corrupted.

Moreover, if it is necessary for a waste product to be made, etc. Here Aristotle puts forward another argument in respect of the same, which is the following: Every contrary has the tendency to change and corrupt; every waste product is a contrary; therefore, every waste product has the tendency to corrupt. He indicates the major premise there: *For change is from a contrary*; the minor premise here: *a waste product is a contrary*. Therefore, he adds: if everything is active because it is a contrary, and understood as referring to natural action, then it follows that everything is corruptible. And this is what Aristotle indicates there: *And if this is corruptible, could it then not be so*. If not everything which is active is a contrary, but something is corrupted by its environment and this not by way of contrariety and it itself, but by way of an accident and because it is a waste product, for this reason Aristotle adds how something is corrupted by a waste product, and this through the action of the more active on the passible, than of the active on the contrary.

For there is a twofold action, as Ibn Rushd says in his commentary on the book, *On the Soul*,[3] an action of the active on the contrary and an action of the active on the passible. And for this reason Aristotle says here: *the lesser flame is destroyed by the greater*; and this *in an accidental way*. And Aristotle concludes from this that *all things are always in motion and become and are corrupted* either from the environment or because of some inhering contrariety. For the environment sometimes works together with a nature itself or sometimes against it; thus sometimes the environment helps a nature in its activities and sometimes works against it. And this is what Aristotle says here: *For sometimes the environment works together*, etc. The rest of what is contained in the text is clear down to that point: *It is necessary to grasp that an animal by nature is warm*, etc.

Again, these four arguments can be summarised as follows: that the first is taken from the essences of the contraries; the second from subjected matter; the third from the effect; the fourth from the action putting forward the effect. That which is in act is not a waste product and destroys a contrary, unless because it is powerful over the passible, and it is not powerful except in that it is a waste product.

---

3 See Averroes, *Commentarium magnum in De anima* II, 213, used here perhaps as an adage.

⟨Questiones⟩
⟨1⟩

Primo dubitatur de hoc quod attribuit corrupcionem per se contrariis, cum in 5 *Physicorum* attribuatur per se corrupcio substancie et corrupcio quedam accidenti. Et similiter in libro *De Generacione* dicit quod corrupcio simplex est entis simplicis, secundum quid autem entis secundum quod quidam. Ens autem simplex est substancia. Cum ergo contrarium non sit substancia, ei non debetur corrupcio per se.

Ad quod dicendum quod motus est actus mobilis et motiui. Vnde potest dici quod motus est motiui et motus est mobilis; quod enim est actus utriusque probatur in 3 *Physicorum*; corrupcio ergo | debetur contrario tanquam mocio; et hoc innuit Aristotiles hic; set in *Physicis* et in libro *De Generatione* intellexit de corrupcione ut actus mobilis suis mutabilibus.

⟨Questio 2⟩

Item, dubitabit aliquis de hoc quod ipse dicit: *Mox enim cum ponitur, inest contrarium passibili materie* [465b 13 *add.*].

Videtur enim quod contrarietas insit per hanc racionem superioribus corporibus. Constat enim quod contrarietas sequitur diuersitatem, et non quamcumque indifferenter, quia si non sit idemptitas ⟨susceptibilis⟩, non potest esse contrarietas; contraria enim nata sunt sese expellere. Item, non sequitur contrarietas diuersitatem numeralem, quia diuerso numero non nata habere idem susceptibile numero, nec similiter contrarietas sequitur diuersitatem generalem, quia omnia genera possunt esse in eodem susceptibili numero simul; ergo contrarietas sequitur diuersitatem specialem set non quamcumque; set diuersitatem specierum que sunt sub eodem genere. Linea enim et superficies sunt diuersa specie et tamen non sunt contraria; species ergo diuerse eiusdem generis habentes idem susceptibile secundum genus uel speciem, sicut habetur in *Predicamentis*, sunt causa sufficiens contrarietatis; ut idem susceptibile secundum speciem habet iusticiam et iniusticiam, secundum genus album et nigrum. Sic igitur in inferioribus corporibus sit reperire diuersitatem specierum contentarum sub eodem genere cum idemptitate susceptibili secundum

Question One

First of all a question arises regarding this, that Aristotle attributes corruption in itself to contraries, since in the fifth book of the *Physics*[4] corruption in itself is attributed to substance and a certain corruption to accident. And similarly in the book *On Generation*[5] Aristotle says that simple corruption is of a simple being, but according to another, however, it is of a being in a certain respect. Simple being, however, is substance. Since, therefore, a contrary is not a substance, corruption in itself is not due to it.

[Solution] To which it should be said that motion is the act of the moved and the mover. Thus, it can be said that motion belongs to the mover and motion belongs to the moved; for that it is the act of both is proved in the third book of the *Physics*;[6] therefore, corruption is due to a contrary like a motion. And Aristotle indicates that here but in the *Physics* and in *On Generation* he has in mind corruption as the act of the moved in its abilities to be changed.

Question Two

Again, someone might have a question regarding what Aristotle says: *For as soon as it is posited a contrary inheres in passible matter.*

Indeed, it would seem that by this argument contrariety would be in the heavenly bodies. For it is clear that contrariety follows from diversity and not in an indifferent manner, because if there is not an identity of the capacity to receive there cannot be contrariety; for contraries have the tendency to expel each other. Again, contrariety does not follow on numerical difference because those which are diverse in number do not have the same capacity to receive in number, nor similarly does contrariety follow upon a diversity of genus, because all genera can be in the same one capable of receiving at the same time. Therefore, contrariety follows on a difference in species but not just any kind, rather the diversity of species that are under the same genus. For a line and a surface are diverse in species and yet are not contraries. Therefore, as is held in the *Categories*,[7] diverse species of the same genus which have the same thing capable of receiving according to genus or species are the efficient causes of contrariety; so that the same thing capable of receiving according to species has justice and injustice, according to genus it has white and black. Therefore, in this way in inferior bodies a diversity is to be found of species contained under the same genus with an identity of the

---

4 See Aristotle, *Physica* V ii, 225b 10–11.
5 See Aristotle, *De generatione et corruptione* I iii, 318b 3–12.
6 Aristotle, *Physica* III iii, 202a 15–18.
7 Aristotle, *Praedicamenta* v, 4a 30–35.

genus uel specierum,[1] cum hoc sit causa sufficiens contrarietatis, uidetur quod in ipsis sit[2] reperire contrarietatem; et si hoc, in ipsis sit reperire causam corruptibilitatis. Quod est ergo quod ipse dicit quod *mox cum ponitur, inest contrarium passibili materie.* Per hoc enim uult proprie innuere quod alia est materia que non est passibilis; hec enim materia non est nisi superiorum corporum.

Ad quod dicendum quod in ueritate generacio et corrupcio, augmentum et diminucio, et alteracio omnis inprimens de qua facit Aristotiles in principio *Celi et Mundi,* sequuntur | motum; motus autem rectus sequitur contrarietatem, contrarietas sequitur diuersitates specierum habencium idem genus et idem susceptibile secundum genus uel speciem, sicut ostensum est. Ita autem reperiuntur in hiis in quibus reperitur potencia antecedens actum. Vnde quidam libri habent hic: *inest contrarium passibili materie*: passibilitas enim recipit semper duo extrema. Vnde a primo, generacio, corrupcio, augmentum, diminucio et alteracio non possunt inueniri nisi in hiis in quibus potencia antecedit actum, nec breuiter aliquis motus rectus nec contrarietas. Igitur, cum in superioribus corporibus potencia non antecedit actum, in hiis non erit possibilitas ad generacionem et corrupcionem uel ad aliquem motum rectum.

Et quod obiciebatur: nonne communicant in materia, set differunt secundum species que sunt sub eoderm genere, et ita uidetur quod tota causa contrarietatis reperitur in hiis, et ita causa paciendi et agendi.

Ad quod dicendum quod non est uerum; ad hoc enim quod fiat accio uel passio, exigitur duplex contrarietas, una materialis que attenditur secundum rarum et densum; altera formalis que attenditur secundum calidum et frigidum; et hic inducit contrarietatem secundum materiam, sicut calidum inducit raritatem et frigidum densitatem. Et hoc est quod dicit Aristotiles in libro *De Generacione.* Et dupliciter dicitur pati: dicitur enim subiectum pati et contrarium pati eciam et nisi calidum simul agat in subiectum frigidi et in ipsum frigidum, numquam a calido corrumpitur frigidum. Quia ergo ista contrarietas materialis non potest reperiri in superioribus corporibus, quamuis alico modo agant in se inuicem secundum species, sicut patet de luna que recipit lumen a sole, secundum diuersas inpressiones quas recipit a sole, diuersimode agit in ista inferiora, propter hoc non possunt sese corrumpere nec eciam est reperire in illis perfec-

---

1 specierum: speciem L.
2 sit: erit L.

one capable of receiving according to genus or species. Since this is the sufficient cause of contrariety it seems that contrariety is to be found in these inferior bodies, and if this is so, the cause of corruptibility will be found in them as well. Which is, therefore, what Aristotle says that *for as soon as it is posited a contrary inheres in possible matter*. For by means of this Aristotle wishes to specifically indicate that there is another matter which is not possible and that matter is that which belongs to the superior bodies.

[Solution] To which it should be said that in truth generation and corruption, growth and decrease, and all change which impresses a form, of which Aristotle makes mention at the beginning of *On the Heavens and the Earth*,[8] follow on from movement. For rectilinear movement follows on from contrariety; contrariety follows on from the varieties of species having the same genus and the same one capable of receiving, as has been shown. Thus, also, they are found in those things in which a potency is found coming before an act. Thus, some books have here: *a contrary inheres in possible matter*; for passability always receives two opposing terms. Thus, from the first, generation, corruption, growth, decrease, and change can only be found in those in which a potency comes before an act, nor indeed any rectilinear movement or contrariety. Thus, since no potency comes before act in the heavenly bodies, no possibility will be found in them neither in respect of generation and corruption nor towards any rectilinear movement.

[A further objection] Again, what was objected: surely they share the matter but differ according to species which come under the same genus, and thus it is clear that the complete cause of contrariety lies in these, and thus the cause of undergoing and acting.

[Response] To which it should be said that this is not true, for in order for action or passion to occur, a twofold contrariety is required, a material contrariety which is to be found in respect of the rare and the dense; and another formal contrariety which is to be found in respect of the hot and the cold; and here this induces a contrariety in respect of matter, just as the hot induces rarity and the cold induces density. And this is what Aristotle says in the book, *On Generation*.[9] And to undergo is said in two ways: for the subject is said to undergo and the contrary is said to undergo even if unless the hot acts at the same time on the subject of cold and on the cold itself, the cold will never be corrupted by the hot. Therefore, because this material contrariety cannot be found in the heavenly bodies, even if in some ways they act upon each other in respect of species, as is clear from the moon which receives the light of the sun according to the different impressions it receives from the sun, (it acts in a different way on these inferior bodies),

---

8 Aristotle, *De caelo* I iii, 270a 13–23.
9 Aristotle, *De generatione et corruptione* II iii, 330b 10–13.

tam causam contrarietatis eo quod non possunt species ille habere esse susceptibile. Simul enim cum erant materie erant et species, unde non erat ibi potencia antecedens actum nec possibilitas in materia existente sub una specie ad aliam speciem. Et hoc est sicut | dicit Auerroys, quod species inmediate insunt suis mediantibus; "inmediate", dico, quia non mediantibus dimensionibus, quia, si mediantibus dimensionibus esset possibilitas uel ad diuisionem [mediantibus dimensionibus esset possibilitas] ⟨uel⟩ ad multiplicacionem et per consequens ad corrupcionem. In istis autem inferioribus insunt species mediantibus dimensionibus, et propter hoc recipiunt species diuisionem secundum diuisionem eorum et diuersificantur species secundum diuersitatem dimensionum in materia; nec tamen dico quod ante aduentum speciei insunt dimensiones terminate materie corporalium, immo simul tempore terminantur dimensiones et recipitur species; non enim potest esse materia que est necessitas sine specie; tamen alica terminacio dimensionum sequitur speciem, sicut est de disposicione omnis accidentis, quod non est subiectum.

⟨Questio 3⟩

Consequenter dubitabit aliquis de accione accident⟨al⟩i in passibile, uidelicet quomodo calor nostri corporis consumit suum subiectum et destruit, cum nullus actus existens in propria potencia siue in propria materia destruit ipsam; si ergo calor uitalis sit in humiditate spermatica sicut in subiecto, non destruet ipsam.

Item quomodo calor naturalis destruitur a calore continentis, cum destructio proprie debet esse a contrario: nichil enim corrumpitur nisi ab incontingenti, nec corrumpitur nisi incontingens, sicut habetur in 1 *Physicorum*. Constat autem quod calor continentis non est incontingens calori innato, eo quod sint isti calores idem nomine et diffinicione, quare idem specie.

Item, si nichil agit physice nisi in suum contingens, cum non sit qualitas actiua incontingens passiue, uidetur quod caliditatis non sit corrumpere humiditatem, et ita uidetur quod per finicionem humidi a calore innato non finiatur uita.

Solucio. In ueritate, si calor uitalis esset in humido naturali sicut in proprio subiecto, non corrumperet ipsum, immo magis conseruaret; quia ergo est sicut subiectum extraneum et quodam modo innaturale, propter hoc inter ista est quodam modo

because of this they cannot corrupt each other nor again is the complete cause of contrariety to be found in them because those species cannot have a being which is capable of receiving. For at the same time as there is matter there will also be species, thus there was not a potency coming before an act there nor a possibility in the matter existing under one species in respect of another species. And this is as Ibn Rushd says, that unmediated species inhere in their intermediaries; "unmediated", I say because they are not mediated by dimensions, because if they were mediated by dimensions there would be a possibility either towards division or to multiplication and as a result towards corruption. However, in these inferior bodies there are species inhering by means of dimensions and because of this the species receive division according to the division of those and species are diversified according to the diversity of the dimensions in matter. Nor, however, do I say that before the arrival of the species that there are dimensions determining the matter of the bodies, rather at the same time both the species is received and the dimensions are determined. For there cannot be matter which is unavoidable without species. Again, some determination of dimensions follows on from species, such as is the situation of every accident that is not a subject.

Question Three

Next someone might wonder about accidental action upon the passible, namely, how the heat of our body consumes its subject and destroys it, since no act existing in its proper potency or in its proper matter destroys it. If, therefore, vital heat is in the spermatic humidity as in a subject, it will not destroy it.

Again, in what way does the heat of the environment destroy natural heat since destruction properly should be from a contrary. For nothing should be corrupted except by what is incompatible, nor is it corrupted except that it is incompatible, as is held in the first book of the *Physics*.[10] It is clear, however, that the heat of the environment is not incompatible with innate heat, because these two have the same name and definition and so are the same species of heat.

Again, if nothing were to act in a physical way except on its environment, since an active quality is not incompatible with a passive quality, it seems that heat would not corrupt humidity and thus it would seem that life would not end through the ending of humidity by innate heat.

Solution. In truth, if vital heat were in natural humidity as in its proper subject, it would not corrupt it but rather it would preserve it. Therefore, because it is like an external subject and unnatural in a certain way, for this reason there is a contrariety in a certain way between them, namely the kind of contrariety which arises

---

10 Aristotle, *Physica* I v, 188b 14.

contrarietas, uidelicet talis contrarietas que attenditur secundum naturam et extra naturam, de qua loquitur Aristotiles in 5 *Physicorum*.

Ad secundum dicendum quod destructio caloris innati a calore continentis non est nisi secundum uiam accidentis sicut innuit Aristotiles in littera, scilicet sicut maior ⟨flamma⟩ destruit minorem, destruendo scilicet nutrimentum minoris flamme cicius quam nutrimentum aliud succedit; nutrimentum enim flamme est fumus, qui continue resoluitur ab uentuoso humido aliquid de sicco; si non enim sicco non potest aliquid inflammari. Vnde nulla pinguedo liquefacta est inflammabilis; nichil enim est inflammabile sine arido; sicut enim habetur in 4 *Metheororum*, continua enim successio fumi est causa generacionis flamme. Et propter hoc ponit Aristotiles in *Posterioribus* istam demonstracionem: Omne quod in multiplici analogia generatur, cito generatur; ignis in multiplici analogia generatur; ergo cito generatur. Et per hoc successiua generacio eius sensu non percipitur. Et ita patet quod multa flamma corrumpit minorem. Et sic corrumpit calor continentis calorem innatum secundum uiam accidentis finiendo suum pabulum antequam aliud nutrimentum succedat.

Ad tercium[3] obiectum dicendum quod, etsi compassibilis sit humiditas cum caliditate, quia tamen non est reperire humiditatem sine materia, sicut habetur in 2 *De Anima*, ubi dicit quod non est possibile sicca corpora tangere se in aqua, eo quod intercidit humiditas, ubicumque est ergo humiditas, ibi est aliquid in quo de necessitate est aliquid de natura contrarietatis, et ubicumque inuenitur de contrario caloris, innuitur de causa duracionis ipsius et permanencie, | sicut habetur in libro *De Animalibus* quod frigus est sicut nutrimentum caloris. Et signum huius est de radiis solaribus, quia recedente luce ex toto in sero, adhuc remanet caliditas in aere; et hoc non est nisi quia caliditas innuit in aere contrarium sibi; hoc facit ad eius commoracionem quod non innuit lux. Dico ergo quod caliditas non agit in humiditate destruendo ipsam racione contrarietatis, quam habet cum ipsa, set quia reperit in materia humiditatis aliquid de contrario quod per se intendit destruere, et per eius corrupcionem accidit quod destruatur humiditas per uiam accidentis.

---

3 tercium: tercio L.

according to nature and apart from nature, of which Aristotle speaks in the fifth book of the *Physics*.[11]

With regard to the second objection, it should be stated that the destruction of innate heat by the heat of the environment is only by way of an accident as Aristotle indicates in the text, namely just as the greater flame destroys the smaller, that is by destroying the fuel of the lesser flame more quickly than more fuel can arrive. For the food of the flame is the smoke which being something of the dry is continually broken down by the windy humidity, for if it were not something of the dry then it could not go on fire. Thus, no liquefied fat is inflammable, for nothing is inflammable without the dry; for as is held in the fourth book of the *Meteorologica*,[12] a continual succession of smoke is the cause of the generation of the flame. And for this reason Aristotle puts forward this proof in the *Posterior Analytics*:[13] Everything that is generated in an increasing proportion is generated quickly; fire is generated in an increasing proportion, therefore it is generated quickly. And for this reason its successive generation is not perceived by the senses. And thus it is clear that the greater flame destroys the lesser. And thus the heat of the environment destroys innate heat in an accidental way by finishing its fuel before further fuel can arrive.

[3.] To the third objection, it should be stated that even if humidity were compatible with heat, humidity cannot be found without matter, as is held in the second book of *On the Soul*[14] where he says that it is not possible for a dry body to touch itself in water because the humidity comes in between. Therefore, wherever there is humidity there is something there in which of necessity is found something of the nature of contrariety, and wherever is found something of the contrary of heat a cause is found of its duration and permanency as is held in the book *On Animals*,[15] that cold is the fuel of heat as it were. And a sign of this is that of the rays of the sun, because when the light has completely gone in the evening, the heat still remains in the air and this can only be because heat finds a contrary to itself in the air and this contrary makes the heat remain with it, a contrary which light does not find. Therefore, I say that heat does not act upon humidity by destroying it by reason of the contrariety which it has with it, but because it finds something of a contrary in the matter of the humidity which it tends to destroy and through its destruction it happens that the humidity is destroyed in an accidental way.

---

11 Ibid., V vi, 230b 15–16.
12 See Aristotle, *Meteorologica* IV ix, 387b–388a 2.
13 Aristotle, *Analytica posteriora* I xii, 78a 1–3.
14 Aristotle, *De anima* II xi, 423a 24–29.
15 Not found but see *De Anima* II iv, 416a 25–26.

Vel aliter potest responderi ad idem quod calor non natus est esse nisi in materia subtili. Vnde cum calor sit fortis [in] materiam subtiliat aliquando, set eciam consumit, si coniunctus sit calor cum siccitate multa; si autem sit debilis, solum resoluit et non destruit, ut talis materia sic subtiliata sit magis conueniens respectu ipsius. Non uideo alico modo quod naturaliter sit contrarietas caliditatis ad humiditatem, ita quod per se racione illius contrarietatis destrueretur humiditas.

Ex predictis patet quod ad conseruacionem uite necessarium est conseruare calorem innatum. Calor enim innatus corrumpitur alico duorum modorum, sicut habetur ab Aristotile in libro *De Sanitatis Regimine ad Alexandrum,* aut naturaliter aut accidentaliter per aliquam uiolentiam intraneam, ut superfluitates multiplicatas in corpore que sunt causa egritudinum: egritudo enim, sicut dictum est superius, non est nisi senectus accidentalis, et omnis senectus sicca. Vnde siue corrumpatur calor naturalis naturaliter siue accidentaliter semper finitur per defectum nutrimenti. Defectus autem nutrimenti fit naturaliter aut propter frigiditatem inpedientem digestionem, et per consequens inpedientem nutrimentum, aut per calorem nimium qui congregatus in se non habet respiracionem uel euentacionem, qui subito finit humidum, sicut patet in carbonibus | ex toto coopertis, cum non possunt habere respiracionem, cito extinguntur; si autem respiracionem habeant, multum possunt conseruari, ut in furnibus propter suam rarefaccionem. Omne ergo uiuens indiget alico modo ut refrigeretur calor innatus; set in plantis sufficit continua successio nutrimenti ad caloris refrigeracionem; continua enim successio nutrimenti continue per motum refrigerat aera et aer refrigerat calorem. Et signum huius est quod ieiunia calefaciunt et generant sitim, propter hoc quod in ieiuniis calor est inmobiis, quod est sue incensionis causa. Quod autem plante indigeant refrigeracione, patet per Aristotilem in libro *De Iuventute:* [4] dicit enim quod in estate arbores in tantum exterius calefiunt quod non sufficit ad refrigeracionem earum humiditas recepta, et propter hoc ponunt rustici lapides frigidos sub radicibus earum et uasa plena frigida aqua. Animalium autem quedam uiuunt in aqua, quedam in aere, et eorum quedam refrigerantur aqua, quedam aere; et eorum que refrigerantur aere, quedam habent pulmonem rarum et parum habent

---

4 *De Iuventute: De Vegetabilibus* L.

Or it can be replied in a different way to the same objection that heat only has the tendency to be in fine material. Thus, when heat is strong it sometimes makes the matter fine and even consumes it if the heat is joined together with a lot of dryness. If, however, the heat is weak it only dissolves and does not destroy so that when such matter becomes fine it is more appropriate to it. I cannot see any way in which there is naturally a contrariety between heat and humidity, such that by reason of that contrariety humidity would be destroyed.

From what has been said it is clear that in order to preserve life it is necessary to preserve innate heat. For innate heat is corrupted in one of two ways, as is held by Aristotle in the book *On the Regimen of Health to Alexander*,[16] either naturally, or accidentally through some inner violence such as waste products multiplied in the body which are the cause of sicknesses. For sickness, as was said above, is nothing but accidental old age, and all old age is dry. Thus, whether natural heat is naturally corrupted or accidentally it is always ended through a lack of nourishment. A lack of nourishment arises naturally either because of coldness impeding digestion and consequently impeding nourishment, or through extreme heat which concentrated in itself does not draw in air or have ventilation and which immediately finishes the humidity. Just as is clear when coals which are completely covered,[17] since they cannot draw in air, are quickly extinguished; if, however, the coals can draw in air they can last for a long time such as in ovens because of their rarefaction. Therefore, every living thing requires that in some way innate heat is cooled down but in plants a continual succession of nourishment suffices in order to cool down heat, for a continual succession of nourishment by means of movement continually cools down the air and the air cools down the heat. And a sign of this is that those fasting become hot and get thirsty because the heat in those who are fasting is immobile which is the cause of its burning. Again, that plants require cooling is clear from Aristotle in the book *On Youth [and Old Age]*. For Aristotle says that in the summer trees can become so hot on the outside that the humidity which they have taken in is not enough to cool them down and for this reason country people put cold stones under their roots and vases full of cold water.[18] Again, some animals live in water some live in the air,[19] some of them are cooled by water and some by air. And of those who are cooled by air, some have a very

---

16 Ps. Aristotle, *De sanitatis regimine ad Alexandrum* (part of the *Secretum secretorum*) in Thomas of Cantimpré, *Liber De Natura Rerum* 79.

17 See Aristotle, *De iuventute et senectute* v, 470a 7–12.

18 Aristotle, *De iuventute et senectute* vi, 470a 32–470b 1.

19 See *De respiratione* ix–x, 474b 25 ff.

de sanguine, et talia non indigent multa refrigeracione; talia autem multum possunt manere sub aqua, set si hic per uiolenciam detineantur, suffocarentur ibi de necessitate sicut testudines, murices et buffones. Que⟨dam⟩ autem habent multum de sanguine et de calore innato, et talia multum indigent refrigeracione, unde non possunt multum esse sub aqua; illa autem que non habent pulmonem et sunt parua non indigent refrigeracione nisi per aerem continentem. Quedam autem sunt que habent multum de calore, etsi sint parua; ad quorum refrigeracionem non sufficit solum aer continens, set habent subtilem pelliculam inferius uersus diafragma qua attrahunt aerem et emittunt interim, quod reddit sonitum, et talia parua animalia multum uiuunt, sicut apes et cicade; apes enim uiuunt per 7 annos. Animalia autem que uiuunt in | aqua, quedam habent pulmones, sicut delfines, et illa refrigerantur per attractionem aeris, et talia animalia non possunt multum uiuere sub aqua. Quidam autem pisces loco pulmonum habent brancas, quibus attrahunt aquam ad infrigidacionem et emittunt. Vnde cum quedam refrigerantur per brancas, quedam per pulmonem, accidit frequenter quod ita indurentur pulmones et brance quod non possunt secundum cursum nature solitum eleuari, et talibus accidit frequenter subita subfocacio.

⟨Questio 4⟩

Set dubitabit aliquis: uidetur enim quod magis debeant animalia refrigerari per recepcionem aque quam per inspiracionem et respiracionem aeris. Omne enim inmoderatum reducitur ad moderatum per inmoderatum. Ynde cum cor sit inmoderate calidum, ut testatur Aristotiles dicens quod cor est principium omnium sensuum et omnis uirtutis animalis, unde ab ipso habent ortum omnes uene, nerui et arterie, et propter nimium suum calorem posuit Dominus ex opposito supra membrum frigidissimum, quod est cerebrum, et sic per inmoderate frigidum debet temperari. Vnde cum cor sit naturaliter calidum, non debet temperari nisi ab eo quod est naturaliter frigidum; set constat quod aer non est naturaliter frigidum, immo magis calidum; ergo per aerem non debet refrigerari cor, set magis per aquam, quod est naturaliter frigidum.

thin lung and have very little blood and such animals do not require much cooling down. Animals like these can stay for a long time under water but if they are forcibly held there they will of necessity suffocate such as turtles, cuttlefish and toads. However, some animals have a lot of blood and innate heat and such animals require a lot of cooling and thus they cannot stay for a long time under water. However, those which do not have lungs and which are small only require cooling down by means of the surrounding air. Again, there are some animals which have a lot of heat even if they are small and the surrounding air alone is not enough to cool them down but they have a very thin membrane underneath near the diaphragm by means of which they draw in air and release it and which makes a sound.[20] Such small animals live for a long time, such as bees and cicadas; for bees live for seven years.[21] Again, some animals that live in water, such as dolphins, have lungs and these are cooled through drawing in air; such animals cannot live for a long time under water. Again, some fish have gills in place of lungs through which they draw in water to cool down and expel it. Thus, since some are cooled down by means of gills, some by lungs, it often happens that the lungs and gills become hardened to such an extent that they cannot be lifted up according to the usual course of nature and frequently it happens that these are quickly suffocated.

Question Four

However, someone will wonder: for it seems that animals should be more cooled down by taking in water than by breathing in and breathing out air. For every excess is led back to moderation by means of an excess. Thus, since the heart is excessively hot, as Aristotle says,[22] saying that the heart is the source of all of the senses and of all animals powers, and so from the heart arise all of the veins, nerves and arteries, and because of the extreme of its heat the Lord placed above it to balance it with the coldest organ which is the brain, and thus through an excessive cold the heat of the heart should be balanced. Thus, since the heart is naturally hot, it should only be balanced by something that is naturally cold. However, it is clear that air is not naturally cold but rather it is hotter, therefore, the heart should not be cooled by means of air but more by means of water which is naturally cold.

---

20 See *Historia animalium* IV ix, 535b 6–10; *De respiratione* ix, 474b 30–475a 21.

21 See Aristotle, *De respiratione* ix, 475a 4–5; Pliny, *Historia naturalis* ix, 22.

22 See Aristotle, *De generatione animalium* II vi, 743b 25–29; *De sensu et sensato* ii, 439a 3–4, 465a 5–7; *De partibus animalium* II vi, 652a 27–30, III vi, 665b 15 ff.

Item, cum aer sit maxime passibilis a qualibet passione, sicut enim de facili infrigidatur, ita de facili calefit; aer ergo attractus ad cor inmutabitur a calore cordis et non econtrario. Et si hoc, tunc reddetur cor magis distemperatum secundum caliditatem per attractionem.

Item, ubi maior est calor, fortiori indiget infrigidacione: set in habentibus sanguinem, forcior est calor; ergo forciori indiget infrigidacione; et econtrario erit in non habentibus. Minus ergo pisces indigent refrigeracione que fit per aquam quam alia habencia multum de sanguine.

125 Solet eciam dubitari, cum indigeat cor refrigeracione, utrum ista refrigeracio debeatur ei racione caloris innati in cartilaginosa substancia eius, aut racione caloris generati ex confricacione parcium, aut racione spirituum contentorum in ipso?

Et uidetur quod racione caloris substancie ipsius cordis, quia cui debetur per se operacio, ei debetur quod est per se sequens operacionem; set uirtuti que est in ipso corde ⟨non⟩ per se debetur operacio neque attraccio aeris. Istud enim fit per dilatacionem ipsius, ergo ⟨cum⟩ per se fit refrigeracio que fit per attractionem aeris, debebitur cordi racione caloris innati in substancia sua.

Contra quod obicitur: quod est maxime calidum in nostro corpore est spiritus; et quod est maxime calidum maxime indiget refrigeracione: ubi enim finis, ibi et operacio, sicut habetur in libro *De Animalibus*; ubi magis de fine, ibi magis de operacione, et de aliis que sunt ad finem; cum igitur in spiritu sit maior indigencia refrigeracionis, propter quod fit attractio aeris, uidetur quod spiritui primo debetur illa refrigeracio.

Hoc iterum non uidetur, quia refrigeracio communis est in plantis et animalibus; ergo propter indigenciam que communis est illis; igitur, cum non communicent in spiritu, plante enim non habent spiritum, set propter refrigeracionem caloris uitalis qui est communis plantis et animalis sicut et uita.

Item: quomodo iuuat aer attractus ad expellendum fumosas superfluitates ipsius corporis? Videtur enim quod magis inpediat: difficilius enim expellitur a uirtute expellente id quod est maius quam id quod est minus. Vnde uidetur quod difficilius debeat expelli commercium ex aere attracto et ⟨spiritu⟩ igneo generato in corde quam alterum illorum.

Solucio. Ad primum dicendum quod uerum est quod omne inmoderatum debet reduci ad moderatum per inmoderatum oppositum. Et concedimus quod aer attractus duplici de causa

Again, since air is capable of being affected to the greatest degree by any action undergone, because just as it can be easily cooled so it can also easily become hot, therefore air which is drawn in to the heart will be changed by the heat of the heart and not the other way around. And if this is the case then the heart will be made even more unbalanced with respect to heat as a result of drawing air in.

Again, where the heat is greater, stronger cooling will be required; but in those who have blood the heat is stronger, therefore, stronger cooling will be needed and it will be the opposite in those who do not have blood. Therefore, fish will need less of the cooling which happens by means of water than others which have a lot of blood.

Again, the question commonly arises, since the heart requires to be cooled whether this cooling down is due to it by reason of innate heat in its cartilaginous substance or by reason of the heat produced in it from the rubbing together of the parts, or is it by reason of the spirits that are contained in the heart?

[Response] And it seems that it is by reason of the hot substance of the heart itself, because that to which an activity in itself is due to it, is also due what follows in itself from the activity. However, neither the activity nor the taking in of air is due to the power which is in the heart itself. For that arises by means of the dilation of the heart. Therefore, since the cooling which arises in itself does so through drawing in of air, this will be required by the heart by reason of the innate heat in its substance.

[Objection] Against which it is objected: that which is most hot in our body is spirit and what is most hot most requires cooling: for where there is a goal, there is also the activity, as is held in the book *On Animals*. [23] Where there is more of a goal, there is more of an activity and of those other things that exist in respect of the goal. Since, therefore, there is in spirit a greater need of cooling, for which the drawing in of air happens, it seems that cooling is due to spirit primarily.

Again, this does not seem to be the case because cooling is common to plants and animals, and therefore because of a need which is common to both. Thus, if they do not share in spirit (for plants do not have spirit), then it is because of the cooling of the vital heat which is common to plants and animals, as is life.

Again, in what way would the drawing in of air help to expel the cloudy waste products of the body itself. For it seems that it would rather impede it, for it would be very difficult for that which is greater to be expelled by an expelling power which is lesser. Thus, it seems that it would be more difficult for the product of the air drawn in and the fiery spirit produced in the heart to be expelled than another of those.

Solution. With regard to the first objection, it should be stated that it is true than all excess should be reduced to moderation through an opposite excess. And

---

23 Aristotle, *De generatione animalium* I viii, 718b 27.

est sufficiens causa mitigandi calorem cordis. Vna causa, quia iste aer qui dicitur res non naturalis multum habet de aqueo admixto; sicut enim habetur in libro *De Vegetabilibus* quod inferior pars aque plus habet | de terreo et superior de aereo et propter hoc est leuior. Similiter inferior pars aeris plus habet de aqueo quam superior uel media. Et propter hoc aliquando cum condensatur inferior pars quod distillat in pluuiam. Vnde racione quam habet de aqueo, habet naturam infrigidandi. Item, ex motu attractionis id quod est subtile est in isto aere qui dicitur res non naturalis acquirit infrigidacionem. Et sic ista duplici de causa potest esse causa sufficiens ad mitigandum calorem innatum in animalibus per aerem, eo quod facilius attrahitur. Vnde cum continua sit refrigerandi necessitas propter maximam ebullicionem sanguinis et cordis animalium et propter continuum motum cordis, illud quod debet fieri infrigidacio, omnino debet esse obediens attractioni, et debet esse iuuans ad expulsionem fumositatum, quod non posset facere aqua; aqua enim non potest subito expelli et subito attrahi, propter sue substancie groscisciem; unde cicius posset suffocari animal quam fieret eius attractio, etsi eciam attrahetur cicius aer currens per uias largiores, scilicet per uias nutrimentales, quam per uias magis angustas ad cor.

Et per hoc patet solucio ad secundum obiectum, [et] quia si aer natura non sit frigida, cum aer qui est res non naturalis ex accidente, scilicet ex motu, et ad mixtionem, sicut dictum est, habet quod infrigidet sufficienter cor, unde etsi aer non sit naturaliter frigidus, tamen ille aer qui est res non naturalis ex alia parte sui est naturaliter frigidus.

Ad tercio quesitum dicendum quod propter hoc quod ille aer qui est res non naturalis est de facili passibilis, propter hoc magis debet esse inspirabilis. Si enim esset ita frigidum quod non posset de facili calefieri ex frequenti sua attractione, posset esse causa extinctionis caloris innati. Vnde magis sequitur oppositum conclusionis quam ipsa conclusio.

Ad aliud quesitum dicendum quod, etsi sit calor in piscibus non habentibus pulmonem, non tamen eorum refrigeracio debet fieri per aerem. Cum enim uiuant in aqua, non esset ipsis possibile attrahere aerem sine aqua. Vnde pisces habentes pulmonem, sicut delfines, eo quod non possunt inspirare aerem dum manent in aqua nisi simul attrahant aquam, non possunt ibi multum uiuere nisi ascendant super aquam. Quia ergo parum est de calore in non habentibus pulmonem sufficit eis

we concede that air drawn in is by a twofold cause, a sufficient cause of reducing the heat of the heart. One cause, because this air which is said to be a non-natural thing has a lot of water mixed with it; just as it is held in the book *On Plants*[24] that the lower part of water has more of the earthy and the higher part has more of the airy and because of this is lighter. Similarly, the lower part of air has more of the watery than the higher or middle part. And because of this, sometimes when the lower part is condensed it is distilled into rain. Thus using the same argument which holds regarding water, it has the nature of cooling down. Again, out of the movement of drawing in that which is subtle in this air (which is called a non-natural thing), it is cooled down. And thus by this twofold cause there can be a sufficient cause to mitigate the innate heat in animals by means of air inasmuch as it can be easily drawn in. Thus, since the need of cooling down is continual because of the great boiling up of the blood and the heart of animals and because of the continual movement of the heart, that which should become the coolant in every way should be responsive to being drawn in and should aid the expulsion of cloudy waste products which water cannot. For water cannot immediately expel and immediately draw in because of its rather thick substance. Thus, an animal will more quickly suffocate before it will become drawn in, even if air would be more quickly drawn in through the larger orifices, namely through the alimentary canals than through the narrower openings to the heart.

And in this way the solution to the second objection is clear because if air is not cold by nature as is the air which is a non-natural thing by accident, namely by motion, as was said, it is held that it would sufficiently cool the heart. Whence, even if air is not naturally cold, yet that air which is a non-natural thing is naturally cold in one part of it.

With regard to the third question, that because of the fact that the air which is a non-natural thing is easily passible, for this reason it should be more breathable. For if it were so cold that it could not be warmed up through it being frequently drawn in, it could be the cause of the extinction of innate heat. Thus, the opposite of the conclusion would more likely follow than this conclusion.

With regard to the other question, it should be stated that even if there is heat in fish that do not have lungs, yet their cooling down does not have to happen by means of air. Since they live in water it is not possible for them to draw in air without water. So it is that fish that have lungs, such as dolphins, because they cannot breath in air while they remain in the water without drawing in water at the same time, cannot live there for a long time unless they come up on top of the water. Therefore, because there is a small amount of heat in those animals which do not

---

24 Nicholaus Damascenus, *De Plantis* II ii.

144 TEXT AND TRANSLATION – LECTIO 5

127 parua refrigeracio, propter hoc quod parum attra|hitur de aqua per brancas ad cor et raro, quia, si multum frequenter, sequeretur extinctio caloris.

Et sciendum quod necessario est inspiracio et respiracio aeris in habentibus pulmonem, non solum propter refrigeracionem caloris innati, set eciam propter hoc ut fiat materia uocis, per quam fit manifestacio affectus cordis. Vnde habetur in fine *De Animalibus* quod uox est materia sermonis; uox enim nichil aliud est, sicut dicit Priscianus, quam aer tenuissimus ictus. Et ita patet quod propter istam necessitatem, ordinauit natura in quibusdam animalibus instrumentum respirandi sicut pulmonem, in quibusdam autem non est ita necessitas, et ideo non ordinauit.

Ad id quod querebatur quod calor in corde indiget refrigeracione, dicendum quod in animalibus calor accidentalis generatur ex confricacione cordis et calor accidentalis spirituum magis indiget refrigeracionem, quia superincensione et calefaccione horum sequeretur superincensio caloris innati ipsius cordis, et festinacio consumpcionis humiditatis que est suum nutrimentum. Vnde isti calores accidentales destruunt calorem innatum, sicut maior flamma destruit minorem, sicut dicit Aristotiles in littera. Finaliter ergo loquendo debetur refrigeracio calori cordis innato.

Ad ultimam questionem dicendum quod in subtilibus cordibus, illud quod maius est, magis est obediens expulsioni quam illud quod minus est eo quod illud quod maius est magis est comprehensibile; set paruum subtile penitus subterfugit accionem expellentis. Et ex hoc patet quomodo aer inspiratus iuuat ad expulsionem fumosarum superfluitatum in corde generatarum.

have lungs a small amount of cooling is enough for them, and because of this a small amount of water is drawn in by means of the gills to the heart, and rarely, because if this were very frequent the extinction of the heat would follow.

Again, it should be known that the breathing in and out of air is necessary in those animals which have lungs, not only because of the cooling of innate heat but also so that it can become the raw material of the voice through which the affections of the heart can become manifest. Thus, it is held at the end of the book, *On Animals*,[25] that the voice is the matter of speech; for as Priscian says,[26] the voice is nothing other than the thinnest air which has been struck. Again, it is clear that because of this need, nature arranged in some animals an organ of breathing such as the lung, and in some however there is not such a need, and so nature did not do so.

With regard to that which was queried, that the heat in the heart needs cooling, it should be stated that in animals an accidental heat is produced by the rubbing together of the heart, and the accidental heat of the spirits more requires cooling because from the flaming up and the heating of these follows the flaming up of the innate heat of the heart itself, and is the speeding up of the consumption of the humidity which is its fuel. Thus, these kinds of accidental heat destroy innate heat, just as the greater flame destroys the lesser, as Aristotle says in the text. Therefore, in finally speaking cooling down is due to the innate heat of the heart.

With regard to the final question it should be said that in very fine hearts, that which is greater is more pliant to expulsion than that which is smaller because that which is greater is more capable of being grasped; but that which is small and fine nearly avoids the action of expulsion. And from this it is clear how air which is breathed in helps to expel the cloudy waste products produced in the heart.

---

25 Aristotle, *De generatione animalium* V viii, 786b 21–22.
26 Priscianus, *Institutiones grammaticae* I, *De voce.*

⟨Lectio 6⟩

[466a 18] Oportet autem accipere quod animal natura est calidum et humidum est et uiuere huiusmodi erit; senium autem est siccum et frigidum [20] et moribidum. Sic enim esse uidetur. Materia autem corporum animalibus hec sunt: calidum et humidum, frigidum et siccum. Necesse est igitur et senectutes siccari. Vnde oportet non leuiter siccabile humidum esse. Et propter hoc imputrescibilia oportet et pinguia esse. Causa enim est quoniam est aeris; aer autem ignis est ad alia; [25] ignis autem non fit putridus. Nec iterum paucum oportet esse humidum. Leuiter siccabile enim est paucum. Vnde magna et animalia et plante, sicut omnino ratio est dicere, longius uiuunt quam parua, quemadmodum dictum est prius; rationabilibus enim est maiora plus habere humidum. Nec tamen propter hoc longioris uite sunt. Due enim sunt causae: [30] quantum et quale, sicut et in terra. Vnde non tantum est multitudo esse humidi sed etiam calidum ut nec leuiter durum nec leuiter siccabile. Et propter hoc homo est longioris uite magis animalium quibusdam [33] maioribus et longioris uite sunt que reliquentur multe [466b 1] humiditatis, si plurima ratione excellant secundum quantitatem; quare relinquuntur secundum qualitatem. Est autem quibusdam calidum pingue quod simul facit, quod non est cito siccari et non cito frigiferi; quibusdam uero est alterum habere humorem. Ideo oportet futurum esse non corruptibile leuiter [5] nec superfluum esse. Interimitur enim huiusmodi aut egritudine aut natura aut dieta aut etate. Contraria enim est superfluitatis potentia etiam corruptiua, hec quidem nature, illa uero partis. Vnde et supereffusa et multa semina senescunt cito; semen enim superfluitas est et amplius exsiccat abiectum. Et propter hoc est mulus longioris uite [10] et equa et asino ex quibus fit, et femine maribus siquidem accedant masculi; ex quo passeres masculi breuioris [12] uite sunt feminis.

Oportet autem accipere quod animal calidum et humidum est natura, et cetera [v, 466a 18]. Hic incipit secunda pars huius tractatus in qua determinat de causis longitudinis et breuitatis uite. Et diuiditur in duas partes principales. In quarum prima determinat causas intrinsecas longioris uite; in secunda determinat causas extrinsecas et magis accidentales. Et quia prius est

Sixth Lecture

Text (466a 18–466b 12)

For it is necessary to understand that an animal by nature is warm and humid and also that living will be of this kind; old age, on the other hand, is dry and cold and moribund. For thus it is seen to be. For the matter of bodies in animals are the following: hot and humid, cold and dry. Thus, it is necessary also for the old to become dry. Thus, the humidity should not be easily dried up. And for this reason they should not be liable to rot and should be fatty. For the cause is because they are airy; air indeed is like fire to the others and fire does not rot. Nor again should the humidity be small for a small amount would be easily dried up. Thus, both large animals and plants, as a general rule, live longer than the smaller as has been said before, for it is more reasonable that the greater would have more humidity. Nor, however, because of this are they longer lived. For there are two causes: quantity and quality, as is also in earth. Thus, it is not enough for there to be a lot of humidity but also heat so that it does not easily become hard nor easily dried up. And for this reason man is longer lived than some of the larger animals; for animals which are lacking in humidity have a longer life; if by reason of having more, they excel according to quantity even if they are lacking according to quality. Again, there is in some a warm fat which does both which is neither quickly dried up nor quickly cooled; in some, however, it has another kind of humor. Thus, it is necessary that it will not be easily destroyed nor be a waste product. For this is destroyed either by sickness or by nature or by diet or by age. For a waste product is contrary and a corruptive power, either of the entire nature or in part. Thus, both a lot of semen and too much emitted ages quickly; for semen is a waste product and moreover its emission dries up. And for this reason the mule is longer lived than the mare and the donkey from which it arises, and females compared to males if indeed the males are active; accordingly male sparrows are shorter-lived than the females.

Division of the Text

For it is necessary to understand that an animal by nature is hot and humid, etc. Here begins the second part of this work in which Aristotle states what are the causes of length and shortness of life. And this is divided into two main parts. In the first of which Aristotle states what are the intrinsic causes of length of life; in the second part he states what are the extrinsic and somewhat accidental causes.

129

essenciale accidentali, | propter hoc ordinantur partes. Et terminatur pars prima ibi: *Amplius autem quecumque fatigancia*, et cetera [v, 466b 12].

Pars prima subdiuiditur in duas partes. In quarum prima determinat in uniuersali causas uite; in secunda determinat de causis longitudinis et breuitatis uite. Et quia longitudo et breuitas sunt sicut passio respectu uite, passio autem naturaliter sequitur id cuius est passio, ergo et causa passionis naturaliter sequitur causam eius cuius est passio; et propter hoc prima pars antecedit secundam. Et terminatur illa prima pars ibi: *Vnde oportet non leuiter humidum*, et cetera [v, 466a 22–23].

Continuacio huius totalis partis ad precedentem est quia in fine precedentis partis dixit quod magna animalia non de necessitate sunt longioris uite quam parua, nec plante de necessitate longioris uite quam animalia, nec sanguinem habencia sunt de necessitate longioris uite quam non habencia, unde quia non assignauit causas horum, propter hoc in hac parte subiungit causas. Vnde sicut hec questio: "Propter quod quedam longioris sunt uite", sequitur naturaliter istam questionem: "Que sunt longioris uite", ita ista pars sequitur precedentem.

Dicit ergo quod *oportet accipere quod* omne *animal est calidum et humidum natura*. Quod ostendit et est demonstracio talis: Omne uiuens, in quantum uiuens, est calidum et humidum, — et hoc accipit ab hoc uerbo: nam *uiuere huiusmodi est* [v, 466a 19], — omne animal est uiuens; ergo omne animal calidum est et humidum natura. Quod autem sit uiuens huiusmodi ostendit per locum a contrariis, quia *senium est frigidum et siccum et moribundum* [v, 466a 19–20]; ergo et uiuere erit calidum et humidum. Concludit ergo quod *necesse est senescentem siccari* [v, 466a 22], eo quod senium est uia in mortem.

Vnde oportet, et cetera [v, 466a 23]. Quia in proximo dixit: *necesse est senescentem siccari* [v, 466a 22] et ita corrumpi, ad hoc ergo quod non corrumpatur de facili *oportet esse humidum non facile siccabile* [v, 466a 23]. Per hoc tangit istam demonstracionem: Quecumque habent humidum non leuiter siccabile sunt longioris uite; set quecumque habent plus de pingui aereo habent plus de humido non leuiter siccabili; ergo quecumque habent plus de aereo pingui sunt longioris uite. Assumpcionem

130

tangit ibi: *Propter hoc inputrescibilia* | *esse pinguia*, et cetera [v, 466a 22–23]. Et reddit causam: quia aeris sunt. Ad hoc subiungit aliam causam, quia *aer est ignis ad alia, ignis autem non putrescit* [v, 466a 24–25], quare nec aerea debent esse in animalibus putrescibilia.

And since what is essential comes before what is accidental the parts are arranged accordingly. And the first part ends here: *Moreover those subject to great toil*, etc.

The first part is subdivided into two parts. In the first of which Aristotle states what are the causes of life in general; in the second he states what are the causes of length and shortness of life. And because length and shortness are like an attribute in respect of life, and an attribute naturally follows that of which it is an attribute, therefore so also the cause of the attribute naturally follows the cause of that of which it is an attribute; and so the first part comes before the second. And that first part finishes there: *Thus, it is necessary that the humidity should not be easily dried up*.

The continuation of all of this part to the previous part is because at the end of the previous part Aristotle said that large animals are not necessarily longer lived than small animals, nor are plants necessarily longer lived than animals, nor those which have blood are not necessarily longer lived than those which do not have blood. Thus, because he did not assign the causes of these, for this reason he adds the causes in this part. Thus, just like this problem: "What is the reason why these are longer lived" naturally follows this question: "Which are those which are longer lived", thus this part follows the preceding.

Literal Explanation of the Text
Therefore, Aristotle says that *it is necessary to understand that* every *animal by nature is warm and humid*. He proves this and his demonstration is like this: Every living thing, inasmuch as it is living, is warm and moist — and this can be got from his words *for living is of this kind* — every animal is living; therefore every animal is warm and moist by nature. Aristotle shows that a living thing is of this kind by making a contrast, because *old age is cold and dry and moribund*; therefore, so living will be warm and moist. He concludes that *it is necessary for an old man to dry up*, since old age is the way to death.

Thus, ... should, etc. Because Aristotle says in the previous sentence that *it is necessary for an old man to become dry* and thus to be corrupted, and so that it is not easily corrupted *the humidity should not be easily dried up*. He indicates this proof as follows: those which have a humidity which is not easily dried up are long-lived; but those who have more of airy fat have more of humidity which is not easily dried up; therefore, those which have more of airy humidity are longer lived. He mentions the minor premise there: *for this reason they should not be liable to rot and should be fatty*, etc. And he gives the cause: for they are airy. To which he adds another cause, because *air is like fire to the others, fire however does not rot*, which is why neither should airy things in animals be capable of rotting.

Nec iterum parum, et cetera [v, 466a 25]. Hic subiungit aliam demonstracionem per quam ostendit quod non omnia uiuencia que habent humidum pingue sunt longe uite, et non est propter qualitatem, set propter quantitatem. Et est demonstracio talis: Omne habens humidum cito siccabile est breuis uite; omne habens parum de humido aereo habet humidum cito siccabile; ergo et cetera. Assumpcionem innuit ibi: *Et propter hoc*, et cetera [v, 466a 23]. Ex hoc, ut dicit, uidetur quod animalia magna et plante debeant esse longioris uite, quia habundant in humido; et quamuis sit probabile, non tamen est necessarium. Quod ostendit ibi: *Nec tamen propter hoc*, et cetera [v, 466a 29]. Et reddit causam propter quam est necessarium, quia non solum quantitas humidi, set qualitas exigitur ad longitudinem uite. Et hoc innuit ibi: *Due enim cause sunt, quantum et quale* [v, 466a 29-30]. Vnde non solum exigit⟨ur⟩ multitudo humidi, set eciam et calidi. Vnde subiungit quod in quibusdam est calidum pingue, quod simul facit ad duo, ad non cito siccari et non cito frigescere; et ex hoc sequitur quod homo sit longioris uite aliis animalibus, excepto tamen elefante, sicut dicitur in libro *De Animalibus*. Et potest formari sic demonstracio: Quibuscumque inest humidum quod non cito siccatur nec cito frigessit, illa sunt longe uite; set quibuscumque inest calidum pingue, inest humidum; ergo non cito siccatur, ergo et cetera. Et patet illatio. Et ulterius infertur: set inter omnia animalia maxime inest pingue homini, excepto elefante; ergo homo et elefans inter omnia animalia sunt longioris uite. Et istam conclusionem innuit ibi: *Et propter hoc homo longioris uite*, et cetera [v, 466a 32]. Vnde dicit quod si multa animalia excellant in plurima quantitate humiditatis secundum quantitatem humiditatis hominis, quia non tamen deficiunt in caliditate, propter hoc non sunt longioris uite: quibusdam enim inest humidum aquosum, quod cito condensatur et infrigidatur. Et hoc innuit ibi: *Quibusdam est alterum habere humorem*, et cetera [v, 466b 3-4], et locum: ⟨*Nec*⟩ | *superfluum esse*, et cetera [v, 466b 5]. Quia dixit quod illa que multum habent de humido, rationabile est quod sint longioris uite, et maxime si habundet calidum pingue. Ostendit hic quod non est necessarium, quia potest esse superfluum. Omne enim superfluum corruptiuum, quia potencia superflua contraria est potencie nature. Et hoc est quod dicit ibi: *Contraria autem est superfluitas potencia et* secundum potencias *corruptiua, hec quidem nature, illa uero partis*, et cetera [v, 466b 6-7]. Demonstracio potest fieri sic: Quicquid est contra-

Nor again should the humidity be small, etc. Here Aristotle adds another proof through which he shows that not all living things which have moist fat are long-lived and it is not on account of quality but on account of quantity. And the proof is like this: Everything which has moisture that is easily dried up is short of life; everything which has a small amount of airy humidity has humidity which is easily dried up; therefore, etc. He indicates the minor premise there: *And for this reason*, etc. From this, as he says, it seems that large animals and plants should be long-lived because they have a lot of moisture; and yet while this is probable, it is, however, not necessary. Which he shows here: *Nor, however, because of this*, etc. And he gives the cause on account of which it is necessary because it is not only quantity of humidity but quality which is required for length of life. And he points that out there: *For there are two causes: quantity and quality*. Thus, not only is a lot of humidity required but also of heat. Thus, he adds that in some there is a warm fat, which does two things at the same time, that it is not easily dried up and not easily cooled down. And from this it follows that man is longer lived than other animals with the exception, however, of the elephant, as is said in the book *On Animals*.[1] And the proof can be formulated in this way: those in which there is a humidity which is not easily dried up or cooled are long lived; but in some there is a warm fat in which there is humidity; therefore, it is not easily dried up, etc. And the inference is clear. And it can be further inferred: but among all animals there is most fat in man, with the exception of the elephant; therefore, among all the animals man and the elephant live longest. And he indicates this conclusion there: *And for this reason man is longer lived*, etc. Thus, he says that if there are some animals which abound in a great quantity of humidity in comparison with the quantity of humidity of man, because, however, they are not lacking in heat, for this reason they are not long lived: for in some there is a watery humidity which is quickly condensed and cooled. And Aristotle points that out there: *in some, however, it has another kind of humor*, etc. and at that place: *Nor be a waste product*. Because he said that it is reasonable that those which have a lot of humidity are long-lived, and above all if they abound in warm fat, here he shows that it is not necessary because it could be a waste product. For every waste product is destructive because the power of a waste product is contrary to the power of nature. And that is what Aristotle says there: *For a waste product is contrary and* in respect of its powers *a corruptive power, either of the entire nature or in part*, etc. The argument can

---

1 Aristotle, *De generatione animalium* IV x, 777b 3–4.

rium secundum potenciam, nature est ipsius corruptiuum; set omnis superfluitas est contraria secundum potenciam nature, ergo omnis superfluitas est nature corruptiua; ex quo concludit dicens: *Vnde superflua et multa semina habencia senescunt cito* [v, 466b 7–8]. Et reddit causam: *Semen enim superfluitas est et ipsum abiectum desiccat* [v, 466b 8–9]. Et potest fieri demonstracio sic: Omne abiectum a corpore ex(s)iccans ipsum est causa breuitatis uite. Et propter hoc dicit quod *mulus longioris uite est equo et asino, ex quibus fit, et femine maribus*, quia minus spermatizant, *si quidam accedant masculi*, supple ad coitum, *ex quo passeres masculi sunt breuiores uite feminis* [v, 466b 9–12].

Et hec est intencio presentis partis usque ad illum locum: *Amplius autem quecumque fatigancia*, et cetera [v, 466b 12].

⟨Questiones⟩
⟨1⟩

Set hic primo dubitatur de hoc quod ipse dicit quod *omne animal est calidum et humidum* [v, 466a 18].

Sillogizetur ergo sic: Omne animal est calidum et humidum; set omne melancolicum est animal; ergo omne melancolicum est calidum et humidum. Et ulterius sequitur quod illud quod est frigidum et siccum per dominium, sit calidum et humidum per dominium, quod est ⟨in⟩possibile; contraria enim per dominium non possunt esse in eodem, immo si unum dominetur, necesse est quod reliquum remittatur: dominari enim dicit fore ad aliquid, et non dicitur ad aliquid nisi respectu unius dominantis.

Item, si omne uiuens est huiusmodi, secundum quod dicit in littera, possum uere dicere quod omne uiuens est calidum et humidum; | set multa sunt uiuencia frigida in 4 gradu que sunt narchotica; ergo frigida in 4 gradu, que sunt narchotica, sunt calida et humida, et non fit denominacio nisi a dominante per dominium; ergo talia sunt calida et frigida.

Item, si *uiuere huiusmodi*; set intelligere et sentire et moueri uoluntarie secundum locum et consimilia sunt uiuere; ergo intelligere et sentire et quodlibet tale est calidum et humidum. Assumpcio patet per illud uerbum secundi *De Anima*: uiuere enim multipliciter dicto, et si unumquodque illorum insit, illud uiuere dicimus, ut intellectus, sensus, motus secundum locum, et cetera. Maior patet in littera. Quod conclusio sit falsa ⟨patet⟩,

be developed as follows: Whatever is contrary in respect of its power is destructive of nature itself; but every waste product is contrary in respect of a power of nature, therefore every waste product is destructive of nature. From which Aristotle concludes by saying: *Thus, both a lot of semen and too much emitted ages quickly; for semen is a waste product and moreover its emission dries up.* And the proof can be developed as follows: Everything ejected from the body which dries it up is a cause of shortness of life. And for this reason Aristotle says that *the mule is longer lived than the mare and the donkey from which it arises, and females compared to males,* because they produce less seed *if indeed the males are active* (add: in respect of coitus); *accordingly male sparrows are shorter-lived than the females.*

And this is the meaning of this part of the text as far at that place: *Moreover those subject to great toil,* etc.

Question One

However, here first of all a doubt arises regarding what Aristotle says, that *every animal is warm and moist.*

[1.] Therefore, this is put into a syllogism as follows: Every animal is warm and moist; but every melancholic is an animal; therefore every melancholic is warm and moist. And further it follows that that which is predominantly wet and dry would be predominantly warm and moist, which is impossible. For predominant contraries cannot be in the same thing, rather if one predominates it is necessary that the remaining decreases; for to predominate means to be in respect of another, and to be in respect of another is not said except in respect of one thing predominating.

[2.] Again, if every living being is of this kind, according to what Aristotle says in the text, I can truly say that every living thing is warm and moist but there are many living things which are cold to the fourth degree and are narcotic; therefore those which are cold in the fourth degree which are narcotic are warm and moist, and the designation only arises from the one dominating by predominating; therefore, animals such as these are warm and moist.

[3.] Again, if *to live is of this kind*; but to understand and to sense and to move voluntarily according to place, and others like these, are to live; therefore, to understand and sense, and whatever is like this, is hot and moist. The minor premise is clear by the words in the second book of *On the Soul*:[2] for living is said in many ways, and if any one of these is present, we say that it is living, such as understanding, sensation, local motion, etc. The major premise is clear in the text. That the conclusion is false is clear because the intellect is not perfected by an

---

2 Aristotle, *De anima* II ii, 413a 21–24.

quia intellectus non perficitur organo corporeo nec est corporeum, set perpetuum et diuinum, sicut habetur in libro *De Anima*.

Ad primum dicendum quod in illo argumento est fallacia accidentis. Cum dico: "Omne animal est calidum et humidum", attribuitur animali secundum quod est uiuens et sic secundum quod non est omnino diuersum; ad hoc quod dico "melancolicum", accidit melancolico esse uiuens secundum quod tale. Vnde cum attribuitur melancolico id quod inest uiuenti secundum quod eciam uiuens, manifestum est quod attribuitur accidenti quod per se inerat subiecto. Talis enim modus argumentandi, secundum quod dicit Aristotiles, tenet in hiis que sunt eadem et indifferencia secundum substanciam. Vnde, cum istud non reperiatur in istis terminis, non tenebit ista argumentacio.

Ad euidenciam huius sciendum quod alia est complexio que debetur uiuenti secundum quod est uiuens in genere, et huiusmodi est materialis respectu omnium complexionum que debentur generibus et speciebus et indiuiduis contentis sub uiuere. Et huiusmodi complexio que debetur uiuenti secundum quod est uiuens habet aliam complexionem antecedentem que est materialis respectu illius, et est illa complexio que ortum habet ex commixtione 4 elementorum, et | dicitur illa complexio innata, relica autem dicitur influens. Et illa que debetur uiuenti secundum quod est uiuens operatur duo: generare et alimento uti. Vnde patet quod illa que debetur animali secundum quod est animal addit differenciam super hanc, quia illa operatur ad sentire et ad presencia opera, sicut dicit Aueroys in commento super librum *De Sensu et Sensato*, quod uirtutes sensitiue mouentur ad interius corporis per motum sui subiecti, scilicet caloris innati. Et ita patet quod sensus perficitur mediante calore. — Item, secundum diuersitatem specierum animalis ⟨et⟩ plantarum diuersantur complexiones. Vnde respectu complexionis humane dicitur asinus frigidus et siccus, et inter homines dicuntur alterius complexionis illi qui sunt in calidis et humidis locis, quam illi qui sunt in frigidis et siccis, et ita locus addit differenciam supra complexionem que debetur speciei. Et similiter sexus: unde femina in eo quod femina dicitur frigida et humida, tamen in eo quod homo, respectu eorum que sunt sub aliis speciebus animalis, debet dici calida et humida. Et similiter indiuiduum addit differenciam complexionum

organised body nor is it corporeal, but is perpetual and divine as is held in the book, *On the Soul*.[3]

[Solution] With regard to the first question it should be said that in there is a fallacy of the accident in that argument. If I say "Every animal is warm and moist", this is attributed to the animal inasmuch as it is living and thus according as it is not at all diverse; with regard to when I say "melancholic" it refers to a melancholic alive inasmuch as it is such. Thus, when one attributes to a melancholic that which is in a living thing inasmuch as it is also living, it is clear that this is attributed to an accident which in itself inheres in a subject. For this way of arguing, according to what Aristotle says,[4] holds in these which are the same and are not different in respect of substance. Thus, since this is not to be found in these terms, this argumentation does not hold.

As evidence of this, it should be known that the constitution which is due to a living thing in respect of what is living as a genus is another, and this type is material with respect to all of the constitutions which are due to genera and species and individuals contained under "living". And a constitution of this type which is due to a living thing inasmuch as it is living has another antecedent constitution which is material with respect of this, and it is that constitution which arises out of a mixture of the four elements, and that constitution is said to be innate, the rest, however, is said to be in flowing. And that which is due to a living thing inasmuch as it is living works in two ways: to reproduce and to take in food. Thus, it is clear that what is due to an animal inasmuch as it is an animal adds a difference onto this, because it works in respect of sensation and acts in respect of present objects, as Ibn Rushd says in the commentary *On Sense and What is Sensed*,[5] that the sensitive powers move to the interior of the body through the movement of its subject, namely, innate heat. And thus it is clear that sensation is completed by means of heat. Again, the constitutions of animals and plants are diversified according to a diversity in species. Thus, with respect to the human constitution a donkey is said to be cold and dry, and among men those who live in warm and moist places are said to be of another constitution than those who are in moist and dry regions, and thus place adds a difference onto the constitution which is due to species. And similarly sex: thus, a female inasmuch as it is female is said to be cold and moist, but inasmuch as she is human she should be said to be hot and moist with respect to those which belong to other species of animals. And similarly an individual adds a difference of constitution according to which it is said that "Socrates cannot live

---

3 Ibid., I iv, 408b 29.
4 Aristotle, *De sophisticis elenchis* xxiv, 179a 37–38.
5 Not found, but see Averroes, *Compendium de somno et vigilia* 78–79.

secundum quod dicitur "Socrates non potest uiuere in complexione Platonis"; et intelligendum de complexione eius fixa, quam habet ex primis generantibus, que merebatur in corpore talem animam, secundum quod dicit Aristotiles quod peccant qui ponunt animam non ponendo in quo et quali. Complexio tamen fluens alicuius indiuidui colerica potest reduci ad temperamentum per exhibicionem 6 rerum non naturalium; et istud tamen est problema apud physicos. Similiter etas addit differenciam super complexionem indiuidui. Vnde, quamuis sicut dicit Auicenna, homo nascatur in summa humiditatis, tamen non debet dici quodlibet indiuiduum hominis humide complexionis, eo quod illud quod est substancia humida natura potest esse sicca. Vnde complexio que debetur indiuiduo secundum se potest dici calida et sicca, tamen racione puericie potest indiuiduum istud dici calide et humide complexionis, et in iuuentute potest dici idem calide et | sicce, et in senio frigide et sicce. Vnde, destructis primis complexionibus potest remanere prima uiuentis secundum quod est uiuens; set ilia destructa, destruuntur et alie. Similiter destructa illa que est materialis ad illam, destruitur ipsa.

Ex hiis patet solucio ad secundo obiectum: cum enim dicitur aliquod uiuens frigidum in 4 gradu, illud respicit complexionem innatam; set cum dicitur quod illud idem uiuens est calidum, id calidum non opponitur tali frigido, eo quod non est calidum simpliciter elementatum, set uitale et currens. Vnde tam illud frigidum quam illud calidum potest inesse per dominium eidem, non tamen secundum idem nec eodem modo.

Ad ultimo obiectum dicendum quod illud uerbum Aristotilis *"uiuere huiusmodi est"* intelligendum est effectiue. Vnde et sentire et intelligere et quelibet uirtus anime perficitur opere calidi. Vnde dicit Philosophus quod frigidum per se non ingreditur opus uirtutis, et quamuis intellectus non operetur mediante corpore, et propter hoc sequitur complexionem corporis, sicut habetur in fine *De Differencia Spiritus et Anime* quod uirtutes anime sequuntur cornplexionem corporis. Vnde

in the constitution of Plato"; and this should be understood regarding his fixed constitution which he has from his parents which merited him such a soul in the body, according to what Aristotle says,[6] that they err who posit a soul without positing in which and in what. However, the choleric flowing constitution of a certain individual can be rebalanced through the use of the six non-natural things; but this is a matter for the medical doctors. Similarly, age adds a difference to the constitution of the individual. Thus, even if it is as Ibn Sīnā says[7] that man is born in utter humidity, yet it is not the case that any individual man is of a humid constitution, because that which is a moist substance by nature can be a dry one. Thus, the constitution which is due to an individual in itself can be said to be hot and dry, yet by reason of childhood this individual can be said to be of a moist and hot constitution, and in youth the same individual can be said to be of a warm and dry constitution and in old age to be of a cold and dry constitution. Thus, when the first constitutions are destroyed, the first constitution of a living thing inasmuch as it is living can remain; but once this is destroyed, so are the others. Similarly, when those are destroyed which are material in respect of it, the first constitution too is destroyed.

[2.] From this it is clear what the solution is to the second objection. For when it is said that some living thing is cold in the fourth degree, that refers to the innate constitution. However, when it is said that that same living thing is hot, that heat is not opposed to such cold because it is not simply elemental heat but is vital and flowing. Thus, both that cold as well as that heat can be in the same thing by predominating, but not, however, according to the same or in the same mode.

[3.] With regard to the final objection, it should be said that those words of Aristotle "and living is of this kind" are to be understood in an effective manner. Thus, both sensation and understanding and any power of the soul whatever is completed by the action of heat. Thus, the Philosopher says,[8] that cold in itself does not enter into the work of a power. And even if the intellect does not work by means of a body, yet for this reason it follows that constitution of a body, as is in held towards the end of *On the Difference Between Spirit and Soul*,[9] that the powers

---

6 Aristotle, *De anima* I iii, 407b, 13–26 *ad sensum*.

7 Not found. See, however, Galen, *De Complexionibus* II ii, 53n: *Alia translatio: homo nascitur in ultimo humiditatis et limositatis.*

8 Not found. See, however, Peter of Spain, *Questiones super libro de Animalibus* XII, 307: *Contrarium autem dicit Philosophus in hoc duodecimo quod frigiditas est priuatio et Auicenna quod frigidum non immiscet se operibus nature.*

9 Costa ben Lucca, *De differentia spiritus et animae* iv, 138.

dicitur quod anima sequitur corpus in suis passionibus et corpus animam in suis accionibus.

(Questio 2)

Consequenter dubitabit de hoc quod ipse dicit, quod pinguia sunt inputrescibilia.

Illud enim uidetur esse falsum, quia due sunt qualitates que per se faciunt ad putrefaccionem, scilicet ille que habent motum a centro, uidelicet caliditas et humiditas: eo enim quod faciunt motum a centro, faciunt ad ingressum caloris extranei preparantis ad consumpcionem humidi substancialis, et ita per consequens ad destructionem calidi innati. Sic ergo pinguedo maxime erit causa putrefaccionis, cum sit calida et humida.

Cum humiditas per se sit causa putrefaccionis, sicut patet per diffinicionem putrefaccionis datam in 4 *Metheororum*: est enim putrefaccio in unoquoque humido proprie et secundum naturam caliditatis a caliditate extranea, pinguia ergo proprie et per se erunt putrescibilia eo quod proprie per se sunt humida. Et quod per se sint humida patet, quia aeris sunt, aer autem primo reperitur humidum.

Item, quod maxime est passibile, maxime debet disponi ad putrefaccionem; set quod maxime est humidum, maxime est passibile; ergo quod maxime est humidum maxime debet disponi ad putrefaccionem. Set aer et aerea inter omnia maxime sunt humida, ergo maxime passibilia et ita ut prius. Non ergo uidetur id quod ipse dicit quod pinguia sunt ⟨in⟩putrescibilia.

Nec uidetur esse causa quam ponit, per causam scilicet quod aeris sunt: ipse enim aer putrescit, singula enim putrescunt preter ignem, sicut habetur in 4 *Metheororum*.

Item, si pinguia essent inputrescibilia, et hoc quia calida et humida, terrestria, que sunt frigida et sicca per locum ab oppositis, essent putrescibilia, quod non uidetur, quia carent causis putrefaccionis, scilicet caliditate et humiditate.

Item, si pinguia que sunt mollia, sunt inputrescibiia, ergo non pinguia que sunt dura sunt putrescibilia. Hoc autem uidemus esse falsum, quia solida corpora ut lapides et metallica corpora non putrefiunt de facili: propter enim soliditatem substancie sue nichil potest dissolui ab eis nec ingredi, quod

of the soul follow the constitution of the body. Thus, it is said that the soul follows the body in its affections and the body follows the soul in its actions.[10]

Question Two

Consequently, a question arises regarding what he says, that fatty things do not rot.

[1.] For that seems to be false, because there are two qualities which in themselves lead to rotting, that is, those which have a centrifugal motion, namely, heat and moisture: for whatever makes a centrifugal motion allows for the entrance of external heat which prepares for the consumption of substantial humidity, and thus as a result for the destruction of innate heat. Thus, therefore, fat will be most likely a cause of rotting since it is hot and moist.

[2.] Since moisture is in itself the cause of rotting, as is clear from the definition of putrefaction given in the fourth book of the *Meteorologica*:[11] for putrefaction is in anything from its own humidity and according to the nature of heat from external heat; therefore, fatty things properly and in themselves will be capable of rotting because properly and in themselves they are humid. And that they are humid in themselves is clear because they are airy, for humidity is to be found first of all in air.

[3.] Again, that which is most passible should be most disposed to putrefaction; but that which is most humid is most passible; therefore, what is most humid should be mostly disposed to putrefaction. But air and airy things are the most moist of all things, therefore they are the most passible, and thus as before. Therefore, it does not seem to be as he says that fatty things are not liable to putrefaction.

Nor does the cause Aristotle posits seem to be the case, namely by reason of the fact that they are airy: for air itself rots, as all individual things rot apart from air, as is held in the fourth book of the *Meteorologica*.[12]

[4.] Again, if fatty things were not liable to rotting, and this because they are hot and humid, earthy things which are cold and dry, to take an opposite example, would be liable to rotting; which does not seem to be the case because they lack the causes of putrefaction, namely, heat and moisture.

[5.] Again, if those fatty things that are soft are not liable to rotting, therefore the non-fatty things which are hard are liable to rotting. This, however, we can see is false because solid bodies such as stones and metallic bodies do not easily rot for because of the solidity of their substance nothing can be dissolved from them or enter into them which would destroy their substance. And accordingly Aristotle

---

10 See Nicholaus Peripateticus, *Quaestiones* VI, 130n; and also below, *Determinatio Magistralis*, 209.
11 Aristoteles, *Meteorologica* IV i, 379a 16–18.
12 Ibid., 379a 14–15.

eorum substanciam corrumpat. Et propter hoc dicit Aristotiles quod non crescunt. Vnde dicit quod lapides et sales et terra unius modi sunt nec crescunt nec augentur.

Quod autem non putrefiat, uidetur illud proprie quod non putrescit nec redit ad suam naturam, sicut caro putrefacta non potest reduci ad suam naturalitatem. Set aer non mutatur a specie aeris per illam inpressionem factam que inpediat effectum eius; non ergo aer purum elementum putrescit. Constat ergo quod putrefaccio aeris non dicitur eius corrupcio substancialis cum unitur in genere ad aliud elementum, set dicitur alteracio quedam uel secundum qualitates primas uel | secundarias, et quocumque modo contingit ut redeat ad naturalitatem suam. Et ita aer qui est purum elementum non putrescit.

Item, cum in omni putrefaccione mutetur sapor et odor, unde dicitur quod omne putrefactum fetidum; sapor autem et odor secundum quod mixtum; purum ergo elementum non potest mutari secundum saporem et odorem; ⟨quod⟩ nullam enim secundariam qualitatem habet, non est possibile putridum fieri.

Item, dicit Aristotiles quod omnia putrefacta ad ultinium fiunt fimus et terra; nullum purum elementum potest conuerti in fimum et terram; nullum ergo elementum purum est putrescibile. Si autem terra per putrefaccionem conuerteretur in fimum et terram, illa iterum terra in qua facta fuit conuersio iterum esset conuertibilis in aliam, cum omnis terra sit putrescibilis, et sic esset procedere in infinitum.

Item, cum unumquodque naturale habeat calorem per cuius existenciam saluetur eius esse et per cuius extraccionem corrumpitur aer, aut est calor eius complexionalis, quem habet ab igne, aut calor celestis; si dicatur quod sit calor complexionalis, hoc non potest esse, quia per eius extraccionem mutaretur ex toto aer secundum substanciam, et non amplius maneret sub contrarietate.

Item, si per extraccionem caloris complexionalis fieret putrefactio, cum in aqua que est purum elementum non sit talis calor neque in terra, non contingeret ita putrefieri, et ita haberetur propositum quod nullum purum elementum putrefieret. Si ergo poterit aer corrumpi per extraccionem a continente, hoc erit per extraccionem caloris celestis per cuius presenciam saluatur cuiuslibet esse; set si hoc, non contingit euitare quin

says that they do not grow.[13] Thus, he says that stones and salts and earth have one mode [of existence] and do not grow or increase.

That something does not become rotten, it seems that it is proper to that which does not become rotten nor returns to its nature, just as corrupted flesh cannot return to its natural state. However, air does not change from the species of air through that impression which has been made which impedes its effect; therefore air which is a pure element does not rot. Therefore, it is clear that the putrefaction of air does not refer to its substantial corruption when it is united in its genus to another element, rather it refers to a certain change either in respect of prime qualities or secondary qualities, and in whatever way it happens to that it returns to its natural state. And thus air which is a pure element does not rot.

[6.] Again, since taste and smell change in all rotting, so that it is said that all rotting is fetid;[14] however, taste and smell exist inasmuch as they are of a composite body; therefore a pure element cannot change in respect of taste and smell; because it does not have any secondary quality it is not possible for it to become rotten.

[7.] Again, Aristotle says[15] that all rotten things in the end become dung and earth; no pure element can be converted into dung and earth; therefore no pure element can become rotten. If, however, earth by means of putrefaction were to be converted into dung and earth, that earth in which the conversion was made would be again convertible into another earth, since all earth is capable of putrefaction, and thus it would be possible to go on into infinity.

[8.] Again, since every natural thing whatsoever has a heat through the existence of which its being is preserved and through the extraction of which the air is corrupted, either this is its constitutional heat which it has from fire, or it is celestial heat. If it is said that it is complexional heat, this cannot be the case because by its extraction air would be completely changed in respect of its substance and moreover would not remain under the classification of contrariety.

[9.] Again, if putrefaction occurred through the extraction of constitutional heat, since this heat would not be in water which is a pure element nor in earth, then it would not happen that putrefaction would occur in this way, and thus one would have the proposition that no pure element would become rotten. If, therefore, air could be corrupted through extraction by the environment, this would be through the extraction of celestial heat through whose presence every being whatever is preserved. However, if this is so, it would not be possible to avoid the fact

---

13 Nicholaus Damascenus, *De plantis* II i.
14 See Aristotle, *Meteorologica* IV i, 379a 5–6.
15 Ibid., 379a 22–23.

ignis putrefiat sicut alia elementa. Constat enim quod quinta essencia que continet omnia in infinitum plus habet de calore celesti quam ignis; in infinitum ergo dominatur quantum ad illum calorem quinta essencia caloris ignis. Sicut ergo ignis extrahit calorem aeris, ita et quinta essencia forcius extrahet calorem per quem conseruatur esse ignis. Et sic male dicit in littera quod ignis non putrescit.

Si autem hic dicatur quod non intelligit hic Aristotiles de aereo elemento, set de aere confuso extra 4, illud adhuc non uidetur, quia si aliquid componitur ex corporibus, de necessitate illud est corruptibile. Et similiter si aliquid ex putrescibilibus, illud est putrescibile; ergo ab oppositis si aliquid est compositum ex inputrescibilibus, illud est inputrescibile. Si ergo elementa sunt inputrescibila, uidetur quod corpus confusum ex ipsis sit inputrescibile. Quicquid enim attribuitur, sicut dicit Aueroys, mixto de generacione et corrupcione, attribuitur ipsi racione alicuius simplicium que ingrediuntur esse eius. Sic ergo uidetur quod aer nullo modo putrefiat.

Solucio. Ad eorum euidenciam sciendum quod quedam pinguedo habet plus de aqueo uel terreo quam aereo, quedam autem plus de aereo. Vnde Aristotiles in libro *De Animalibus* ponit differenciam inter zirbum et pinguedinem puram, dicens quod zirbus coagolatur et puluerizatur, pinguedo autem pura non; unde brodium equi numquam potest coagolari. Et pinguedo autem est in habentibus dentes in utraque mandibula, zirbus autem est in habentibus solum dentes in inferiori. Quamuis dicat alibi quod in animalibus omnibus habentibus sanguinem est zirbus. Talis autem pinguedo que est zirbus non conseruat a putrefaccione nec est difficile siccabile eo quod habet humidum grossum et terrestre, quod de facili potest sublimari per calidum extraneum. Propter hoc dicit Aristotiles quod puluerizatur.

Item, pinguedo in animali, secundum quod uult Aristotiles ibidem, aliquando est admixta cum carne, aliquando sola; animalia autem habencia pinguedinem maximam cum carne parum habent pinguedinis circa uentrem, et talis pinguedo est pinguedo uentuosa, nec de facili desiccatur, et est generata per calorem fortem et ulteriorem digestionem quam sit caro; set illa que est circa uentrem est coagolata debili calore, cuius signum

that fire would become rotten like the other elements. For it is clear that the fifth element which contains everything in an infinite way has more of celestial heat than fire; therefore, the fifth element predominates over the heat of fire in an infinite way in respect of that heat. Therefore, just as fire extracts the heat of air, so also the fifth element more forcibly extracts the heat through which the being of fire is preserved. And thus Aristotle says incorrectly in the text that fire does not rot.

However, if it were said here that Aristotle does not have air which is an element in mind here, but air which is mixed up outside of the four elements, then this does not seem to be the case because if anything is composed of bodies, of necessity it is corruptible. And similarly if anything is composed of things which can rot, that is capable of rotting. Therefore, on the other hand, if anything is composed of things which cannot rot, it will be incapable of rotting. If, therefore, the elements are incapable of rotting, it seems that a body mixed up of these will be incapable of corruption. As Ibn Rushd says,[16] whatever is attributed to a mixed body regarding generation and corruption is attributed to it by reason of some simple bodies which enter into its being. Thus, therefore, it is clear that air can in no way rot.

Solution. In order to make these clear, it should be known that some fat has more of the watery or the earthy than the airy, some however have more of the airy. Thus Aristotle in the book *On Animals*[17] puts forward a difference between zirbus[18] and pure fattiness, saying that omentum becomes thick and is pulverized, pure fat does not; thus horse broth can never thicken. Again, fat is to be found in those which have teeth in both jaws, but zirbus is to be found in those which only have teeth in the lower jaw (even if Aristotle says elsewhere that zirbus is to be found in all animals which have blood). The kind of fat, however, which is zirbus does not protect against putrefaction nor is it easily dried up because it has a gross and earthy kind of humidity, which can easily be sublimated by external heat. For this reason, Aristotle says that it can be pulverized.

[1.] Again, the fat which is in an animal, according to what Aristotle says in the same place,[19] is sometimes mixed with flesh and sometimes is on its own. Those animals which have the most fat with flesh have a small amount of fat around the stomach and such fat is windy nor is it easily dried up, and it is produced by strong heat and a further digestion than flesh is. But that which is near the stomach is

---

16 See Averroes, *De causis longitudinis et brevitatis vitae*, 129.
17 See Aristotle, *Historia animalium* III xvii, 520a 4 ff.; also *De partibus animalium* II v, 651a 20–36.
18 Zirbus seems to include omentum but to be more as well. See Albert the Great, *Questions Concerning Aristotle's On Animals* XII, q. 12, 372 and note 42.
19 See Aristotle, *Historia animalium* III xvii, 520a 21–22.

est quod dissoluitur a facili de calido, quia fuit coagolata a frigido, ut appelletur frigidum calor | debilis. In quibusdam autem animalibus, zirbus est mixtus cum pinguedine, et propter hoc zirbus piscium non coagolatur.

Sciendum iterum quod non est idem unctuositas ex toto et pinguedo, quod patet per Ysaac dicentem quod in animalibus gressibilibus plus est de unctuositate et minus de pinguedine, et in natabilibus econtrario. Probat experimento et racione; experimento, qua magis inuiscat pinguedo gressibilis si tangatur quam natabilis. Aliam differenciam ponit quod unctuositas magis est calida et humida quam pinguedo; pinguia ergo inunctuosa plus habent de calido et humido quam alia pinguia, et talia proprie sunt aerea. Vnde dicit Aristotiles quod in pinguedine nichil est de aqua et terra, set supernatat aquam, eo quod multum includitur in ipsa de aere, sicut si includentur in utre; talis enim pinguedo, etsi sit irritatiua flamme, non tamen hoc facit secundum se nisi admisceatur siccum; flamma enim non generatur nisi in fumo, fumus autem non generatur nisi ex humido admixto cum sicco. Et propter hoc cera secundum se non inflammatur nec alia pinguedo liquida; et propter hoc additur licinium, ut ex siccitate licinii et ex humiditate pinguedinis fiat temperamentum, quod potest fieri materia fumi. Set pinguia grossa que multum habent de aqueo et terreo per se sunt inflammabilia, eo quod possunt resolui in fumum. Ex quo patet quod pinguedo pura aerea non potest desiccari a calore. Et hoc est quod dicit Aristotiles in littera: *Oportet pingue non de facili esse siccabile* [Cf. 466a 23] nec a frigido. Constat enim quod pinguedo pura non coagolatur a frigido, sicut patet per Aristotilem in 4 *Metheororum*, ubi dicit quod ambiguissime ⟨nature⟩ se habet oleum, et cetera, et hoc est propter multitudinem sue caliditatis et sue unctuositatis uiscose, que facit firmam adherenciam parcium et ad retentionem parcium aerearum et caloris per quem conseruatur eius esse. Vnde ⟨cum⟩ calidum agit in oleum non coagolatur set operatur ad conuersionem parcium aquearum in aereas; uiscositas enim non permittit partes aqueas exalare, nisi totum ipsum oleum exalet ex toto. Similiter cum frigidum agit in ipsum partes aereas condempsatim aqueas nec possunt exprimi prop|ter uiscositatem. Et sic semper, siue calidum siue frigidum agat in ipsum, rema-

thickened by weak heat, a sign of which is that it is dissolved as easily by heat as it was coagulated by cold, so that cold is called weak heat. However, in some animals zirbus is mixed with fat and for this reason the zirbus of fish does not thicken.

[2.] Again, it should be known that oiliness is not completely the same as fattiness, as is clear from what Isaac ben Solomon Israeli says,[20] that in walking animals there is more oiliness and less of fattiness whereas in swimming animals it is the opposite. He proves this both from experience and by argument: by experience, because the fat of a walking animal is stickier when it is touched than that of a swimming animal. Another difference which he posits is that oiliness is more hot and moist than fattiness; therefore, fatty animals which are oily have more of warmth and moisture than other fatty animals, and such animals are properly speaking airy. Thus, Aristotle says[21] that there is nothing of water and earth in fat but rather it floats on water because there is a lot of air enclosed in it, just as if it were enclosed in a vase. For such fat, even if it triggers flame, yet it does not do this in itself but only if it is mixed with the dry; for flame is only produced in smoke and smoke is only produced from humidity mixed with the dry. And for this reason a candle in itself will not go on fire nor will any other liquid fat; and for this reason a wick is added so that from the dryness of the wick and the humidity of the fat a balance arises which can become the raw matter of the smoke. However, thick fats that have a lot of water and earth are inflammable in themselves because they can be dissolved into smoke. From which it is clear that a pure airy fat cannot be dried up by heat. And this is what Aristotle says in the text: the fat should not be easily dried up nor from cold. For it is clear that pure fat is not thickened by cold, as is clear from Aristotle in the fourth book of the *Meteorologica* where he says[22] that oil has a most ambiguous nature, etc., and this is because of the extent of its heat and viscous oiliness which makes for a firm adhesion of the parts and for a retention of the airy parts and of the heat through which its being is preserved. Thus, when heat acts upon the oil it is not thickened but it brings about a change of the watery parts into airy parts; for the viscosity does not allow the watery parts to be given off unless the oil itself is completely given off. Similarly, when cold acts upon those airy parts condensing them into watery parts, again they cannot be expressed because of the viscosity. And thus it is all the time, whether the hot or the cold acts on it, it remains in a liquid form, and that happens, as Aristotle says,[23]

---

20 Isaac Israeli, *De dietis universalibus* xxxviii, f. 71ra-rb.
21 Aristotle, *De generatione animalium* II ii, 735b 25–27.
22 Aristotle, *Meteorologica* IV vii, 383b 20–21.
23 See ibid., 383b 24–25.

net in sua liquiditate; et illud accidit, sicut dicit Aristotiles, non solum quia uiscosum, set quia plenum aeris. Et sic patet quare pinguia aerea non de facili desiccantur. Et eciam patet causa quare non putrefiunt de facili, eo quod habent multum de calore, qui non potest exalare propter uiscositatem inpedientem. Vnde uiscositas prohibet ingressum calori extraneo et egressum calori innato. Quotiens enim non potest uinci calor rei contente a calore continentis, non accidit putrefaccio. Vnde dicit Aristotiles quod feruens, prout calidum est, non putrefit; et reddit causam, quia minor est calor in aere quam in re contenta, qua de causa nequaquam uincit nec facit permutacionem quamlibet. Pinguia ergo inputrescibilia sunt eo quod eorum calor non uincitur a calore continentis.

Hiis uisis, facile ⟨est⟩ respondere ad obiecta.

Quod obiciebatur primo, quod pinguia sunt calida et humida, et ita habent duas causas que faciunt ad putrefaccionem, dicendum quod quecumque caliditas non operatur ad putrefaccionem; set caliditas extranea. Calor enim naturalis facit ad congregacionem parcium, sicut dicit Auicenna, et ad commoracionem parcium, nisi calor extraneus faciat contrarium. — Vel potest dici, quod, etsi calidum et humidum habeant de se facere motum a centro, tamen inpediunt⟨ur⟩ in quibusdam propter uiscositatem, que non patitur separacionem parcium, et ita nec, per consequens, ingressio caloris extrinseci continentis.

Ad id quod obiciebatur quod, cum humiditas per se sit causa putrefaccionis, non tamen propter hoc sequitur quod quodlibet humidum de facili sit putrescibile. Dicit enim Aristotiles quod putrefaccio est communis passio geliditatis proprie et caliditatis aliene. Vnde, cum sit multum de humido in re contenta cum habundancia geliditatis naturalis, tunc de facili incidit putrefaccio. Et similiter cum est humiditas cum habundancia caliditatis extranee; | set cum est cum habundancia caliditatis innate, non de facili uincitur a calore continentis, et tunc fit conseruacio a putrefaccione.

Ad tercio obiectum dicendum quod, etsi humiditas sit maxime passibilis, non tamen sequitur quod quodcumque humidum sit maxime passibile a quocumque; accio enim potest inpediri, ne de facili patiatur per aliquod adiunctum ei. Si aliquis debilis de facili expungnatur a quolibet forciori; set si iuuetur ab alio, non ita de facili expungnatur; similiter, etsi humiditas de facili sit passibilis, non tamen cum forti calore est

not only because it is viscous but because it is full of air. And thus it is clear why airy fatty things are not easily dried up. Again, the cause is clear why they do not easily rot because they have a lot of heat which cannot be given off because of the viscosity impeding this. Thus, viscosity does not allow the incoming of external heat and the outgoing of innate heat. For rotting will not occur as long as the heat contained in the heat of the environment cannot overcome the thing. Thus, Aristotle says,[24] something which is boiling inasmuch as it is hot, does not rot; and he gives the reason, because the heat in the environment is less than that contained in the thing, and because of that cause it can in no way overcome nor bring about any change whatsoever. Therefore, fatty things cannot become rotten because the heat of the environment cannot overcome their heat.

Having seen these things, it is easy to respond to the objections.

[1.] With regard to that which was objected first, that fatty things are warm and moist and thus they have two causes which bring about rotting, it should be stated that it is not just any heat which brings about putrefaction but rather external heat. For natural heat brings about a coming together of the parts, as Ibn Sīna says, and a remaining together of the parts unless the external heat does the opposite. Or it can be said that even if heat and humidity in themselves have the tendency to bring about a centrifugal motion, yet this is impeded in some because of viscosity, which does not undergo the separation of parts and thus, neither, as a consequence, does it undergo the coming in of the extrinsic heat of the environment.

[2.] With regard to that which was objected that since humidity in itself is the cause of rotting, it does not, however, follow that any kind of humidity can easily become capable of rotting. For Aristotle says[25] that putrefaction is a common attribute of extreme cold in itself and the heat of another. Thus, when there is a lot of humidity contained in a thing with an abundance of natural extreme cold, the rotting easily occurs. And similarly when there is humidity with an abundance of external heat; but when it is with an abundance of innate heat, the heat of the environment does not easily overcome it and thus a preservation occurs from putrefaction.

[3.] With regard to the third objection it should be said that even if humidity is most passible yet it does not follow that any humidity whatsoever is most passible by anything whatever; for an action can be impeded lest it be easily affected by something which has been added to it. If something weak is easily beaten by something stronger, yet if it is aided by another it is not so easily beaten. Similarly, even if humidity is easily passible, yet with a strong heat it is not passible by the environ-

---

24 Ibid., IV i, 379a 31–33.
25 Ibid., 379a 20–22.

passibilis a continente. Vnde patet quod non sequitur quod pinguia, quamuis sint per se humida, sint putrescibilia. Vnde per interempcionem assumpcionis potest solui illud argumentum.

Ad 4 dicendum quod in oppositis sese includentibus non tenet consequenter in ipso, set magis econtrario: pinguia enim mollia, illud contrarium continet ista duo contraria, putrescibile et inputrescibile. Quedam enim pinguia mollia sunt putrescibilia et quedam pinguia mollia sunt inputrescibilia. Vnde, sicut non ualet istud argumentum: Omne euectum est sanum, ergo, omne chathochiuum est egrum; sicut non ualet istud argumentum: si pinguia mollia sunt putrescibilia, quod non pinguia dura sunt putrescibilia; et est in omni tali argumento fallacia consequentis.

Ad hoc quod querebatur, utrum aer putrefiat, dicendum sicut ostensum erat, quod aer elementum non putrefit. Et concedimus raciones que inducte fuerunt ad hoc. — Raciones autem inducte ad oppositum soluuntur in primo capitulo 4 *Metheororum*. Vnde non oportet hic eas ponere.

⟨Questio 3⟩

Item, dubitabit aliquis ad hoc quod ipse dicit quod *multa semina senescant cito* [v, 466b 8], et redit causam quare *semen superfluitas est et ex⟨s⟩iccat abiectum* [v, 466b 8–9].

Videtur enim quod emissio seminis, cum sit superfluitas, sit causa salubris, quia cuiuscumque retencio infert nocumentum corpori, expulsio eius erit iuuamentum, cuius contrarium dicit in littera. | Veritas assumpcionis patet per id quod dicit in littera quod *contraria est superfluitas potencia et corruptiua* [v, 466b 6]; quod autem retencio superflui siue seminis inferat nocumentum, patet, quia aliquando redundat sperma retentum super epar, et corrumpitur uirtus digestiua; aliquando resoluitur in fumos uenenosos, ex quo accidit aliquando mania et melancolia et multe alie egritudines; et aliquando fiunt apost⟨em⟩ata uenenosa per eius residenciam et putrefaccionem in aliquo membro.

De decisione spermatis dubitauerunt antiqui. Dicebant enim quidam quod deciditur a toto corpore ad quod induxerunt, sicut dicit Aristotiles in libro *De Animalibus*, 3 raciones: prima sumitur a delectacione, que maior est propter deci-

ment. Thus, it is clear that it does not follow that fatty things are liable to rot even if they are humid. Thus, it is clear that by the removal of the minor premise the argument can be destroyed.

[4.] With regard to the fourth argument it should be stated that in opposing things which include themselves that it does not hold consequently in this but rather the other way around: for soft fatty things, that contrary contains these two contraries, liable to rotting and not liable to rotting. For some soft fatty things are liable to rotting and some soft fatty things are not liable to rotting. Thus, just as this argument is not valid: "All vomiting is healthy, therefore every antiemetic is unhealthy" so that argument is not valid either: "If soft fats are liable to rotting, that hard fats are not liable to rotting"; and in all such arguments there is a fallacy of the consequent.

[5.] With regard to that which was asked, whether air rots, it should be said as was shown that air which is a pure element does not rot. And we concede the arguments which were brought forward in this regard. The arguments which were brought forward against are solved in the first chapter of the fourth book of the *Meteorologica*.[26] Thus, it is not necessary to put them forward here.

Question Three

Again, somebody will doubt with regard to what Aristotle says that *a lot of semen and too much emitted ages quickly*, and he gives the reason why: *for semen is a waste product and moreover its emission dries up*.

For it seems that the emission of semen, since it is a waste product, would be a cause of health because the retention of anything causes harm to the body and its expulsion will be helpful, the opposite of which Aristotle says in the text. The truth of the minor premise is clear from what Aristotle says in the text that *a waste product is contrary and a corruptive power*. However, that the retention of a waste product or semen causes harm is clear because sometimes sperm which is retained backs up over the liver and destroys the digestive power; sometimes it dissolves into poisonous fumes from which sometimes madness and melancholy and many other diseases arises. And sometimes poisonous abscesses arise because of its presence and putrefaction in some organs.

The Ancients wondered concerning the descent of sperm for some said that it descended from the entire body and in respect of which they introduced three arguments, as Aristotle says in the book *On Animals*.[27] The first argument is taken

---

26 See ibid., 379a 11–b 6.
27 See *De generatione animalium* I xvii, 721b 6–24.

sionem a toto corpore quam a parte; secunda sumitur a similitudine generantis et generati in inperfeccione, quia filius inperfectus generatur frequenter ex inperfecto; tercia racio sumitur a similitudine inperfeccionum, quia a generante habente membra ⟨in⟩ perfecta generatur filius habens membra inperfecta, et non potest esse nisi membrum ex quo fit generacio decidatur a quolibet membro. Etsi iste raciones essent sufficientes, falsum esset quod dicit Aristotiles hic, quod semen est superfluitas, cum sit decisio a substanciis membrorum. Et respondet Aristotiles istis racionibus. Et primo prime, dicens quod summa delectacio que est in emissione spermatis, non est propter decisionem aliquam que fit a membris, set propter confricacionem omnium membrorum in corpore. Vnde qui multum utuntur coitu non multum delectantur. — Ad aliud dicit quod semen non est id quod deciditur a toto, set est aliquid quod est conueniens et adsimilabile toti. Vnde dicit quod est ultimum quod additur supra totum corpus assimilabile. Et quia est illud superfluum cibi quod est in ultima potencia ut assimiletur corpori, propter hoc in potencia habet in se omnia membra, nullum tamen actu, eo quod illa superfluitas non actualiter habebat speciem membrorum nec erat | conuersa in species membrorum, set facta tamen est sicut necessitas, et propter hoc sigillata est potencia in ipso ad species omnium, et propter hoc filii non frequenter assimilantur generantibus.

Set adhuc restat dubitacio quomodo ex mutilatis generantur filii perfecti.

Si enim nichil de superfluo ultimi cibi sit in ultima potencia assimilandi membris que deficiunt, quod patet quod unicuique membro appropriata est sua ⟨uirtus⟩ digestiua et sua uirtus conuersiua conuertenti in suam speciem. Tercia enim digestiva digerit carnem in carne et os in osse, et alius est cibus ossis quam carnis, quia si non esset diuersus, non esset os diuersum a carne. Deficiente ergo uirtute adaptante materiam, deficit materia que debet esse necessitas respectu membrorum deficiencium in generante; et si hoc, ut uidetur, inpossibile esset ex mutilato generari perfectum.

Ad quod dicendum quod ex superfluitate cibi ossuum aliorum membrorum generatur os membri mutilati et ex superfluitate cibi ⟨carnis aliorum membrorum generatur caro membri

from pleasure which is greater because of its descent from all of the body rather than from a part; the second argument is taken from the similarity in imperfection between the parent and the offspring, because frequently an imperfect son is produced from an imperfect parent; the third argument is taken from the similarity of imperfections because from a parent who has an imperfect organ a son is produced who has imperfect organs, and this can only be the case if the organ from which the production takes place descends from a certain organ. And even if these arguments are sufficient, it is false what Aristotle says here,[28] that semen is a waste product since it is something which descends from the substances of the organs. And Aristotle would respond with these arguments. And first of all, he replies by saying that the height of pleasure that is in the emission of sperm is not because of a certain descent which occurs from all of the organs but is because of the rubbing together of all of the organs in the body. Thus, those who have a lot of sexual intercourse do not have much pleasure.[29] With respect to the other point, Aristotle says[30] that semen is not that which descends from the whole but is something which is connected and assimilated to the whole. Thus, Aristotle says[31] that it is the final thing which is added to what can be assimilated to the body. And since it is that waste product of food that is in its final potency so that it can be assimilated to the body, it has because of that the potential in itself to be all organs but none in act. Because that waste product does not actually have the form of the organs nor was it changed into the form of the organs, but it has, however, been made into a kind of a necessity and because of this there is a potency sealed in it in respect of all forms. And for this reason children not infrequently resemble their parents.

However, a doubt remains as to how complete children are produced from those who are mutilated.

For if nothing of the waste product of the finally digested food is in the final potency to be assimilated to the organs which are missing, which is clear because to each organ is assigned its proper digestive power and its transformative power to convert into its own form. The third stage of digestion digests flesh into flesh and bone into bone,[32] and the food of bone is different from the food of flesh, because if it were not diverse, bone would not be different from flesh. Therefore, if the power to adapt the matter is lacking, the matter will be lacking which should be a necessity with respect to the deficiencies of the organs in the parent; and if this is the case, as it seems, it will be impossible for a complete being to be produced by a mutilated one.

To which it should be said that from the waste produce of the food of the bones of other limbs is produced the bone of the mutilated limb and from the waste produce of the food of the flesh of the other limbs is produced the flesh of

---

28 Ibid., 721b 23–24; 28 ff.
29 Ibid., 723b 33–724a 1.
30 Ibid., 725a 21–22.
31 Ibid., 725a 24–25.
32 See Isaac Israeli, *Liber urinarum*, f. 160vb.

mutilati). Ad hoc inducuntur 3 raciones Aristotilis in libro *De Animalibus*. Prima est quod animalia magni corporis sunt causa parue generacionis et parui corporis multe. Causa autem huius non potest esse nisi quia superfluitas cibi in magnis animalibus parua est, eo quod conuertitur in crementum corporis; set corpora parua indigent nutrimento pauco, et propter hoc ex cibo ultimo derelinquuntur multe superfluitates, que possunt esse materia multiplicis generacionis. Et hec est causa quare animalia magni corporis sunt paucorum filiorum et parui corporis multorum. — Alia causa est quia in etate puericie non emittitur sperma, et causa non est nisi quia cibus quartus totum conuertitur in crementum corporis. Vnde dicit Aristotiles quod 5 annis recipit puer medietatem crementi quod recipit in toto tempore residuo. — Tercia racio est quod homines multe pinguedinis et multe carnis non generant, quia superfluitas que est in eis digeritur et | conuertitur in carnem et pinguedinem. Ex hiis ergo patet quod sperma est superfluitas cibi. Vnde patet falsitas eorum qui posuerunt quod sperma decidatur a cerebro proprie, quod uoluerunt probare per hoc quod cerebrum est illud membrum quod maxime incurrit nocumentum et priusquam aliud aliquod membrum ex coitu. Et dicit Aristotiles quod oculus est locus aptissimus ad generacionem spermatis, cuius signum est quod per eius emissionem debilitatur uisus. Causa autem huius est, sicut dicit Aristotiles, eo quod eius natura est similis nature cerebri, et ita per hoc uidetur quod sperma decidatur a cerebro. Non tamen ilud de necessitate sequitur per illam racionem, quia, quod in coytu prius incurrit nocumentum cerebrum quam aliud membrum, hoc est quia in coytu cum spermate extrahitur calor naturalis purus et mundus, sicut dicit Aristotiles. Vnde cum cerebrum sit frigidissimum in toto corpore, per deperdicionem caloris naturalis, cicius incurrit nocumentum, quia, cum totum corpus depauperetur a calore naturali et spirituali, quia spiritus gignitiuus componitur ex triplici spiritu, calidi, spirituali et naturali, propter hoc totum corpus incurrit debilitatem ex frequenti einissione seminis; et quia

the mutilated limb. In respect of this Aristotle puts forward three arguments in the book, *On Animals*.[33] The first is that animals with a large body are the cause of little production and those with small bodies produce many. The cause of this cannot be other than the waste product of food in large animals is small because it is transformed into the increase in size of the body; but small bodies require a small amount of food and because of this there remain a lot of waste products from the finally digested food which can be the matter of many productions. And this is the reason why animals with a large body have few offspring and those with a small body have many. Another cause is because during the time of childhood sperm is not emitted and the reason for this can only be that the fourthly digested food is converted into the growth of the body. Thus Aristotle says[34] that a child gets in five years half of the growth that it gets in all of the remaining time. The third reason is that men who have a lot of fat and a lot of flesh do not reproduce[35] because the waste product that is in them is digested and converted into flesh and fat.[36] From these things it is clear that sperm is a waste product of food. Thus, the falsity is clear of those who posit that the sperm descends from the brain itself, which they wanted to prove by the fact that the brain is that organ which most incurs damage as a result of sexual intercourse and before any other member. Again, Aristotle says[37] that the eye is the most apt place for the generation of sperm, a sign of which is that because of its emission sight is weakened. The cause of this is, as Aristotle says,[38] that its nature is similar to that of the brain and thus because of this it seems that sperm descends from the brain. However, this does not necessarily follow because of that argument since what firstly gets harmed in sexual intercourse is the brain more than any other organ and this is because, as Aristotle says,[39] in sexual intercourse pure and clean natural heat is extracted together with the sperm. Thus, since the brain is the coldest part of the entire body, as a result of the loss of natural heat, it more quickly incurs harm because the whole body is deprived of natural and spiritual heat. Since the generative spirit is composed of a threefold spirit, of the hot, the spiritual and the natural, for this reason the whole body incurs a weakening from the frequent emission of semen;[40] and because semen is not just any

---

33 Aristotle, *De generatione animalium* I xviii, 725a 28–30.
34 Ibid., 725b 19–25.
35 Ibid., 725b 29–33.
36 Aristotle, *De Partibus Animalium* II v, 651b 13–15.
37 Aristotle, *De Generatione Animalium* II vii, 747a 13–16.
38 Ibid., 747a 17–19.
39 Ibid., V iii, 783b 28–31.
40 Ibid., I xviii, 725b 6–7.

non est quecumque superfluitas semen, set superfluitas qua indigetur, sicut dicit Aristotiles, propter hoc per frequentem emissionem depauperatur corpus ab humiditate, et sic semen abiectum desiccat. Et hoc est quod dicit in littera.

Ex hiis patet solucio ad id quod obiciebatur, quod retencio seminis infert nocumentum ubi sit multum superfluum, et tunc est superfluum, cum destruitur a regimine nature.

kind of waste product but a waste product which is needed, as Aristotle says, [41] for this reason by frequent emission the body is deprived of humidity and thus when semen is ejected this causes dryness. And this is what Aristotle says in the text.

From this the solution is clear to that which was objected because the retention of semen causes harm where there is a lot of waste product, and then there is a waste product, since this is destroyed by the rule of nature.

---

41 Ibid., 725a 24.

⟨Lectio 7⟩

[466b 12] Amplius autem, quecumque fatigantia sunt masculorum, et propter laborem senescunt magis; desiccat enim labor, senectus autem sicca. Natura enim in omne est [15] dicere, masculina feminis longius uiuunt, quoniam maioris caloris est masculus femina. Sed que sunt in calidis, longioris uite sunt quam que in frigidis locis propter eamdem causam propter quam uere et maxime permanifesta est magnitudo secundum naturam frigidorum animalium et propter hoc serpentes [20] et talpe et pelle uaria magna sunt in calidis locis et in mari Rubro ostracoderma, ut sunt ostrea post alia. Augmenti enim calida humiditas causa est uite. In humidis autem locis magis aquosum est humidum quod est in animalibus; unde leuius densatur. Quare hec quidem non omnino fiunt [25] animalium, nec quantitatis magne, que sunt pauci sanguinis in locis ad Arctum, nec gressibilia nec aquosa in mari. Hec quidem fiunt minora quidem et uite breuioris. Aufert enim gelu augmentum. Alimentum non accipientia et plante et animalia corrumpuntur. Consummunt [30] enim ipsa se ipsa. Sicut enim multa flamma obruit et corrumpit paruam in alimento consumendo, sic et physicus calor primum digestiuus et cuius est digestio, consumit materiam [33] in qua est. Aquatica autem pedibus ambulantibus minus longioris uite sunt, non quoniam [467a 1] humida simpliciter, sed quoniam aquosa sunt. Huiusmodi autem humidum uelociter corrumpitur, quoniam frigidum et densibile est. Et etiam quod est sine sanguine, propter idem, nisi magnitudine protendatur. Nec enim pinguedinem nec dulcedinem habet. In animali enim pinguedo dulcedo est. Vnde apes [5] longioris uite sunt aliis animalibus maioribus.

6. [467a 6] Et in plantis sunt que longius uiuunt et magis quam in animalibus, primum quidem quoniam minus aquosa sunt. Quare non cito densatur. Postea dulcedinem habent et pinguedinem; ex quo etiam sicca et terrea sunt. Tamen non habent humorem leuiter exsiccabilem. [10] De eo autem quod multo tempore est esse arborum naturam, oportet causam aggredi. Habent enim ad animalia proprium, nisi ad incisa. Noue enim semper plante fiunt; ex quo multo tempore sunt. Semper enim altere productiones fiunt nec senescunt; et radices similiter et | non simul, sed, quando productio [15] et rami

Seventh Lecture

Text (466b 12–467a 25)

Moreover, it is the case regarding those males that are subject to great toil and because of their work to become old more quickly; for work dries up and old age is dry. For by nature as a general rule, the male lives longer than the female because the male has a greater heat than the female. However, those who are in warmer places are longer-lived than those who are in cold places; for the same reason why truly and most clearly there is the large size according to nature of cold animals. And because of this snakes and moles and those with scaly skin are of a large size in hot regions and so are the shellfish in the Red Sea such as those which after others are oysters. For the warm moisture is a cause of growth as well as life. However, in humid places there is a more watery humidity that is in the animals and so it congeals more easily. For this reason, in northerly places either there are no animals at all which have little blood, nor those of a large size, nor those which walk on dry land nor animals which swim in the sea; or if there are animals they are small and short-lived; for the icy cold takes away growth. For both animals and plants are destroyed if they do not take in food, for they consume themselves. For just as the large flame destroys and corrupts the small flame by consuming the fuel, so also the natural heat which is primarily digestive and that of which there is digestion, consumes the matter in which it is. Water animals are shorter-lived than land animals not because they are simply humid but because they are watery. Humidity of this kind is swiftly destroyed because it is cold and is easily congealed. And again, that which is without blood, for the same reason, is swiftly destroyed unless it is protected by size. For it has neither fatness nor sweetness. For in an animal there is sweet fat. Thus, bees are longer-lived than other larger animals.

Those which are longest-lived are among plants and more than among animals, for, first of all, they are less watery which is the reason why they are not quickly congealed. Further, they have sweetness and fatness; from which also they are dry and earthy. However, they do not have a moisture which can be easily dried up. It is necessary, however, to ascertain the cause of that which is why it is the nature of trees to exist for a long time. For in respect of animals they have something proper to themselves, except with regard to insects. For new plants always arise, for which reason they exist for a long time. For other shoots always arise nor do they age;

perduntur,[1] alteri autem germinant. Cum autem sic faciunt, radices alie ex eo quod est, fiunt et sic semper perficiunt; hoc quidem corruptum, id uero factum totum, propter quod hec quidem longius uiuunt. Comparantur enim plante decisis sicut dictum est. Decisa enim uiuunt et duo et multa fiunt [20] ex uno. Decisa autem usque ad id quod est uiuere, ueniunt, multo autem non possum tempore, nec enim habent organa, non possunt ipsa facere principium quod in unoquodque est, sed quod est in planta potest. Vndique enim radices habent et germen potentia; unde et ab hac semper prouenit, hoc quidem nouum, illud autem uetus. Parum [25] autem est aliqua differentia in eo quod est sic semper esse longioris uite ⟨...⟩ [desunt 467a 26–467b 9].

Amplius autem quecumque fatigancia, et cetera [v, 466b 12]. Continuacio huius partis et ordo ad precedentem patet per precedencia.

Et diuiditur ista pars in duas[2] partes, in quarum prima ponit causas longitudinis et breuitatis uite repertas in animalibus tantum; in secunda parte ponit causas communiter repertas in plantis. Et patet ordo et sufficiencia.

Quantum ad primam partem procedit hoc modo. Dicit quod *quecumque sunt fatigancia masculorum et per laborem senescunt magis* [v, 466b 12–13]. Et subiungit causam dicens: *Desiccat enim labor, senectus autem sicca est* [v, 466b 13–14]. Et est demonstracio talis: Omne desiccans corpus est causa breuitatis uite; labor et fatigacio desiccant corpus; ergo sunt causa breuitatis uite.

Maiorem probat ibi: *Senectus autem sicca est. Natura autem sicut in homine est dicere masculina feminis* [v, 466b 14–15]. Istud medium sumitur a sexu, et tenet in specie hominis. Et est demonstracio talis: Quecumque habent plus de calore innato sunt longioris uite; masculi hominum habent plus de calore innato; ergo sunt longioris uite. Assumpcionem assignat ibi: *Amplius autem quoniam calidior est masculus femina* [v, 466b 15–16].

Et sic terminatur prima pars huius partis.

Secunda pars incipit ibi: *Set que sunt in calidis locis longioris sunt uite quam que in frigidis*, et cetera [v, 466b 16–17].

---

1 perduntur: producuntur L.
2 duas: tres L.

and similarly roots, but not at the same time, but when shoots and branches are lost others grow up. For when they do this other roots arise from what is there, they arise and thus always compete; this one destroyed and this one made whole, because of which this is the longest-lived. For there is a similarity between plants and insects as has already been said, for they live even if divided and two or more arise from one. However, having been divided they succeed in reaching that which is to live but they cannot live for a long time for they do not have organs, nor can they make the principle which is in every part but that which is in a plant can. For they have roots and stem everywhere in potency; whence from this always arises, this one which is new, this one which is old. For there is hardly any difference in that which is always thus, to be long-lived.[1]

Division of the Text

Moreover, it is the case regarding those which are subject to great toil, etc. The continuation of this part in respect to the proceeding and its arrangement is clear by what has come before.

And this part is divided into two parts, in the first of which Aristotle puts forward the causes of length and shortness of life which are found in animals alone; in the second part he puts forward the causes which are commonly found in plants. And the order and sufficiency is clear.

Literal Explanation of the Text

With regard to the first part, Aristotle proceeds in the following way. He says that *those males which are subject to great toil and because of their work become old more quickly*. And he adds the cause, saying: *for work dries up and old age is dry*. And the proof is like this: Everything which dries out a body is a cause of shortness of life; work and tiredness dry out the body; therefore, they are a cause of shortness of life.

He proves the minor premise there: *For old age is dry. For by nature as a general rule, the male lives longer than the female.* This middle term is taken from gender and holds in the human species. And the proof is of this kind: Those which have more of innate heat are longer-lived; the males of humans have more innate heat; therefore they are longer-lived. Aristotle assigns the minor premise there *because the male has a greater heat than the female.*

And thus, the first part of this part ends.

The second part begins here: *However, those who are in warmer places are longer-lived than those who are in cold places*, etc.

---

1 Note that the *translatio vetus* finishes at this point, i.e., lines 467a 26–467b 9 are missing.

180 TEXT AND TRANSLATION – LECTIO 7

146   Et debet esse demonstracio talis: Omne habens plus de calido et humido est longioris uite; set omnis uiuens existens in calidis locis plus habent de calido et humido; ergo omne uiuens existens in calidis locis secundum quod tale debet esse longioris uite quam quod est in frigidis. — Maiorem innuit ibi: *Propter que uidetur magis*, et cetera [v, 466b 18?]. Et est signum talis, quia maiora sunt animalia que sunt frigida secundum naturam in talibus locis quam in frigidis, ut serpentes et talpe et animalia que sunt uaria pelle; in locis autem oppositis, scilicet frigidis et humidis, in animalibus autem multiplicatur humidum aquosum. Vnde *in locis ad Arcton*, id est sub polo Archico, *nec gressibilia nec aquosa in mari* [v, 466b 25–26] sunt longe uite, et sunt minora quam ea que sunt in locis calidis. Et reddit causam: *Aufert enim gelu augmentum*, et cetera [v, 466b 28].

    Hic ponit causam quare gressibilia sunt longioris uite quam aquatica. Et est demonstracio talis: Omne habens plus de humido aquoso, quod est frigidum et desiccabile, est breuioris uite; set aquatica habent plus de humido aquoso quam gressibilia; ergo sunt breuioris uite. Et reddit causam aliam quare sunt breuioris uite, quoniam sunt sine sanguine, et quia non habent pinguedinem neque dulcedinem. *Vnde apes sunt longioris uite aliis animalibus maioribus* [v, 467a 4–5] propter pinguedinem et dulcedinem quam habent, etsi sint sine sanguine.

    Set in plantis est quod longius uiuunt, et cetera [vi, 467a 6]. Hic incipit uitima pars. Que iterum subdiuiditur in duas partes, in quarum prima ponit causas in uniuersali quare plante sunt longioris uite animalibus; et in secunda parte ponit causas appropriatas quantum ad arbores; et terminatur ibi: *De eo autem quod multo tempore*, et cetera [vi, 467a 10].

    Dicit ergo quod plante sunt longioris uite, eo quod *minus aquosa sunt* [vi, 467a 7] et *habent humorem non leuiter exsiccabilem* [vi, 467a 9]. Reliqua in littera plana sunt.

    Quantum ad secundam partem procedit hoc modo. Dicit enim quod oportet determinare causam propriam quare arbores sunt longioris uite. Et hec causa facit differenciam inter arborem proprie et animalia [et] quorum partes uiuunt per aliquantulum temporis post abscisionem. Et hoc tangit ibi: 147 *Causam enim non habent pro|pria animalia si incisa*, et cetera [vi, 467a 11–12]. Dicit ergo quod cum *perduntur rami, alteri germinantur* [vi, 467a 15], et sic *semper altere producciones fiunt* [vi, 467a 13]. Vnde hec est causa quare longius uiuunt quam animalia, in quibus, cum perduntur membra, altere producciones non fiunt.

And the proof should be as follows: Everything which has more of heat and humidity is longer-lived; but every living thing which exists in warm places has more of heat and humidity; therefore, every living thing existing in warm places as such must be longer lived than that which is in cold places. He puts forward the major premise there: *For the same reason clearly there is the large size*, etc. And the sign of this is as follows: because animals are bigger which are cold according to nature in such places than in cold places, such as snakes and moles and animals with multicolored skin. In opposite places, however, namely those which are cold and moist, watery moisture is however increased in animals. Thus, *in northerly places*, that is under the north pole, *neither those which walk on dry land nor animals which swim in the sea* are long-lived, and they are smaller than those which are in warm places. And he gives the cause: *For the icy cold takes away growth*, etc.

Here Aristotle puts forward the reason why land animals are longer-lived than water animals. And the proof is of this kind: Everything which has more of watery humidity, which is cold and liable to being dried up, is shorter-lived; but water animals have more of watery humidity than land animals; therefore, they are shorter-lived. And Aristotle gives another cause why they are shorter-lived, because they are without blood and because they do not have fatness nor sweetness. *Thus, bees are longer-lived that other larger animals* because of the fatness and sweetness which they have, even if they are without blood.

Those which are longest-lived are among plants, etc. Here begins the final part which is once again divided into two parts, in the first of which Aristotle puts forward the causes in general why plants are longer-lived than animals; and in the second part he puts forward the appropriate causes in respect of trees. And it ends there: *It is necessary, however ... to exist for a long time*, etc.

Therefore, he says that plants are longer-lived because *they are less watery* and *have a moisture which is not easily dried up*. The rest of the text is clear.

With regard to the second part Aristotle proceeds in this way. For he says that it is necessary to identify the specific cause why trees are long-lived. And this cause makes a difference between a tree properly speaking and animals whose parts live for a short amount of time after being cut off. And he mentions this here: *For in respect of animals they have something proper to themselves, except with regard to insects*, etc. Therefore, he says that when *shoots and branches are lost others grow up*, and thus *other shoots always arise*. Whence, this is the cause why they live longer than animals, in which, if they lose limbs, new ones do not arise.

Comparantur autem plante decisis, et cetera [vi, 467a 18]. Hic comparat plantas ad animalia que deciduntur. — Dicit enim quod, sicut in arboribus multa fiunt ex uno, ita et in animalibus. Vnde dicit quod decisa animalia, *usque ad id quod est uiuere uenerunt, non tamen possunt* uiuere *multo tempore* [vi, 467a 20–21]. Et reddit causam, quia *non habent organa* [vi, 467a 21], et propter hoc *non possunt facere ipsum principium* uiuendi *quod est in unoquoque* [vi, 467a 21–22]. *Set quod est in planta potest,* et reddit causam, quia *undique* planta *habet germen et radicem potencia* [vi, 467a 22–23]: germen, racione cuius potest fieri noua produccio, radicem per quam potest fieri attraccio nutrimenti. *Vnde et ab hac,* id est a planta, *semper prouenit, hoc quidem nouum, illud uero uetus* [vi, 467a 23–24]. Et potest formari sic argumentacio: Omne habens in se principium secundum quamlibet partem producendi nouum loco ueterati, longioris est uite quam illud quod non habet hoc; set planta secundum quamlibet partem habet principium per quod potest producere nouum loco ueterati, quod non habet animal; ergo planta est longioris uite quam animal. — Maior non indiget multum probacione. Set minorem ostendit: *Set quod est in planta potest, undique enim habet germen potencia,*[3] et cetera [vi, 467a 22–23]. Quod autem animalia non undique habent illud principium producendi, scilicet nouum ex ueteri, probat ibi: *Decisa autem usque ad id quod est uiuere uenerunt* [vi, 467a 20].

Et sic finitur iste liber.

⟨Questiones⟩
⟨1⟩

Hic primo dubitatur quare dicit: *Quecumque fatigancia masculorum* [v, 466b 12–13], et cetera. Videtur enim quod fatigacio et labor desiccant feminas sicut masculos; senectus autem sicca est; unde non solum fatigancia masculorum propter laborem senescunt, set | eciam feminarum. Inconuenienter ergo, ut uidetur, posuit istam determinacionem "masculorum".

Ad hoc dicendum quod femine naturaliter frigide sunt, unde ex indigestione multiplicantur superfluitates crude in ipsis; quia ergo per laborem confortaretur calor in ipsis mulieribus quod esset causa melioris digestionis et consumendi superfluitates, et propter hoc labor in mulieribus non operatur ad corrupcionem, set magis ad uite conseruacionem. Set quia in masculis est calor fortis, et ita uirtus digestiua fortis, pauce

---

3 germen potencia: generacionem L.

For there is a similarity between plants and insects, etc. Here Aristotle compares plants to animals which are divided. For he says that, as in the case of trees, many arise from one, so it is in animals. Thus, he says that animals which are divided *succeed in reaching that which is to live but they cannot live for a long time*. And he gives the cause: because *they do not have organs*, and because of this *they cannot make the principle* of living *which is in every part. But that which is in a plant can*, and he gives the cause, because a plant has *a root and stem everywhere in potency*: a shoot, by reason of which a new production can arise, a root through which the drawing in of food can occur. *Whence from this*, that is from a plant, always arises, this one which is new, this one which is old. And the argument can be constructed as follows: everything which has a principle in itself in respect of any part to produce the new in the place of the old, is longer-lived than that which does not have this; but a plant in respect of any part has a principle whereby it can produce the new in the place of the old, which an animal does not have; therefore a plant is longer lived than an animal. The major premise does not require much proof. However, Aristotle points out the minor premise: *But that which is in a plant can, for it has generation everywhere*, etc. However, that animals do not have that principle of producing everywhere, namely the new from the old, Aristotle proves here: *Having been divided they succeed in reaching that which is to live.*

And thus this book is finished.

Question One[2]

Here first of all the question arises why Aristotle says that: *Males which are subject to great toil*, etc. For it seems that toil and labour dry up females just like males; for old age is dry; therefore, not just the great toil of males due to work causing aging, but also that of females. Therefore, it seems that Aristotle mistakenly puts forward this distinction "of males".

[Solution] To which it should be stated that females are naturally cold and so from indigestion thick waste products are multiplied in them. Therefore, because heat is strengthened in these women by means of work which would be a cause of better digestion and of the consumption of waste products, and because of this, work in women does not bring about corruption but rather it works more to preserve life. However, because there is a strong heat in males and thus a strong

---

2 Finishing off the seventh lecture with seven questions seems more than coincidence.

generantur superfluitates in illis; unde augmentato calore per exercitium et laborem, de necessitate sequetur festinac(i)o consumpcionis humiditatis naturalis, et ita senium.

⟨Questio 2⟩

Consequenter queritur de hoc quod ipse dicit quod *masculina in specie hominis longius uiuunt* [v, 466b 14–15]; et reddit causam quia *calidior est masculus femina* [v, 466b 16], unde est distinctio maris a femina, et utrum ex natura operante naturaliter est quod femina est frigidior uiro?

Aristotiles enim repetit in libro *De Animalibus* diuersas opiniones distinctionis maris a femina; quidam enim posuerunt quod ex diuersis locis matricum accidit distinctio maris a femina, quia ex semine uel spermate cadente in dextram partem matricis, generatur masculus, in sinistra femina. Empedocles autem posuit generacionem maris ex spermate cadente in matricem calidam, et femine in frigidam. Tercia oppinio fuit quod ex spermate desciso a testiculo dextro generatur mas, et ex sinistro femina; unde accidit quod, si ligetur sinister testiculus, quod generetur mas, et si dexter, femina. Duas primas opiniones falsificat Aristotiles per hoc quod in eadem matrice aliquando concipiuntur mas et femina, et quando⟨que⟩ in dextra parte generatur femina et in sinistra mas. Tercia opinio similiter non est necessaria, quia, sicut dicit, contingit generacionem esse sine testiculis, sicut patet in piscibus. Vnde dicit Aristotiles quod id quod natura facit, facit quia necessaria est ut | illud facit, aut facit propter hoc quod meliori modo faciat. Vnde testiculos non facit natura quia sint necessarii ad generacionem: sine enim illis potest esse generacio; set in quibusdam facit testiculos ut per illis meliori modo fiat generacio. Nulla enim istarum causarum est necessaria distinguendi marem a femina. Necessarium est ergo quod fiat distinctio maris a femina propter fortitudinem uirtutis eius spermatis quod deciditur a generante. Vnde, cum in eo quod deciditur sit uirtus fortis, quia a patre est forma et principium motus, tunc de necessitate dat speciem similem speciei generantis. Vnde cum principium motus et digestionis sit in eo quod est a patre, necessarium est uirum esse calidiorem femina. Semen enim oportet esse digestiuum. Omne autem quod digeritur, decoquetur; decoctio autem

SEVENTH LECTURE – TEXT AND TRANSLATION   185

digestive power, very few waste products are produced in them; thus, when heat is raised as a result of exercise and work, of necessity there follows a consumption of natural humidity, and then old age.

Question Two

Consequently, the question arises regarding that which Aristotle says, that *the males in the human species live longer*; and he gives the cause because *the male is warmer than the female*; from where does the distinction between male and female arise, and whether from nature working naturally is it case that the female is colder than the man?

In the book, *On Animals*,[3] Aristotle repeats the various opinions regarding the distinction between male and female. For some held that the distinction between male and female arose from different places in the womb, so that a male was produced by seed or semen falling into the right part of the womb, and a female into the left. Empedocles, however, held that the production of a male was due to sperm falling into a warm womb, and of a female into a cold womb. The third opinion was that a male was produced from sperm coming down from the right testicle and a female from the left; thus, it would happen that if the right testicle is tied that a male will be produced and that if the left is tied that a female will be produced. Aristotle disproves the first two opinions by the fact that sometimes both a male and a female are conceived in the same womb, and sometimes a female is produced in the right part of the womb and sometimes a male in the left. Similarly, the third opinion is not necessary, because, as Aristotle says, it happens that reproduction takes place without testicles as is clear in fish. Thus, Aristotle says[4] that what nature does, it does either because it is necessary that it does so, or it does so so that what it does is done in the best way. Thus, nature does not make testicles because they are necessary for reproduction because reproduction can take place without them; but in some nature does make testicles so that by means of them reproduction can take place in the best way. However, none of these causes is necessary for the distinction between male and female. Therefore, it is necessary that the distinction of male from female happens because of the strength of the power of the sperm which comes from the parent. Thus, since there is a strong power in that which comes from the parent, because the form and principle of motion is from the father, then of necessity he imparts a likeness that is similar to the likeness of the parent. Thus, since the principle of motion and digestion is in that which is from the father, it is necessary for a man to be warmer than the female.[5] For it is necessary that semen digests. For everything that is digested is

---

3 See Aristotle, *De generatione animalium* IV i, 763b 29 ff.; 765a 22–24.

4 Ibid., IV i, 766a 6.

5 Ibid., 765b 16–17.

seminis est a calore spermatis in quo est principium motus. ⟨Si ergo sperma⟩ non potest uincere nec sufficienter digerere materiam propter defectum caloris, tunc necesse est quod mutetur in contrarium, et tunc fit femina; femina enim contraria est uiro; unde non est femina nisi uir occasionatus; et propter hoc, cum uirtutes sint contrarie, et secundum contrarietatem uirtutum necesse est diuersitatem ⟨esse⟩ instrumentorum quibus utuntur uirtutes, patet quod distinctio maris a femina est secundum contrarietatem uirtutum spermatum et instrumentorum uirtutum ipsarum.

Et sic patent raciones Aristotilis per quas probat distinctionem[4] maris a femina et per quas sequitur de necessitate quod masculus calidior est femina. Vnde dicit Aristotiles quod cum mari [non] debetur fortitudo et femina inbecillitas, ita non sunt nisi digestio et indigestio, fortitudo et inbecillitas; diuersitas autem digestionum [ex indigestione] ex diuersitate prouenit reperta in membro quod est fons et principium caloris, a quo est destructio uite tam in mari quam in femina. Ex hiis patet quod ex natura naturaliter operante non est quod fiat femina, set occasionaliter, et patet eciam quod de necessitate frigidior est uiro.

⟨Questio 3⟩

Consequenter obicitur contra hoc quod dicit quod *que sunt in calidis locis sunt longioris uite quam que sunt in frigidis* [v, 466b 16–17].

Illud non uidetur esse necessarium. In locis enim calidis magis accidit putrefaccio quam in locis frigidis. Dicit enim Aristotiles in 4 *Metheororum* quod frigiditas continentis inpedit putrefaccionem, unde minus accidit corrupcio per putrefaccionem in yeme quam in estate. Sic ergo male ponit Aristotiles pro causa illud longioris uite.

Etsi adhuc saluatur per distinctionem, quod quedam corrupcio fit per uiam putrefaccionis, et quedam per uiam arefactionis, et non intelligit Aristotiles hic quod in locis calidis minus incurrunt uiuencia corrupcionem que fit per uiam putrefaccionis, set intelligit de alia que fit per uiam arefactionis, adhuc hoc nichil est. Dixit enim Aristotiles quod cum *continens simul agit* [iii, 465b 26–27] cum natura, cicius accidit consump-

---

4 distinctionem: diffiniciones L.

decocted; the decoction, however, of semen is from the heat of sperm in which there is the principle of motion. If, however, the sperm cannot overcome or sufficiently break down the matter because of a lack of heat, then it necessarily changes into its contrary and then a female arises; for the female is contrary to the male; thus the female is nothing other than a man changed by certain circumstances.[6] And because of this, since the powers are contrary, and following from a contrariety of powers it is necessary that there is a diversity of the instruments which are used by the powers, it is clear that the distinction of male from female is in respect of the contrariety of the powers of the sperm and of the instruments of the powers themselves.

And thus the arguments of Aristotle are clear by which he proves the distinction of male from female and from which it follows of necessity that the male is warmer than the female. Thus, Aristotle says[7] that since strength is due to the male and weakness to the female, thus they are only due to digestion and indigestion, strength and weakness. For a diversity of digestion arises from a diversity that is found in the organ which is the source and principle of heat, from which is the destruction of life in both the male as well as the female. From these it is clear that from nature working naturally a female should not arise, but only in certain circumstances, and it is also clear that of necessity the female is colder than the male.

Question Three

Consequently, it is objected against what Aristotle says that *those who are in hot places are longer-lived than those who are in cold places.*

This does not seem to be necessary, for in hot places rotting occurs more than in cold places. Indeed, Aristotle says in the fourth book of the *Meteorologica*[8] that the cold of the environment impedes rotting and so corruption by rotting happens less in winter than in summer. So, therefore, Aristotle is wrong in putting that forward as a cause of length of life.

And even if this argument is saved by the distinction, that some corruption occurs by way of putrefaction and some by way of withering up, and Aristotle does not mean here that in hot places living things incur less of the corruption which happens by way of putrefaction, but he means the other that happens by withering, yet this is of no relevance. For Aristotle says that since *the environment works together* with nature, the consumption of substantial humidity happens more

---

6 Ibid., II iii, 737a 27–28.
7 Ibid., IV i, 765b 8–10.
8 Aristotle, *Meteorologica* IV i, 379a 29–30.

cio humiditatis substancialis, et ita corrupcio per arefactionem; sicut cum maior flamma simul agit cum minori in pabulum minoris, accidit quod cicius consummatur nutrimentum minoris quam aliud nutrimentum succedat, et sic subito corrumpitur minor flamma. In loco ergo calido festinatur utraque corrupcio, que fit per uiam putrefactionis et per uia arefaccionis.

Propter hoc dicendum quod sermo eius non est uniuersalis, set solum extendit sermonem illum ad uiuencia que secundum naturam[5] sunt frigida; talia enim recipiunt temperamentum ex caliditate loci; et istud patet per suum exemplum: dicit enim quod in locis calidis sunt maiora animalia que secundum naturam sunt frigida, ut serpentes et talpe, et que sunt sub pelle uaria. In quibusdam tamen locis calidis, inpossibile est quod sit uiuens, sicut sub torrida uel in locis uicinis utrique tropico, sicut exposito, in locis propinquis utrique polo infra ambitus utriusque circuli Artici non est possibile per gelu uiuere et in locis uicinis circulum[6] Architum parum uiuunt siue sint in mari siue non, nec recipiunt magnum crementum, sicut dicit Aristotiles in littera.

⟨Questio 4⟩

Consequenter dubitatur de hoc quod ipse dicit, quod *aquatica sunt minus longe uite pedibus ambulantibus, non quoniam humida,* | *set quia aquosa* [v, 466b 33–467a 1]. Et reddit causam, quoniam *tale humidum uelociter corrumpitur, quia frigidum et densabile* [v, 467a 1–2].

Super hoc est questio, cum humidum in aere et in aqua non accipiatur equiuoce, quia, si sic, non essent tantum 4 qualitates prime, immo plures: alia enim humiditas esset in aqua quam in aere secundum speciem, et alia siccitas in terra quam in igne. Quod cum falsum sit, oportet quod eadem sit secundum speciem humiditas aque cum humiditate aeris; humidum ergo utrobique idem est secundum speciem. Set quecumque sunt eadem secundum speciem, cuicumque contrariatur unum, et reliquum, et a quocumque natum est unum corrumpi, et reliquum; a quocumque ergo natum est desiccari humidum aquosum, et aereum et econtrario, et non erit unum humidum magis densabile quam reliquum in quantum humidum, nec cicius conseruetur unum a calido quam reliquum, in quantum utrumque est humidum.

---

5 naturam: natura L.

6 circulum: circa L.

quickly, and thus corruption by means of withering up; just as the greater flame works together with the smaller flame on the fuel of the smaller, it happens that the nourishment of the smaller is consumed more quickly than further fuel can follow, and thus the smaller flame is immediately destroyed. Therefore, in a hot place both corruptions that happen by way of rotting and by way of withering are hastened.

[Solution] Accordingly, it should be stated that Aristotle's statement is not universal but that he only extends his statement to those living things that are cold by nature. Indeed, such living things are balanced by the heat of the environment and this is clear from his example, for he says that animals which are cold by nature are bigger in warm places, such as snakes and moles and those which have scaly skin. Yet in some hot places it is impossible for anything to be living, such as in the torrid regions or in the places near both tropics, as has been explained. In places which are near both poles and within the zone of the Arctic circle it is not possible to live because of the ice and in places near the arctic circle very few live whether in the sea or not, nor do they gain a large growth, as Aristotle says in the text.

Question Four

Consequently, what he says is questioned, that *water animals are shorter-lived than land animals not because they are simply humid but because they are watery*. And he gives the cause, because *humidity of this kind is swiftly destroyed because it is cold and is easily congealed*.

In relation to this there is a question, since the moisture in air and in water are not taken in an equivocal manner, because if so there would not just be four primary qualities but rather more: there would be another humidity in water than in air with respect to species, and another dryness in earth than in fire. However, since this is false, it is necessary that the humidity of the water is the same in respect of species with the humidity of the air; therefore, the humidity in both is the same in respect of species. However, some things are the same in respect of species where one is opposed to the other and to the rest, and there is a tendency from both to destroy the other and the rest. Therefore, there is a tendency from whichever to dry up watery humidity, as well as airy humidity and the other way around, and there will not be one humidity which is more likely to be coagulated, nor will one be preserved more quickly by heat than the rest, inasmuch as both are humid.

Et hoc est quod intendit Aristotiles in littera, cum dicit *quod* aquosa *minus longe uite sunt, non quoniam humida sunt simpliciter, set quoniam aquosa;* humidum enim aquosum est frigidum naturaliter, et propter hoc de facili inmutatur a frigido, quia in genere proporcionali facilior est conuersio; et iterum grossum est in substancia, propter hoc de facili condensatur a frigido et euaporat a calido. Set humidum aereum, quia subtile in substancia, non de facili condensatur, et quia calidum natura non de facili infrigidatur nec de facili patitur a suo simili, scilicet a calore continentis, nisi sit continens multum uincens in caliditate. Tunc enim non agit quia simile, set quia superfluum; omnis enim superfluitas contraria est secundum potenciam et corruptiua nature, propter hoc hec animalia humida humiditate calida siue aerea sunt longioris uite quam humida aquosa. — Quomodo autem caliditas in humiditate agat, cum sint qualitates contingentes, hoc relinquo sub probante, quasi de hoc aliquantulum sit tactum superius.

(Questio 5)

Consequenter dubitabit aliquis de hoc quod ipse dicit quod aquatica sine sanguine sunt, propter hoc minus longe uite sunt. Per hoc innuit ipse quod habencia sanguinem sunt longioris uite.

Istud autem uidetur esse falsum. Dicit enim in libro *De Animalibus* quod corpora sanguinea maxime sunt putrescibilia et maxime racione parcium uicinancium ossibus. Et sic uidetur quod habencia sanguinem cicius incurrunt corrupcionem, que fit per uiam putrefaccionis, quam non habencia.

Id uidetur per hoc quia sanguis habet duas qualitates que habent motum a centro, et ita habent causam que per se disponit ad putrefactionem.

Ad quod dicendum quod in ueritate, quantum est de natura sanguinis, corpora sanguinea de facili incurrunt corrupcionem que fit per uiam putrefactionis; set quia non est aliquis humor ita amicabilis nature sicut sanguis, quia calidus et humidus, et *uiuere huiusmodi est,* et quia dulcis propter hoc ap⟨p⟩etitur et trahitur ad membra nutrienda, manifestum est quod natura magis est solicita circa regimen eius quam circa regimen aliorum humorum. Set cum destruitur a regimine nature propter eius multiplicacionem in corpore aut propter qualitatem aliam malam generatam in ipso ex indigestione, si fiat nimis liquidus

And this is what Aristotle means in the text, when he says that *water animals are shorter-lived than land animals not because they are simply humid but because they are watery*; for watery humidity is naturally cold and accordingly is easily changed by cold, because conversion is easier into a proportional genus; and again it is thicker in substance and because of this it is easily condensed by cold and evaporated by heat. However, airy humidity because it is subtle in substance is not easily condensed and because it is warm by nature it is not easily cooled down nor easily acted upon by something similar to it, namely by the heat of the environment, unless the environment is overwhelming in heat. For then it does not act because it is similar but because it is a waste product, for every waste product is a contrary in respect of its power and is destructive of a nature. For this reason, these animals which are humid with a warm or airy humidity are longer-lived than those with a watery humidity. However, as to how heat acts on humidity since they are adjoining qualities, I leave here unproved, as I touched upon this just above.

Question Five

Consequently someone might wonder about what Aristotle says that water animals which are without blood, for this reason are less long-lived. In this, Aristotle suggests that those which have blood are longer-lived.

This seems to be false. For Aristotle says in the book *On Animals*[9] that bodies which have blood are most liable to rotting and especially by reason of the parts close to the bones. And thus it is clear that those which have blood incur the corruption which occurs by way of putrefaction more quickly than those which do not have blood.

This seems to be the case inasmuch as blood has two qualities which have a centrifugal motion, and thus they have a cause which in itself predisposes towards putrefaction.

[Solution] To which it should be said that in truth, insofar as it is in the nature of blood, bodies which have blood do more easily incur the corruption which arises by way of putrefaction; but because there is no other humor as friendly to nature than blood, because it is warm and moist, and *living is of this kind*, because it is sweet and so it is desired and drawn in to nourish the organs, it is clear that nature is more concerned about its regimen than regarding the regimen of the other humors. However, as it is destroyed by the regimen of nature because of its multiplication throughout the body or because of another bad quality produced in it out of indigestion if it becomes extremely liquid or watery, then it is as a result of

---

9 Aristotle, *Historia animalium* III xix, 521a 1–2.

uel aquosus, tunc est ex causa uiarum putridarum egritudinum. Sanguis ergo, cum non habeat excessum in qualitate uel quantitate, alia est causa lo⟨n⟩ge uite, non quia sanguis, sicut dicit Aueroys supra istum locum, set quia calidus et humidus. Signum autem huius est, sicut dicit Aristotiles in littera quod *apes sunt longioris uite animalibus maioribus* [v, 467a 4–5], quamuis sanguinem ⟨non⟩ habeant. Et quia sanguis est calidus et humidus, propter hoc dicit Aristotiles quod salus sanguinis uniuersaliter reperitur in corpore animalis et est semper in corpore dum uiuit; et cum sanguis in corpore embrionis in matrice et post in corde, antequam recipiat embrio figuracionem completam et postquam caruerit sanguine, corrumpitur et accidit mors; et inde accidit quod propter euacuacionem sanguinis moriuntur multa animalia. Et cum generatur in corpore sanguis aquosus subtilis multus, tunc accidit quod | homines sudant sanguinem in tempore calido, et maxime in tempore in quo incurrit homo iram uehementem uel uerecundiam. — Et ex hoc patet quod possibilis fuit Ihesum sudare sanguinem, et inde manifestatur quod fuit uerus homo. — Tamen mortem naturalem que fit per arefactionem, tardius incurrunt sanguinea quam sanguinem non habencia, et causa huius assignata fuit superius, non tamen propter hoc quod sanguinea, set quia calida et humida.

⟨Questio 6⟩

Consequenter dubitabit aliquis de hoc quod dicit Aristotiles quod causa longioris uite in plantis quam in animalibus, est quod loco perditarum parcium producuntur semper noue. Vnde est hoc quod similiter non accidit in animalibus quod loco membrorum, si perdantur, non nascantur alia, cum magis sint perfecta quam plante, et perfectiores habent uirtutes quam plante. Vnde cum perfectum sit quod proprie attingit uirtuti, quia ⟨quod⟩ maxime perfectum est maxime deberet attingere proprie uirtuti, et tunc maxime attingit aliquid proprie uirtuti cum potest facere quale ipsum est, sicut habetur in 4 *Metheororum* quod tunc pepansis completa est in fructibus cum semina ualuerint facere quale ipsum fructiferum est; sic ergo uidetur quod cum animalia suis partibus magis sint perfecta quam plan-

the sicknesses of putrid veins and arteries. Blood, therefore, since it does not have an extreme in either quality or quantity, is another cause of a long life, not because it is blood, as Ibn Rushd says[10] with regard to this place in the text, but because it is warm and moist. A sign of this, as Aristotle says in the text, is that *bees are longer lived than larger animals*, even if they do not have blood. And because blood is warm and moist, Aristotle says accordingly[11] that the welfare of blood is to be found everywhere in the body of an animal and is always in the body as long as it lives; and as the blood in the body of the embryo in the womb and later in the heart, before the embryo receives complete formation and afterwards it lacked blood, it is corrupted and death occurs; and thus it happens that because of loss of blood many animals die. And since a lot of subtle watery blood is produced in the body, then it happens that men sweat blood in hot weather, and especially at a time when a man incurs strong anger or shame. And from this it was possible for Jesus to sweat blood and thus it was made clear that he was truly a man. However, the natural death which occurs through withering up, is more slowly incurred by sanguineous animals than those which do not have blood, and the cause of this was assigned above: not indeed because of the fact that they are sanguineous but because they are warm and humid.

Question Six

Next the question arises regarding that which Aristotle says that a cause of length of life in plants rather than in animals is that new parts are always produced in the place of those which are lost. Thus, there is this that it does not happen in the same way in animals that new limbs grow in the place of others if they are lost since they are more complete than plants and have more perfect powers than plants. Thus, since that which is perfect is one which achieves its own power because that which is perfect to the greatest degree is that which should most achieve its own power, and then something achieves its own power when it can do what it is, as is held in the fourth book of the *Meteorologica*[12] that then digestion is complete in fruits when the seeds succeed in making what the fruit tree is. So, therefore, it seems that since animals are more perfect in their parts than plants

---

10 Averroes, *De causis longitudinis et brevitatis vitae*, 148–49.
11 Aristotle, *Historia animalium* III xix, 520b 23–24; 521a 7–9.
12 Aristotle, *Meteorologica* IV iii, 380a 13–15.

te quod magis deberent habere uirtutem loco ueteris deperditi ⟨producere nouum⟩ quam plante.

Ad quod dicendum quod non est simile de animalibus et uegetabilibus, quia in genere animalium tota potencia materie ex qua generantur membra est finita; unde, cum sit tota potencia materie finita in generacione ex qua generantur membra radicalia, ut os membrum et consimilia, deperditis talibus, non est possibilitas in animalibus ad illa innouanda; deficiente enim propria generacionis materia, de | necessitate deficit ipsa generacio. Sunt tamen alia membra in animalibus que non procreantur ex spermate, set ex sanguine, sicut caro et pinguedo, et talia si deperdantur possunt restaurari, quia eorum materia in corpore animalis, manente uita, semper potest esse presens. Sunt alia membra, ut dentes et caude serpentium, que possunt regenerari. Et dentes enim generantur non ex spermate, set ex superfluitatibus cibi ossuum, et propter hoc dicit Aristotiles quod si homo uiueret per CCC annos, haberet plures dentes tunc quam in iuuentute. Similiter caude serpentium renascuntur, quia habent materiam presentem, quia nascuntur ex superfluitate cibi uicinancium parcium, et caude aliorum animalium ex superfluitate cibi cossarum; propter hoc ⟨homines⟩ carent caudis, exceptis quibusdam hominibus quorum superfluitates cossarum conuertuntur in caudis; et si ille caude amputarentur, renascerentur alie. Set in plantis, sicut dicit Aristotiles in libro *Vegetabilium*, materia ex qua generantur est eis uicina, et propter hoc dicit quod cito generantur, et cicius subtiles quam dempse, propter multitudinem figurarum que sunt in dempsitate. Similiter dico quod materia, ex qua generantur partes plantarum est eis presens; propter hoc natura in loco ueteris potest producere ⟨nouum⟩.

⟨Questio 7⟩

Quare autem partes plantarum, si decidantur, possunt uiuere per multum tempus et partes animalium decise non, causam huius sufficienter assignat Aristotiles in littera. Dicit enim quod

that they should be more likely than plants to have a new production in the place of the older one which is lost.

[Solution] To which it should be said that it is not the same thing regarding animals and plants because in the genus of animals all of the potential of the matter from which the parts of the body are developed is finished; thus, since all of the potential of the matter is finished in the generation whereby the basic parts of the body are produced, such as the bones and others like these, when these are lost there is no possibility in animals for these to be renewed. For when the specific material of generation is lacking, of necessity the production itself is lacking. However, there are other parts of the body in the animals which are not produced from sperm but from blood such as flesh and fat and these, if lost, can be restored because their matter in the body of the animal, as long as it is alive, can always be present. There are other parts of the body such as teeth and the tails of serpents that can grow again. Again, teeth indeed are produced not from sperm but from waste products of the food of bones[13] and because of this Aristotle says[14] that if a man were to live for three hundred years he would have as many teeth as in his youth. Similarly, the tails of serpents grow again[15] because they have the matter present because they grow from an excess of food near the parts, and the tails of other animals from an excess of the food of the hips. For this reason men do not have tails with the exception of some men whose waste products of the hips is converted into tails, and if these tails are amputated more grow. However, in plants, as Aristotle says in the book *On Plants*,[16] the material from which they are produced is close by to them and accordingly he says that they are quickly produced, and the subtle more quickly than the dense, because of the multitude of shapes which are in density. Similarly, I say that the matter from which the parts of plants are produced is present to them; because of this nature can produce something new in place of the old.

Question Seven

The reason why the parts of plants if cut off can live for a long time whereas the parts of animals if cut off cannot, is satisfactorily assigned by Aristotle in the text. For he says that in plants there is a shoot everywhere and a potential root, thus

---

13 Aristotle, *De generatione animalium* II vi, 745b 6–7.
14 Ibid., 745a 33–35.
15 Aristotle, *Historia animalium* II xvii, 508b 7–8.
16 Nicholaus Damascenus, *De Plantis* II i.

in plantis est germen ubique et radix in potencia, unde cum ubique sit germen, quod appellat Auensereth filium nature, ubique est causa uiuendi.

155 Item, quia ubique est radix in potencia, quam appellauerunt antiqui, sicut dicit Aristotiles in libro *De Animalibus*, mediatricem inter cibum et plantam; et similiter appellauerunt ipsam causam uite, id est causam dietans uite in tempus. Propter hoc partes plantarum possunt uiuere longo tempore post abscisionem.

Set, quamuis partes animalium permaneant usque ad uiuere, quia tamen non habent causam duracionis[7] uite in tempus, propter hoc non possunt uiuere longo tempore; deficiunt enim organa que necessaria sunt ad conseruacionem uite.

Si quis querat si radix in planta est mediatrix inter ipsam plantam et cibum sibiipsi in dimittendo inconuenientem, quod non contingit cum discreptione, quod non uidetur fieri sine sensu; et sic uidetur quod attraccio cibi tam in plantis quam in animalibus fiat cum sensu. Quod negat Aristotiles in libro *De Vegetabilibus*, dicens quod attraccio cibi est a principio naturali, et istud est commune animalibus et plantis, nec est attraccio cibi omnino cum sensu.

Propter hoc sciendum quod dicitur triplex sensus: animalis, racionalis et naturalis; sensu nature sentit adamas ferrum et ipsum attrahit cum electione; et hoc sensu sentit quod hoc naturale quod est sibi conueniens et inconueniens, et cum hoc sensu attrahit omne nutribile nutriens. Verum est ergo quod attractio cibi non fit omnino cum sensu quod fit anima racionali uel sensibili, set eius attractio fit de necessitate cum sensu nature, sicut ostensum est.

> HEC SUFFICIANT AD PRESENS DE MORTE ET UITA.
> DEO GRACIAS.
> MAGISTER PETRUS DE YBERNIA FECIT HOC OPUS.

---

7 duracionis: deduccionis L.

SEVENTH LECTURE – TEXT AND TRANSLATION   197

since there is a shoot everywhere which Ibn Zur'a[17] calls a child of nature, the cause of life is also everywhere.

Again, because there is potentially a root everywhere, which according to Aristotle in the book *On Animals*,[18] the ancients called a mediator between the food and the plant; and similarly they called it the cause of life, that is the cause of the persistence of life in time. Accordingly, the parts of plants can live for a long time after being cut off.

However, even if the parts of animals *succeed in reaching that which is to live* because, however, they do not have a cause of the duration of life in time *accordingly they cannot live for a long time for they do not have organs* which are necessary for the preservation of life.

If someone were to wonder if the root in a plant is the mediator between the plant itself and the food by eliminating what is inappropriate to itself, that could only happen with discrimination, which does not seem to happen without sensation; and thus it seems that the drawing in of food both in plants and animals occurs with sensation. This is denied by Aristotle in the book *On Plants*,[19] saying that the drawing in of food is from a natural principle and that is common to animals and plants, nor is the drawing in of food accompanied at all by sensation.

Accordingly, it should be known that sensation is said in three ways: animal, rational and natural. The magnet senses the iron by natural sensation and draws it to itself with choice; and by sense it senses that this natural thing is appropriate or not appropriate to it, and by this sense it attracts everything which is nourishing and nourishes. Thus, it is true that the drawing in of food does not happen at all with the sensation which arises from a rational or sensible soul, but its attraction arises of necessity with the sensation of nature, as has been shown.

THESE WORDS ARE ENOUGH FOR THE MOMENT CONCERNING DEATH AND LIFE.
THANKS BE TO GOD.
MASTER PETER OF IRELAND COMPOSED THIS WORK.

---

17 The Avenzoreth referred to here, namely Abū 'Alī 'Isā Ibn Zur'a Ibn Yuhannā (d. 1008), is still not well documented in Western sources nor do we know how his thought was transmitted to the West. The only other use of this author discovered so far is an aphorism found in Albert the Great: see Bertolacci (2103).
18 Not found. However, see Nicholaus Damacenus (Ps. Aristotle), *De Plantis* I iv.
19 Nicholaus Damacenus, *De Plantis* I i.

Magistri Petri de Ybernia

Determinatio Magistralis Rege coram Manfredo quaestionis disputatae

"Utrum membra essent facta propter operationes vel operationes factae propter membra"[1]

---

1 Edition in C. Baeumker (1920), 41-49.

Master Peter of Ireland

Solution to a Disputed Question Posed by King Manfred (*c.* 1260)

Whether the Bodily Organs are Made on Account of their Functions or Whether the Functions Happen Because of the Organs

Dubitauit Rex Manfridus et quesiuit a magistris utrum menbra essent facta propter operaciones uel operaciones essent facte propter menbra. Et fuerunt raciones ducte pro et contra, sed determinauit magister Petrus de Ybernia, gemma magistrorum et laurea morum.

Dixit ergo quod questio ista plus esset metaphisicalis pocius quam naturalis, et esset determinata in fine undecimi *Prime Phylosophie*; et quod esset questio de sollicitudine cause prime circa res que sunt in uniuerso, quia non est sapientis et omnipotentis relinquere malum nec facere aliquid iniuste, sed omnia disponere meliori modo quo possunt saluari ad permanenciam eternam uniuersitatis.

Et sunt duo sermones hic qui sunt in fine contradictionis: habere scilicet sollicitudinem circa omnes species, et reliquere aliquod malum uel mala multa; et illud non est sapientis artificis. Aut ergo non est sollicitudo, aut non erit aliqua species ordinata ad destruendum aliam speciem, quia si hoc esset, esset malum. Supponimus ergo quod sollicitudo est, et si aliquis error accidit uel malum, hoc non est ex diminucione contingente agenti, sed ex necessitate solum materie. Et propter uirtutem huius questionis ponebant quidem duo principia in rebus, prin-

King Manfred[1] pondered and asked the professors[2] whether the bodily organs are made on account of their functions or whether the functions are made with reference to the bodily organs.[3] And the arguments were developed for and against. The solution was, however, given by Master Peter of Ireland, outstanding of all the professors and glorious in his reputation.

He said therefore that this problem is one which is more metaphysical than natural and that its solution has been given at the end of Book Twelve of the *Metaphysics*[4] and that it refers to the question of the care which the First Cause[5] has for those things which are in the universe; for it would not be the act of the One who is Wise and Omnipotent to allow evil, nor to do anything which is unjust, but rather it is to arrange everything in the best way possible by which all will be preserved in respect of the eternal permanency of the universe.[6]

Again, there are two positions here which are completely contradictory: namely, to have concern with regard to all species; or to allow some evil or many evils to exist — for that is inconsistent with being a wise Maker. So therefore, either there is no providence, or no species will be disposed towards the destruction of another, since if this were the case, it would be evil. Let us suppose then that there is providence, and if it happens that there is error or evil, this is not because of a lack of on the part of a contingent agent, but only due to some material necessity. And on account of the difficulty of these questions, some posited two principles in things, a principle of evil and a principle of good, which is both heresy and

---

1 Manfred of Sicily (1258–1266) was a notable proponent of Aristotelianism in Southern Italy, having himself translated the *De pomo* or *De morte Aristotelis*. The illegitimate son of Emperor Frederick II Hohenstaufen, though recognised by him, Manfred inherited the throne after the death of Frederick's legitimate son, Conrad IV and the unsuccessful attempt to place Conrad's infant child Conradin on the throne. Manfred became king in 1258. The papacy was opposed to Manfred since he had made alliances with the Muslims and instead papal support was given to Charles of Anjou who defeated Manfred at the battle of Beneventum. Dante encounters Manfred in *Purgatory* (Canto III) where Manfred reveals that he repented before dying and now has the hope of heaven even though he was excommunicated.

2 Baeumker (1920) suggested that this formal occasion may have been to mark when Manfred brought the *studium generale* back from Salerno to Naples.

3 A standard theme for debate in the universities of the time but perhaps proposed with a view to Manfred's interest in birds of prey as Manfred was editing and completing his father's, Frederick II's treatise, the *De arte venandi cum avibus*.

4 Aristotle, *Metaphysics* XII x, 1075a 12–25. Peter calls this Book Lambda, Book XI of the *Metaphysics* since the translation he was using (the Arabic-Latin translation taken from the Long Commentary of Averroes which was translated by Michael Scot and quoted at Paris by 1231) did not have Book Kappa. Book Kappa was reintroduced by Moerbeke in his Greek-Latin translation, thereby making Book Lambda, Book XII and cited as such by, e.g., Aquinas, after 1271 when the translation of Moerbeke began to circulate.

5 Averroes, *Long Commentary on the Metaphysics* XI (XII), comm. 52.

6 The question of the eternity of the world was already exercising minds both at Paris and also here obviously at Naples.

cipium mali et principium boni, quod est heresis | et absurdum. Et hoc non oportet, quia inpossibile est malum esse nisi in priuacione que contingit materie passibili. Et propter hoc non est possibile separari malum a bono, immo semper concomitantur sese siue simpliciter siue secundum quid, et omne quod est, in eo quod est, bonum est.

Si ergo aues uiuentes de raptura sunt ordinate ad interficiendum alias aues, uel lupi ad interficiendum oues, id non debet esse ex ordine nature et natura ordinante; natura enim est causa tocius ordinacionis; et omne quod est preter ordinem, extra naturam est, sicut habetur in libro *Celi et Mundi*. Ista questio soluitur in XI° *Prime Phylosophie* sic, et abbreuio sentenciam [que] uerborum Aristotelis, ubi querit quo modo est bonum et nobile in natura tocius, utrum bonum aliquod sit distinctum per se et est id | propter quod sunt omnia, aut est bonum propter ordinem partium uniuersi in toto quem habent ad inuicem, aut utroque modo. Et ponit exemplum de duce in exercitu et de rectore in ciuitate. In ciuitate enim est bonum et propter ordinacionem eorum ad inuicem que sunt in ciuitate, et propter rectorem qui distinctus est ab hiis que ordinantur ab ipso. Et similiter partes exercitus habent ordinem inter se in diuidendo sese, unde quedam pars ordinatur ad alteram, et habent in exercitu multa officia et utilitates multas propter multas uirtutes, que tamen omnes utilitates ordinantur ad unum finem in ordine, ergo per eum est bonum. Et bonum distinctum dicitur dux, qui est causa tocius ordinacionis; unde dux non dicitur bonus propter ordinem, sed ordo dicitur bonus propter ducem; ordo enim non est causa ducis, sed dux magis est causa ordinis. Et id bonum quod dicitur de ordine, dicitur secundum magis et minus, et per se et per accidens.

Et secundum ponit Phylosophus exemplum de familia eiusdem domus: quidam enim sunt liberi et quidam serui, et quidam sunt seruientes et quidam sunt custodes et defensores domus; sed liberi non licenciantur malas acciones facere, sed omnes acciones sunt propter utilitatem; acciones autem

absurd.[7] Indeed, this cannot be the case since it is impossible for evil to exist except in a privation which arises from matter's capacity of being acted upon. And because of this it is not possible to separate evil from good; rather they are always found together whether absolutely or relatively; and yet everything which is, insofar as it is, is good.[8]

If therefore birds which live by preying are disposed to kill other birds, or wolves to kill sheep, this should not be from the arrangement of nature or from the way nature orders things; yet nature is the complete cause of order, and all that is contrary to order is outside of nature, as is held in the book *On the Heavens and the Earth*.[9]

This problem is solved in the *Metaphysics*, book XI [XII] as follows and I summarise the words of Aristotle[10] where he asks in what manner are the good and the noble in the nature of all: whether the good is something distinct in itself and is that on account of which all things are; or is the good due to the order of the totality of the parts of the universe which they have in respect of each other? Or is it in some way due to both? And Aristotle gives the example of the leader of an army and of the ruler of a city. Now in the city the good exists both on account of the reciprocal relations between those who are in the city, as well as because of the ruler who is distinct from those who are ordered by him. And similarly the parts of the army have an order among themselves by being distinguished from each other, and so one part is ordered in respect of another. Again, in the army there are many tasks and many advantages on account of many strengths, and yet all the advantages are ordained towards one goal in the arrangement; thus there is good by means of it. And the leader, he who is the cause of all of the order, is said to be a distinct good; so the leader is not said to be good because of the order but the order is said to be good because of the leader; for the order is not the cause of the leader but rather the leader is the cause of the order.[11] And that good which is said of the order is said to a greater or lesser extent, and in itself and in an accidental manner.

And next Aristotle[12] gives the example of a family belonging to the same house, for some are freeborn and some are slaves, and some are servants and some are protectors and defenders of the house. However, the freeborn are not allowed to commit bad actions, but all actions are on account of usefulness. However, the actions of those who serve share very little with the actions of the freeborn. And in

---

7 Averroes in his text had referred to two gods, one good and one evil, moderated here by Peter to two opposing "principles". This position is rejected as absurd since evil as a privation cannot be opposed to the good, and as heresy because opposed to the teachings of the Church. Peter would also have been aware of the contemporary situation where the Cathars maintained this ancient dualism.

8 Boethius, *Quod substantia in eo quod sint bonae sint* (*De hebdomadibus*) 44, 72–73.

9 Aristotle, *De caelo* III, ii, 301a 4–5.

10 Aristotle, *Metaphysics* XI (XII) x, 1075a 12 ff.

11 Averroes, *Long Commentary on the Metaphysics* XI (XII) x, comm. 52.

12 Aristotle, *Metaphysics* XI (XII) x, 1075a 19–21.

204 TEXT AND TRANSLATION – DETERMINATIO QUAESTIONIS DISPUTATAE

44 seruientium de paucis communicant cum accionibus libero-
rum. Et eciam in uniuerso sunt liberi, sicut superiora | corpora,
que semper propter aliquam utilitatem mouentur et sine errore.
Et hoc respondeo ad primum, id est ad intencionem primi.

Acciones autem rerum corruptibilum minime sunt conuenientes et ordinate, et sic non inueniuntur in eodem ordine, sed
quedam eorum tenent magis ordinem et quedam minus, sicut
dicit Phylosophus de lupis et animalibus uiuentibus de rapina.
Et non inueniuntur aliqua in uniuerso sine ordine, quia omnia
sunt ordinata respectu alicuius, et omnes acciones sunt propter
unum, et respiciunt omnia agencia ordinem propter unum. Et
illud est prima causa, quem ad modum omnia que sunt in
domo sunt propter dominium domus. Et sunt acciones
omnium que sunt in ordine uniuersi communicantes secundum magis et minus ad inuicem; sicut pauce sunt acciones
seruiencium in domo communicantes cum acciones liberorum,
et pauciores sunt acciones luporum uel canum, ita est de hiis
que sunt sub celestibus quod pauce sunt acciones eorum communicantes cum celestibus, quia modicum habet unumquodque corruptibilium de bono celestium, siue sit naturale siue
uoluntarium. Et inpossibile est quod habeant plus, cum limitate
sint potentie ad aliquid isto modo.

45 Vnde in toto uniuerso sunt quedam propter quedam, id est
uiliora propter nobiliora. Et istud *propter quid* diuersificatur, |
quia quedam sunt que iuuant acciones aliorum, et quedam sunt
que faciunt acciones conpletas magis et quedam minus. Et quedam sunt sic ordinata ad inuicem inter species corruptibilium,
ut sint quedam in istis speciebus corruptibilibus propter cibum
et sustentaciones uite aliorum, sicut plante propter animalia, et
quedam animalia sustentant se ad inuicem. Et hoc est causa
pugne animalium. Vnde animalia curuorum unguium et come-
dencia carnes crudas pugnant cum omnibus animalibus, et hoc
et quia inueniunt cibum et iuuamentum uite in eis. Et ita ordinauit natura uniuersalis omnia propter aliquod iuuamentum et
maxime propter iuuamentum et sustentamenta hominum. Et
propter hoc dicit Phylosophus: sumus et nos finis omnium,
non finis propter quem omnia sunt, sed ut illud cuius dicunt
esse omnia propter aliquam utilitatem; sed omnia sunt propter

the universe the spheres are free, namely[13] the heavenly bodies,[14] which on account of some advantage are always moved and without error. And I answer this to the first objection, that is, in respect of what was intended by the first objection.[15]

The actions however of corruptible things are connected and ordered to the least extent, and thus they are not found in the same order, but some of them tend more to order and some to less, as Aristotle says of wolves and animals which live by preying. However nothing in the universe is to be found without order because everything is ordered with respect to the other, and all actions are on account of the one thing, and all agents have regard for order on account of one thing. And that is the First Cause, just as in the way everything which is the house is because of the lordship of the house. Again, the actions of all those which are in the order of the universe are connected to each other to a lesser or greater degree, just as few of the actions of those who serve in the house are connected with the actions of the freeborn, and even less so the actions of wolves and dogs. This is the case of those who are under the heavens because few of their actions are connected with those of the heavens, because any of those which are corruptible only share in a small part of the good of the heavens, whether this is natural or voluntary. And it is impossible that they could have more, because of the limits to the potential of anything in this manner.

Thus, in all of the universe there are some who exist because of others, that is, the lower for the higher. And this *because of which* is varied, for there are some who help the actions of others and there are some who carry out actions, some more complete and some less. And there are some who are thus ordered in respect of one another among the species of corruptible things, so that there are some in these species of corruptible things which exist as the food and the sustenance of the lives of others, such as plants for animals, and some animals sustain themselves from each other. And this is the cause of the struggle between the animals. Thus animals with sharp claws and which consume raw meat, fight with all animals and this because they find food and the sustenance of their life in them. And so nature in general arranged everything on account of some assistance and especially for the nourishing and sustaining of human beings. And because of this Aristotle says:[16] we are the goal of everything, not the goal on account of which all things are, but as that of which all are said to exist because of some advantage. However,

---

13 Baeumker points out here in his critical apparatus that this sentence was difficult to interpret. It is possible that we could read "the stars" (stelle) here instead of "namely" (scilicet).

14 Averroes, *Long Commentary on the Metaphysics* XI (XII) x, comm. 52.

15 This, of course, indicates that this is the record of the conclusion of actual debate, the *determinatio*, where Peter is responding to an objection put forward by another professor.

16 Aristotle, *Physica* II, ii, 194a 35.

46 unum motorem omnium, primum | scilicet. Et dicitur bonum distinctum, propter quod sunt omnia.

⟨Et⟩ propter hoc, si sustinentur indiuidua unius speciei per indiuidua alterius speciei uel generis, hoc non est contra naturam ordinantem, sed totum est de bonitate ordinis et de sollicitudine ordinantis datum. Et non est inconueniens quod magis appareat beniuolencia nature in una specie quam in alia: quamuis ex se natura se habet equaliter ad influendum, tamen non equaliter res sunt preparate ad recipiendum influenciam; unde relegata est inuidia ex toto a primo, sicut ait Plato. Bonum ergo quod dicitur bonum ordinis non inuenitur nisi secundum magis et minus, secundum prius et posterius, et secundum nobilius et uilius; et semper posterius est propter prius, et uilius propter nobilius, et imperfectius propter perfectius, et materia propter formam et motus propter motorem.

Et quia in animalibus motor est anima et instrumentum est corpus, et inuencio instrumenti est propter motorem, necesse est quod corpus organicum sit propter animam, et non anima que est motor propter organum. Qualis ergo est anima, tale facit natura corporis, ut conueniat operacionibus anime; qualis ergo est anima, tales debent esse operaciones eius, et quales sunt operaciones talis anime, talia oportet esse organa exercentia operaciones illas. Si ergo est anima irascibilis et furiosa, oportet quod natura faciat menbra et organa deseruientia ire; non est enim esse corporis nisi ab anima, neque organum potest moueri per se nisi moueatur a motore, et motor non mouet nisi propter finem. Et [propter hoc] ⟨quia⟩ quedam

47 animalia | habent animas indiscretas et rudes, propter hoc habent corpora forcia conueniencia ruditati anime et simplicitati eius, sicut asinus, unde habet soleas in pedibus, et quia anima irascibilis et gulosa inuenitur in leone, propter hoc ordinauit natura ut haberet magnum os et ungues curuos. Et quia quedam animalia naturaliter habent artem, propter hoc habent naturaliter instrumentum aliquod conueniens illi arti per quod exercent operaciones illius artis; et quia anima humana est in potencia ad omnes artes, propter hoc habet aliquod instrumentum quod est in potencia omnia instrumenta omnium arcium, et hoc est manus. Vnde manus est organum organorum, sicut

all exist because of the one mover of all, namely the First; and it is said to be the separate Good on account of which all things are.

And because of this, if individuals of one species are sustained by means of individuals from another species or genus, this is not against nature which orders, but all is from the good of order and is given from the care of the one that orders. Again, there is nothing incongruous if the benevolence of nature appears more in one species rather than in another, even nature in itself is constituted so as to influence equally, yet things are not equally prepared in order to receive that influence. Thus, envy is something which is completely removed from the First, as Plato says.[17] The good therefore which is called the good of the order is not found except according to a greater or lesser extent, according to a before and after, and according to a higher and a lower. And what comes after is always because of what comes first, and the lower because of the higher, and the less complete because of the more complete and the matter because of the form and the moved because of the mover.

Again because in animals the mover is the soul,[18] and the body is the instrument, and the design of the instrument is because of the mover, it is necessary that an organic body is for the sake of the soul, and the soul which is the mover does not exist because of an organ. Therefore depending on what the soul is, nature makes a certain body, so that it conforms in its operations with the soul. Therefore, whatever the soul is, such must be its operations, and whatever are the operations of such a soul, such must be the organs to exercise those functions. If therefore the soul is angry and furious it is necessary that nature makes the limbs and organs to serve anger, for the existence of the body is only from the soul, nor can an organ move itself unless it is moved by a mover, and the mover does not move except on account of an end. And since some animals have undistinguished and coarse souls, because of this they have strong bodies well suited to the roughness and simplicity of the souls, such as the ass, and so he has hoofs on his feet. And since an angry and gluttonous soul is to be found in the lion, because of this nature has arranged it that he has a big mouth and curved claws. And because some animals naturally have a skill, because of this they naturally have an instrument well suited to that skill by means of which they exercise the activities of that skill. And since the human soul is capable of all the arts, because of this human beings have an instrument which is potentially all of the instruments of all the skills, and this is the hand. So it is that the hand is the organ of all organs, as Aristotle says,[19] since it is potentially a hammer, a sword and a dagger.

---

17 Plato, *Timaeus*, 29 e. In Calcidius, 26: *Optimus erat; ab optimo porro longe relegata est invidia.*
18 Aristotle, *De anima* II iv, 415b 21.
19 Aristotle, *De anima* III viii, 432a 1–2.

ait Phylosophus, quia est in potencia malleus et ensis et sica. Patet ergo quod menbra sunt animalis propter uirtutes, et menbrum et uirtus propter operacionem; menbrum enim non habens operacionem non debet dici menbrum nisi equiuoce.

Dico ergo: non quia ungues sunt curue, rapiunt aues, sed quia habent animam talem irascibilem et iracundam, cuius organum non potest sustentari nisi per usum carnium crudorum, etiam necessarium fuit nature ut faceret organa que faciliori modo possunt capire et retinere, et hoc est per curuitatem | in rostro et unguibus. Vnde illud non est ex necessitate materie neque debet attribui casui, sed habent ista organa ex necessitate condicionis finis, non absolute ex necessitate materie que attribuitur casui.

Vnde non concedo quod sit conclusio, si aliqua auis habet curuas ungues et rostrum curuum et forte aptum ad retinendum et capiendum, quin sit interficiens secundum modum suum. Vnde miluus et aquila et uultur et sparuius et astur et breuiter omnia que sic se habent sunt rapacia secundum magis et minus. Et hoc est quia secundum quod anima est magis uel minus iracunda, et complexio corporis fit colerica secundum magis et minus; anima enim sequitur conplexionem corporis in passionibus suis, et corpus animam in accionibus suis.

Patet ergo, domine mi Rex, quod menbra et uirtutes sunt propter operaciones, et non e conuerso. Patet solucio questionis, sicut michi uidetur.

It is clear therefore that the organs of an animal exist because of the powers, and an organ and a power on account of an activity. Organs which do not have a function should not be called an organ except in an equivocal manner.[20]

I STATE THEREFORE: it is not because their talons are curved that birds prey on others but because they have such an irrational and angry soul whose bodily organ cannot be sustained except by making use of raw meat. And so it was necessary for nature to make organs which could seize and hold in an easy manner, and this by means of the curvature in the beak and talons. Thus, this does not come from a material necessity[21] nor must it be ascribed to chance, but they have these organs due to the necessity of the manner of the goal, absolutely not out of the necessity of matter or of chance.

Thus, I do not concede that it is the case that if some bird has curved talons and a curved beak and is well adapted to seizing and holding, that this is why it kills according to its own manner. The kite and the eagle, the vulture, the sparrow hawk and the goshawk and the like, and all that are thus constituted, are rapacious to a greater or lesser extent. And this is according as their soul is ferocious to a greater or lesser extent, and the temperament of the body becomes choleric to a greater or lesser extent. For the soul follows the constitution of the body in its passions, and body follows the soul in its actions.[22]

It is clear therefore, Lord my King, that the organs and powers are on behalf of the activities and not the other way round. The solution to the problem is clear, as it seems to me.

---

20 Aristotle, *De anima* II i, 412b 20–24.
21 Aristotle, *Physica* II ix, 200a 30–34.
22 Nicholaus Peripateticus, *Quaestiones* VI, 130n. This last quotation links this work with the commentary on the *De longitudine et brevitate vitae* (see above, lect. 6, q. 2, 159), but the quotation itself may have already achieved the status of a popular saying: *corpus animam in sua action sequitur, anima corpus in sua passione comitatur* as it is to be found in the *Viaticus* of Constantine the African, who is himself quoting Galen.

Bibliography

Ancient and Medieval Authors

Adam de Belle Femme (de Puteorum Villa), (1908) *Memoriale Rerum Difficilium seu De Intelligentiis*, [Baeumker, C., ed., but mistakenly attribued to Witelo], Münster.

Albert the Great, (1890) *Commentarius Super Aristotelis Librum de Longitudine et Brevitate Vitae* [A Borgnet ed.], *Opera Omnia* IX, Paris.

—, (2008) *Questions Concerning Aristotle's On Animals* [Resnick I. M. and Kitchell K. E. Jr transl.], Washington.

Alfred of Sarachel, (1988) *Commentary on the* Metheora *of Aristotle* [Otte, J. K., ed.], Leiden.

Algazel, (1933) *Metaphysica* [Muckle, J. T. ed.], Toronto.

Anon., (1966), *Liber sex principiorum* [ed. Minio-Paluello, *Aristoteles Latinus* I, 6–7], Leiden.

Arnald of Villanova (1975), Opera Medica Omnia [Garcia-Ballester, L., Paniagua, J. A., and McVaugh, M. R], Granada-Barcellona.

Averroes, (1592) *Commentarium Super Metaphysicam*, Venice.

—, (1949) *Compendium librorum qui parva naturalia vocuntur* [Shields, A. L. ed.], Cambridge, Mass.

—, (1953) *Commentarium Magnum in De Anima* [Crawford, F. S., ed.], Cambridge, Mass.

Avicenna, (1508) *Sufficentia*, Venice.

—, (1968–1972), *Liber De Anima (Sextus De Naturalibus)* [Van Riet, S., ed.], Leiden.

Boethius, (1978) *The Theological Tractates* [Loeb, No. 74], Cambridge Mass.-London.

Calcidius, (1876) *Platonis Timaeus interprete Calcidio* [Wrobel, I., ed.], Leipzig.

Constantine the African, (1515) *De gradibus medicinarum*, Lyons.

Costa ben Lucca, (1878) *De Differentia Spiritus et Animae* [ed. Barach, C. S.], Innsbruck.

Frederick II Hohenstaufen, (2007) *De arte venandi cum avibus* [Trombetti Budriesi A. L., ed.], Rome-Bari.

Galen, (1490) *Opera*, Venice.

—, (1506) *Tegni*, Pavia.

—, (1821–1823) *Opera Omnia* [Kuhn, C. G., ed.], Leipzig.

—, (1976) *De Complexionibus* [*Galenus Latinus*, 1, Durling, R. J., ed.], Berlin.

—, (2011) *Method of Medicine*, Volume III: Books 10–14 [Johnston, I., and Horsley, G. H. R., (eds)], Cambridge Mass.

Haly Abbas, (1515) *Pantechne*, in *Opera Omnia Ysaac*, Lyons.

Isaac Israeli (1515), *De Dietis Universalibus, Liber Urinarum* [in *Opera Omnia Ysaac*], Lyons.

212   BIBLIOGRAPHY

Maurus Servius Honoratus, (1881) *In Vergilii carmina comentarii. Servii Grammatici qui feruntur in Vergilii carmina commentarii* [Thilo, G. and Hagen, H. eds], Leipzig.

Nicholas of Damascus, (1989) *De plantis* [Drossart Lulofs, H. J., and Poortman, E. L. J., eds], Amsterdam.

Nicholas Peripateticus, (1973) *Quaestiones* [ed. Wielgus, S.] in "Quaestiones Nicolai peripatetici", *Medievalia Philosophica Polonorum* 17, 57–155.

Petrus Calo, (1911) *Vita S. Thomae Aquinatis*, in *Fontes Vitae S. Thomae Aquinatis*, Fasc. I, [Prümmer D. ed.], Toulouse.

Peter of Ireland, (1920) *Determinatio Magistralis*, in C. Baeumker, 'Petrus de Hibernia. Der Jugendlehrer des Thomas von Aquino und seine Disputation vor König Manfred'. *Sitzungsberichte der Bayerischen Akademie der Wissenschaften*, Philos.-philolog. Und hist. Klasse. Heft 8.

—, (1993) *Expositio et Quaestiones in Aristotelis librum De longitudine et brevitate vitae* [Dunne, M., ed.], *Philosophes Médiévaux* 30, Louvain-Paris.

—, (1996) *Expositio et Quaestiones in Peryermenias Aristotelis* [Dunne. M., ed.], *Determinatio Magistralis* [Baeumker, C. ed., reprint of 1920 edition], *Philosophes Médiévaux* 34, Louvain-Paris.

Peter of Spain, (1951–1952) *Obras Filosóficas*, [Alonso, M. ed.], Madrid.

—, (2015) *Questiones super libro De animalibus* [Navarro Sanchez, F., ed.], Farnham.

Thomas Aquinas, (2002) *Super librum De causis Expositio* [ed. Saffrey, H. D.], Paris.

Thomas of Cantimpré (1973), *Liber De Natura Rerum* [ed. Boese, H.], Berlin.

Urso of Salerno (Calabria), (1936) *Aphorismi* [*Die medizinisch-naturphilosophischen Aphorismen und Kommentare* [*Aphorismi*] *des Magister Urso Salernitanus*, Creutz, R. ed.], Berlin.

Modern Authors

Bertolacci, A., (2013) 'Albertus Magnus and "Avenzoreth" (Ibn Zur'a, d. 1008): Legend or Reality?' in *The Medieval Legends of Philosophers and Scholars, Micrologus* 21, 369–96.

Bydén B. and Radovic F., eds, (2018) *The Parva naturalia in Greek, Arabic and Latin Aristotelianism*, New York.

Crisciani, C., (2004–2005) 'Aspetti del dibattito sull'umido radicale nella cultura del tardo medioevo (secoli xiii–xv)', *Arxiu de Textos Catalans Antics* 23/24, 333–80.

—, (2018) 'Death as a Destiny and the Hope of Long Life in the Latin Middle Ages', in *Longevity and Immortality: Europe-Islam-Asia*, Micrologus 26 5–25, Florence.

Crowe, M. B., (1956) 'Peter of Ireland. Teacher of Thomas Aquinas', *Studies, An Irish Quarterly Review of Letters, Philosophy, and Science* 45, 443–56.

—, (1963) 'Peter of Ireland's Approach to Metaphysics', *Miscellanea Medievalia* 2, 154–60.

—, (1969) 'Peter of Ireland. Aquinas' Teacher of the *Artes Liberales*', in *Arts libéraux et philosophie au moyen âge. Actes du IVe Congrès international de Philosophie médiévale*, Montréal-Paris, 619–26.

Dalgaard, K. E., (1982) 'Peter of Ireland's Commentary on Aristotle's *Peri Hermeneias*', *Cahiers de l'Institut du Moyen-Âge Grec et Latin* 43, 3–44.

Delle Donne, F., (2009) '"*Per scientiarum haustum et seminarium doctrinam*": edizione e studio dei documenti dello *Studium* di Napoli in età sveva', *Bulletino dell'Istituto Storico Italiano per il Medio Evo* 111, 101–225.

Donati, S., (2012) 'The Critical Edition of Albert the Great's Commentaries on the *De sensu et sensato* and *De memoria et reminiscentia*', in *The Letter Before the Spirit: The Importance of Text Editions for the Study of the Reception of Aristotle* [van Oppenraay, A. M. I. and Fontaine, R., eds] 345–99, Leiden.

Dunne, M., (1991–1992) 'Petrus de Hibernia – A Thirteenth-Century Irish Philosopher', *Philosophical Studies* 33, 201–30.

—, (2002) 'The Commentary of Peter of Auvergne on Aristotle's *On Length and Shortness of Life*', *Archives d'histoire doctrinale et littéraire du moyen âge* 69, 153–200.

—, (2003) 'Concerning "Neapolitan Gold": William of Tocco and Peter of Ireland', *Bulletin de la Société internationale pour l'étude de la philosophie médiévale* 45, 61–65.

—, (2003) 'Thirteenth and Fourteenth-Century Commentaries on Aristotle's *De longitudine et brevitate vitae*', *Early Science and Medicine* 8: 320–35.

—, (2004) 'Peter of Ireland', in *Dictionary of Irish Philosophers*, Bristol.

—, (2006) 'Peter of Ireland, the University of Naples and Thomas Aquinas' Early Education', *Yearbook of the Irish Philosophical Society*, 84–96.

—, (2009a) 'Peter of Ireland and Aristotelianism in Southern Italy', *The Irish Contribution to European Scholastic Thought* [M. Dunne and J. McEvoy, eds], 49–59, Dublin.

—, (2009b) '"The causes of the length and brevity of life call for investigation": Aristotle's *De longitudine et brevitate vitae* in the 13th and 14th Century Commentaries', in *Vita longa. Durata della vita e vecchiaia nella tradizione medica e aristotelica antica e medievale* [C. Crisciani, L. Repici, P. B. Rossi, eds], 121–48, Florence.

—, (2014) '*Dubitauit rex Manfridus* … King Manfred and the *Determinatio Magistralis* of Peter of Ireland', in *Translating at the Court. Bartholomew of Messina and Cultural Life at the Court of Manfred, King of Sicily* [P. De Leemans, ed.], 49–64, Leuven.

—, (2015) 'Pietro d'Ibernia [Peter of Ireland]', in *Dizionario Biografico degli Italiani*, Rome.

—, (2018) 'Aristotle's Natural Philosophy in the writings of Peter of Ireland (Petrus de Hibernia)', in *Edizioni, Traduzioni e Tradizioni Filosofiche (Secoli XII–XVI). Studi per Pietro B. Rossi a cura di L. Bianchi, O. Grassi, C. Panti*, II, 245–56, Rome.

—, (2021) 'From *longitudo vitae* to *prolungatio vitae*: Peter of Ireland and Roger Bacon on life and death', in *The Philosophy of Roger Bacon. Studies in Honour of Jeremiah Hackett* [Poloni, N. and Kadar Y., eds], 1–20, Abingdon.

—, (2022a) 'Peter of Ireland and Berthold of Moosburg on First Being, First Life, and First Mind', in *The Renewal of Metaphysics. Berthold of Moosburg on Proclus' Elements of Theology* [Calma, D. and King, E., eds], 429–52, Leiden.

—, (2022b) 'Death, the Intellect and the Resurrection of the Dog: Goeffrey of Aspall's *Questions on the De Longitudine et Brevitate Vitae*', in *The Embodied Soul: Aristotelian Psychology and Physiology in Medieval Europe Between 1200 and 1400* [Gensler, M., Mansfeld, M., Michałowska, M., eds], 163–90, Cham.

Federici Vescovini, G., (2004) 'La tradizione dei *Parva Naturalia* nell'insegnamento universitario medievale *(secoli XIII e XIV)*', in *Parva Naturalia. Saperi medievali, natura e vita* [Crisciani, C., Lambertini R., Martorelli Vico R., eds], 125–41, Pisa–Roma.

BIBLIOGRAPHY

Freudenthal, G., (1995) *Aristotle's Theory of Material Substance*, Oxford.

Gauthier, R.-A., (1989) 'Preface', Sancti Thomae de Aquino, *Expositio Libri Peryermenias*, Opera Omnia iussu Leonis XIII P. M. edita, Tomus I* 1, Rome-Paris.

Gill, M. L., (1988) 'Aristotle on Matters of Life and Death', *Proceedings of the Boston Area Colloquium in Ancient Philosophy* 4, 187–205.

Grabmann, M., (1926) 'Magister Petrus de Hibernia, der Jugendlehrer des Heiligen Thomas von Aquin. Seine Disputation vor König Manfred und seine Aristoteles-Kommentare', *Mittelalterliches Geistesleben* I, 249–65, Munich.

Haddad, C., (1971) *'Īsā Ibn Zurʻa, philosophe arabe et apologiste chrétien*, Beirut.

Haskins, H., (1924) *Studies in the History of Medieval Science*, Cambridge Mass.

Imbach, R. (1996) *Dante, la philosophie et les laics*, Fribourg-Paris.

King, R. A. H., (2001) *Aristotle on Life and Death*, London.

Lohr, C. H., (2010) *Latin Aristotle Commentaries*, I.2 Medieval Authors M-Z, Florence.

Luper, S., ed., (2014) *The Cambridge Companion to Life and Death*, Cambridge.

McEvoy, J., (1994) 'Maître Pierre d'Irlande, professeur *in naturalibus* à l'université de Naples', in, *Actualité de la pensée médiévale* [Follon J. and McEvoy J., eds], 146–58, Louvain.

Repici, L., (2007) 'Aristotele, l'anima e l'incorruttibilità: note su *De longitudine et brevitate vitae*, 1–3', *Antiquorum Philosophia* 1, 283–305.

Robiglio, A., (2002) '"Neapolitan Gold": A Note on William of Tocco and Peter of Ireland', in *Bulletin de la SIEPM* 44, 107–11.

Sermoneta, G., (1969) *Un glossario filosofico ebraico italiano del XIII secolo*, Florence.

Starr, P., (2006) 'Ibn Zurʻa Abu 'Ali 'Isa Ishaq', in *Medieval Islamic Civilisation: An Encyclopedia* [Meri, J. W., ed.] vol. 1, 376b–377b, New York–Abingdon.

Weijers, O. (2002) *La 'disputatio' dans les Facultés des arts au moyen âge*, La Haye.

Index nominum (ab ipso auctore citatorum)

Algezel, 62

Anaxagoras, 62

Arcton, 180

Aristotiles, 40, 42, 44, 46, 52, 54, 56, 60,
62, 64, 66, 70, 76, 78, 80, 84, 86, 90,
94, 96, 102, 104, 106, 108, 126, 128,
130, 134, 136, 138, 144, 154, 156,
160, 162, 164, 166, 168, 170, 172,
174, 184, 186, 188, 190, 192, 194,
196, 202
auctor (Aristoteles), 84, 98

Auensereth, 70

Auerroes, 90, 114, 126, 132

Auicenna, 80, 100, 114, 156, 166

Circulus Articus, 188

Commentator (Auerroes), 58, 92, 108

Constantinus (Africanus), 76, 80

Dominus, 138

Empedocles, 184

Galenus, 56, 60, 78, 96

Haly (Abbas), 70

Ihesus, 192

medici, 64

Manfridus, Rex, 208

Philosophus (Aristoteles), 156, 202, 204

physici, 156

Plato, 206

Priscianus, 144

Rasis, 70

Socrates, 156

Ysaac, 164

Index operum (ab editore citatorum)

Adam de Puteorum Villa,
    Memoriale rerum difficilium (seu *De Intelligentiis*): VI; 111

Alfredus Anglicus,
    In Metheorum Aristotelis: IV; 109

Algazel,
    Metaphysica: 63

Anonymous,
    Liber de Sex Principiis, A.L., I, 6-7: II, 29: 47

Aristoteles,
    Praedicamenta, a Boethio transl. (editio composita), A.L., 1 1-5:
        v, 2a 11-12; 123
        v, 4a 30-35; 129
        x, 13a 19-20; 77
        xi, 14a 8-9; 77, 81
    Analytica Posteriora, a Jacobo Veneto transl., A.L., IV 1-4:
        I xii, 78a 1-3; 135
    Topica, a Boethio transl., A.L., V 1-3:
        VI ii, 140a 18-19; 83
        VII i, 152a 1-3; 79
    De Sophisticis Elenchis, a Boethio transl., A.L., VI 1-3:
        i, 165a 24-27; 53, 75
        xxiv, 179a 37-38; 155
    Physica, a Jacobo Veneto transl., A.L., VII 1.2:
        I v, 188b 14; 133
        I vii, 190b 5-9; 103
        II i, 192b 21-22; 81 — 192b 34 – 193a 1; 81

II ii, 194a 35; 205
II ix, 200a 30-34; 209
III iii, 202a 15-18; 129
V i, 224a 35; 53
V i, 225a 6-7; 123
V ii, 225b 10-11; 129
V iv, 228a 7-20; 77, 51
V iv, 228a 10-13; 79
V iv, 228a 13-16; 81
V iv, 228b 1-2; 79
V vi, 230b 15-16; 135
VII ii, 244a 27-28; 111
VII iii, 245b 19-21; 111
VII iii, 247a 29; 111
VII iii, 247b 23-24; 111
De Caelo a Geraldo Cremonensi transl.:
    I iii, 270a 13-23; 131
    II i, 284a 14-15; 43
    II iii, 286a 9; 20
    II iii, 286a 32; 20
    II iv, 286a 9; 23
    II vi, 288b 12; 79
    II vi, 288b 18-19; 81
    II vi, 288b 30 – 289a 1; 53
    III, ii, 301a 4-5; 203
De Generatione et Corruptione, a Burgundio Pisano transl., A.L., IX 1:
    I ii, 317a 24-25; 107
    I iii, 318b 3-12; 129
    II ii, 329b 26; 21
    II iii, 330b 10-13; 131
    II vii, 334b 23-24; 19, 20
    II viii, 335a 1-4; 57
    II viii, 335a 10-11; 61

II viii, 335a 18-20; 111
II x, 336b 12-16; 49
Meteorologica, a Henrico Aristippo transl
  IV i, 379a 1-2; 93
  IV i, 379a 5-6; 161
  IV i, 379a 11 – 379b 6; 169
  IV i, 379a 14-15; 159
  IV i, 379a 16-18; 107, 159
  IV i, 379a 20-22; 167
  IV i, 379a 22-23; 161
  IV i, 379a 24; 22
  IV i, 379a 29-30; 187
  IV i, 379a 31-33; 167
  IV ii, 379b 18; 59
  IV ii, 379b 25; 21
  IV ii, 379b 35; 19, 20
  IV iii, 380a 13-15; 193
  IV iii, 381b 7-9; 59
  IV iv, 381b 31 – 382a 1; 57
  IV v, 382b 8-10; 107
  IV vi, 383a 6-13; 97
  IV vii, 383b 20-21; 165
  IV vii, 383b 24-25; 165
  IV vii, 383b 20-25; 57
  IV vii, 383b 34; 22
  IV vii, 384a 10; 109.
  IV ix, 387b 31 – 388a 2; 135
De Anima, a Jacobo Veneto transl.:
  I iii, 407b 13-26; 157
  I iv 408b 21-23; 87
  I iv, 408b 29; 155
  II i, 412a 8-9; 43
  II i, 412b 20-24; 209
  II ii, 413a 22-25; 45
  II ii, 413a 21-24; 153
  II ii, 413a 26-27; 45
  II ii, 413a 30-31; 45, 59, 61
  II ii, 413a 31-32; 45
  II ii, 413a 32 — 413b 2; 45
  II ii, 413b 4-7; 47
  II iv, 415b 21; 207
  II iv, 415a 26 – 415b 7; 20, 23
  II iii, 414b 7-8; 61

II iv, 415b 13; 41
II iv, 416a 6-9; 21
II iv, 416a 9-15; 21
II iv, 416a 25-26; 135
II iv, 416a 27-28; 47
II iv, 416b 27-29; 59
II xi, 423a 24-29; 135
III, viii, 432a 1-2; 207
De Anima, a Michaele Scoto transl.:
  I iv, 408b 21-22; 87
  II iv, 416a 25-26; 135
De Sensu et Sensato, ab anonymo transl.:
  i, 436a 13-15; 85
  ii, 439a 3-4; 139
  ii, 465a 5-7; 139
De Somno et Vigilia, ab anonymo transl.:
  i, 454a 26-28; 87
  ii, 456a 3-6; 65
De Iuventute et Senectute, a Iacobo Veneto transl.:
  iii, 468b 28; 67
  v, 470a 7-12; 137
  vi, 470a 32 — 470b 1; 137
De Respiratione, a Iacobo Veneto transl.:
  ix-x, 474b 25; 137
  ix, 474b 30 — 475a 21; 139
  ix, 475a 4-5; 139
  xx, 480a 11-12; 67
De Animalibus, a Michaele Scoto transl.:
  (*Historia animalium*)
  II, 508b 7-8; 195
  III, 520a 4; 163
  III, 520a 21-22; 163
  III, 520b 23-24; 193
  III, 521a 1-2; 191
  III, 521a 7-9; 193.
  IV, 535b 6-10; 139.
  (*De partibus animalium*)
  XII, 651a 20-36; 163
  XII, 651b 13-15; 173

INDEX OPERUM

XII, 652a 27-30; 139.
XIII, 665b 15; 65, 139
XIII, 656b 17; 27
XIII, 666a 6-8, 11-13; 65
(*De generatione animalium*)
XV, 718b 27; 141
XV, 721b 6-24; 169
XV, 723b 33 — 724a 1; 171.
XV, 725a 21-22; 171
XV, 725a 24; 175
XV, 725a 24-25; 171
XV, 725a 23-24; 28; 171
XV, 725a 28-30; 173
XV, 725b 6-7; 173
XV, 725b 19-25; 173
XV, 725b 29-33; 173
XVI, 735b 25-27; 165
XVI, 737a 27-28; 187.
XVI, 741b 15; 63
XVI, 741b 22; 63
XVI, 742b 35-36; 65, 67
XVI, 743b 25-29; 124, 139
XVI, 744a 2; 27
XVI, 745a 33-35; 124
XVI, 745b 6-7; 195
XVI, 747a 13-16; 173
XVI, 747a 17-19; 173
XVIII, 763b 29; 185
XVIII, 765a 22-24; 185
XVIII, 765b 2; 21
XVIII, 765b 8-10; 187
XVIII, 765b 16-17; 185
XVIII, 766a 6; 185
XVIII, 766b 31; 21
XVIII, 767b 6; 21
XVIII, 777b 3-4; 151
XVIII, 777b 16-20; 95
XIX, 778b 25-32; 87
XIX, 778b 27-32; 85
XIX, 781a 21-23; 65
XIX, 783b 28-31; 173
XIX, 784b 32-35; 85
XIX, 786b 21-22; 145

Metaphysica:
IV ii, 1004b 4-17: 49
XII, x, 1075a 12-15; 201, 203
XII, x, 1075a 19-21; 203

Pseudo-Aristoteles,
Liber De Causis: prop. XVII (XVIII);
41, 49

Pseudo-Aristoteles (Avicenna),
De Mineralibus (seu *De Congelatione
et Conglutatione Lapidum*), ab
Alfredo Anglico transl.,
(Meteorologica vetus, IV xiii): 57

Ps. Aristoteles (Nicholaus Damascenus),
De Plantis, ab Alfredo Anglico transl.:
I i; 47, 197
I ii; 53, 63, 71
I iv; 197
II i; 161, 195
II ii; 143
II vi; 97

Ps. Aristoteles, *De Sanitatis Regimine ad
Alexandrum*, a Johanne Hispalensi
transl.: 137

Avicenna,
Liber De Anima (seu Sextus De
Naturalibus):
II i; 101
V iv; 115, 117
Sufficientia, ed. Venice 1508:
I vii; 81

Averroes,
*Commentarium Magnum in De
Anima*:
I; 87
II; 127
*Compendium De Causis Longitudinis et
Brevitatis Vitae*:
61, 91, 93, 109, 163, 193

INDEX OPERUM

Compendium De Memoria et
   Reminiscentia:
   113, 115
Commentarium Super Metaphysicam,
   ed. Ven. 1562: XI (Lambda); 61,
   201, 203, 205
Compendium De Somno et Vigilia: 155

Boethius,
   De Trinitate:
   ii; 41, 43
   Quomodo Substantiae: 68
   De Hebdomadibus: 68, 203

Costa ben Lucca,
   De Differentia Spiritus et Animae:
   II; 69, 115
   III; 69
   IV; 157

Galenus,
   Tegni:
   III; 57, 79

Haly Abbas,
   Pantegni, a Constantino Africano
   transl.:
   IV v; 71

IV xix; 69

Isaac Israeli,
   De Dietis Universalibus:
   xxxviii; 165
   Liber Urinarum: 171

Nicolaus Peripateticus (Pseudo-
   Averroes),
   Quaestiones:
   VI; 69, 71, 159, 209

Plato,
   Timaeus, 29e; 207

Plinius,
   Historia Naturalis:
   xi, 22; 139

Priscianus,
   Institutiones Grammaticae:
   I; 127

Rasis,
   Liber Almansoris (*Physiognomia*
   Rasis):
   II; 71

Index rerum

accio, 52, 78, 88, 100, 124, 126, 130, 132, 144, 158, 166, 202, 204, 208

ad aliquid, 110, 114, 116, 152, 204

adamas, 196

aer, 56, 92, 104, 110, 134, 136, 138, 140, 142, 144, 146, 148, 158, 160, 162, 164, 166, 168, 188

aereus, 56, 96, 142, 148, 150, 158, 162, 164, 166, 188, 190

alteracio, 110, 112, 130, 160

analogia, 134

anima, 26, 35, 42, 44, 46, 48, 62, 66, 68, 69, 70, 72, 76, 82, 86, 98, 102, 104, 110, 114, 116, 118, 156, 158, 196, 206, 208, *passim*, – actus corporis organici, 46

animal, *passim*, – calidum et humidum natura, 146, 148, – que sunt uaria pelle, 176, 180, 188

apis, 120, 138, 176, 180, 192

apoplexia, 64

aqua, 56, 92, 96, 98, 100, 102, 104, 106, 108, 110, 134, 136, 138, 140, 142, 160, 164, 188

aquaticus, 176, 180, 188, 190

arbor, 66, 136, 176, 180, 182

arefactio, 186, 188, 192

arteria, 70, 138

artifex, 60

asinus, 146, 152, 154, 206

assumpcio, 42, 124, 126, 148, 150, 152, 178

auis, 66, 202, 208

bonus, 82, 202, 206

branca, 127, 138

brodium, 162

buffo, 138

caliditas 54, 56, 58, 92, 100, 104, 106, 108, 132, 134, 136, 140, 150, 158, 164, 166, 188, 190, – naturalis, 92, – uitalis, 54

calidum, 58, 152 – 158, *passim*, – celeste, 56, – complexionabile, 56, – innatum, 96, 106, 134, 136, 142, 144, – pingue, 146, 150, – uitale, 54, 156

calor, 88, 166, *passim*, – celestis, 56, 60 160, – complexionabilis, 56, 60, 160, – continentis, 132, 134, – elementorum siue ignis, 56, – innatus, 96, 106, 132, 134, 136, 138, 142, 144, 166, 178,- naturalis, 66, 88, 106, 132, 136, 172, – uitalis, 58, 132, 140

causa, 40, 44, 56, 60, 62, 88, 94, 100, 118, 130, 134, 136, 142, 158, 166, 172, 182, 192, 202, 204, *passim*, – efficiens, 116, – essencialis, 116, – materialis, 116, – sufficiens, 128, 130, 142

celestis, 204

cerebrum, 64, 66, 68, 108, 138, 172, – posterior cellula cerebri, 112

chathochiuum, 168

cibarium, 94

cibum, 204

cicada, 138

colericus, 90, 156, 208

commixtio, 154

complexio, 66, 82, 84, 88, 92, 112, 114, 154, 156, 208, – innata, 156

composicio, 88, 102, 116

INDEX RERUM 221

compositus, 98, 102, 106

conseruacio, 112, 114, 166

continens, 82, 88, 96, 120, 126, 132, 134,
138, 160, 166, 168, 186, 190

contrarium, 122 –117, 132, 152, *passim*

contrarietas, 58, 86, 96, 110, 118, 124,
126, 128, 130, 132, 134, 136, 160, ,
186, – materialis, 130

conuersio, 102, 160, 164, 190

cor, 52, 62, 64, 66, 68, 70, 138, 140, 142,
144, proporcionale cordi, 66,
– affectus cordis, 144

corpus, 156, *passim*, – uermi simile, 114,
– inferiora, 130, – metallica, 158,
– supercelestia, 48, – superiora, 48,
128, 130, 204

corruptio, 58, 92, 94, 98, 100, 102, 104,
106, 108, 110, 112, 114, 118, 122,
124, 128, 130, 132, 134, 162, 182,
186, 188, 190 – naturalis, 108,
– physica, 112, – substancialis, 160

corruptiuus, 146, 150, 152, 168, 190

coytus, 172

crasis, 96

creacio, 40, 116

cristallus, 108

dator – formarum, 106

decisio 170, – spermatis, 168

decoctio, 58, 184

delectacio, 168, 170

delfines, 138, 142

demonstracio, 100, 118, 122, 124, 126,
134, 148, 150, 152, 178, 180

densitas, 104, 130

dentes, 162, 194

diastole, 70

digestio, 58, 136, 144, 162, 182, 184, 186

dimensiones, 106, 132

distancia, 108

diuinus, 154

docibilitas, 102, 108, 114

dominium, 54, 58, 90, 96, 152, 156, 204

dux, 202

ecclesia, 64

effectus – permanendi, 118

egritudo, 64, 76, 78, 82, 84, 86, 98, 102,
104, 110, 112, 136, 146, 192

elementum, 56, 60, 92, 100, 110, 116,
154, 160, 162, 168, 192

embrio, 192

epar, 60, 168

es, 102, 116

esse, 40, 92, 100, 132, 160, 162, 164, 176,
passim – in termino, 110,
– susceptibile, 132, ens, 40, 48, 92,
128, Ens Primum, 40
essencia, 40, 86, 114, 116, 118, 162,
– quinta, 162

essentialis, 116, 148

euectum, 168

exercitus, 202

existencia, 92, 122, 160

experiencia, 70

fallacia – accidentis, 154 – consequentis,
168

femina, 146, 152, 154, 176, 178, 182, 184,
186

fetidum, 160

fieri, 102, *passim*

fimus, 160

finis, 116, 125

flamma, 134, 188

flegmatici, 90

fluxus, 76, – humorum, 68, 108

forma, 40, 42, 60, 70, 106, 116, 118, 184,
206 – inpressa, 116

generacio, 58, 60, 78, 100, 130, 134, 162,
170, 172, 184, 194

germen, 178, 182, 196

glacies, 108

gressibilis, 120, 122, 164, 176, 180

INDEX RERUM

habitus, 76, 80, 82
habitualiter, 82
heresis, 202
hoc aliquid, 40, 42, – quidem, 106, 113,
    178, 182
homo, 70, 90, 92, 94, 108, 122, 146, 150,
    154, 156, 172, 178, 192, 194, 204
humidum, 54, 152, *passim* – aereum, 56,
    96, 150, 188, 190, – aqueum, 56, 96,
    188, – nutrimentale, 58,
    – oleoginosum, 58, – pingue, 96, 150,
    – substanciale, 58, 158, 188
humor 68, 88, 92, 108, 146, 150, 176, 180,
    190

ieiunia, 136
ignis, 56, 60, 92, 100, 102, 106, 108, 110,
    136, 146, 158, 160, 162, 188
igneus, 140
igneitas, 106
ignorancia, 102, 104, 112, 114
illatio, 150
imaginacio, 112
incontingens, 132
indigestio, 92, 114, 182, 186, 190
inmaterialis, 116, 118
intellectus, 44, 46, 78, 152, 154, 156
intellectivus, 64, 68
intencio, 52, 74, 76, 80, 112, 118, 152, 204
interempcio, 168
inuestigacio – per rememoracionem, 112
iudicium, 78
iuuenis, 86
iuuentus, 84, 156, 194

lapis, 56, 102, 136, 158, 160
leccio, 104
leo, 206
leprosus, 84
licinium, 58, 164
linea, 124, 128
littera, 104, 180
luna, 48, 130

lupus, 202, 204
lux, 110, 134
luxuria, 70

malus, 82, 114, 190, 200, 201
manus, 70, 206
materia, 200, 203
melancolia, 168
melancolicus, 90, 152, 154
menbrum, 208
metaphisicalis, 200
mixtio, 92, 142
mixtum (mistum), 108, 160, 162
molensis, 92
mors, 46, 66, 82, 84, 86, 148, 192
motor, 44, 206, – celi, 44, – coniunctus,
    44, primum, 206
motus, 40, 42, 44, 46, 62, 64, 66, 68, 70,
    78, 80, 100, 106, 110, 114, 120, 126,
    128, 130, 136, 142, 152, 154, 158,
    166, 184, 186, 190, 206, – a centro,
    110, 158, 166, 190, – spirituum, 68
mulieres, 70, 182
murices, 138
mutilati, 170

narchotica, 152
natura, 52, 66, 80, 82, 128, 144, 184, 186,
    194, 202, 204, 206, *passim*, – contra
    naturam, 206, – extra naturam, 134,
    202, – preter naturam, 78, 92,
    – secundum naturam, 52, 58, 74, 76,
    78, 80, 86, 92, 94, 106, 134, 144, 158,
    180, 188
naturalis, 42, 66, 58, 80, 86, 88, 92, 100,
    102, 106, 108, 114, 132, 136, 142,
    160, 166, 172, 184, 192, 196, 200, 204
necessitas, 60, 106, 132, 144, 170, 200
    passim
nerui, 64, 138
nobilis, 202, 204, 206

obediencia, 68

INDEX RERUM 223

oculus, 86, 172
odor, 160
oleoginosus, 58
oleum, 56, 96, 164
omnipotens, 200
operacio, 80,86, 88, 100, 126, 140, 206, 208
organum, 116, 206, 208
os, 60, 170, 190, 194, 206
ouis, 202

pepansis, 192
per, *passim*, – accidens, 98, 100, 102, 104, 202 – se, 46, 48, 86, 94, 98, 100, 102, 104, 110, 112, 116, 122, 124, 126, 128, 134, 136, 140, 154, 156, 158, 164, 166, 168, 190, 202, 206
permanencia, 78, 92, 134, 200
permaneo, 118
peryodus (periodus), 48, 52, 94
pinguedo, 134, 158, 162, 164, 172, 176, 180, 194
pinguis, 96, 146, 148, 150, 158, 164, 166, 168
piscis, 138, 140, 142, 164, 184
planta, 44, 46, 50, 52, 54, 62, 64, 66, 86, 90, 96, 120, 122, 136, 140, 146, 148, 150, 176, 178, 180, 182, 192, 194, 195, 196, 204
pluuium, 142
pori, 64, 68
potencia, *passim*, – ad agendum, 110, 147, assimilandi, 170, – materie, 194, – uegetatiua, 44, 106
principium, 44, 52, 64, 80, 82, 138, 178, 182, 184, 186, 200, 202, *passim*, – principia materialia uiuentis, 48
propter *passim*, – quid, 94, 204
processio, 40, 44, 48
puer, 114
puericia, 156, 172
pulmo, 136, 138, 142, 144
putredo, 106

putrefaccio, 106, 158, 160, 162, 166, 168, 186
putrescibilis, 148, 158, 168, 190

quadre (anni), 94
qualitas 54, 60, 86, 106, 150, 158, – actiua, 90, 92, 100, 132, – contingens, 190, –sensibilis, 110, – prima, 108, 112, 114, 188, – prima uel secundaria, 88, 160, – secundaria, 88, 108

racio, 58, 60, 82, 106, 122, 124, 126, 128, 134, 136, 140, 142, 156, 162, 164, 168, 170, 172, 182, 186, 190, 200
racionabilis, 46, 100, 178
radii (solares), 134
radicalis, 194
radix, 182, 198
raptura, 202
raritas, 104, 130
rector, 202
refrigeracio, 136, 138, 140, 142, 144
regimen, 92, 190, – nature, 174, 190
rememoracio, 112, 114
reminiscibilitas, 98, 102, 112, 114
res, 40, 56, 68, 78, 80, 166, 204, 206 – res non naturalis, 142, 156
reuma, 68, 108
reuoluciones, 48, 94
risibilis, 118
rustici, 136

sales, 160
sanguineus, 90, 96, 190, 192
sanguis, 64, 66, 120, 122, 140, 142, 148, 162, 190, 192
sanitas, 76, 78, 80, 82, 98, 102, 104, 108, 110
sapiens, 200, – duplex opus sapientis, 52, 74
sapor, 160
sciencia, 46, 48, 102, 104, 110, 112

224 INDEX RERUM

scolares, 68

secundum, *passim*, – quid, 52, 128, 202

semen, 146, 168, 170, 172, 174, 184, 192

senectus, 82, 84, 86, 128, 136, 176, 178, 182

senex, 86, 114

senium, 86, 128, 184

sensus, 46, 52, 64, 78, 84, 134, 138, 152, 154, 196

serpentes, 176, 180, 188, – caude serpentium, 194

sexus, 154, 178

simplex, 106, 118, 128, 162, – simpliciter, 84, 86, 156, 176, 190, 202

sistole, 70

sol, 48, 96, 130

solicitudo, 200, 206

solicitus, 190

sompnus, 46, 58, 76, 84, 86

species, 90, 110, 106, 114, 124, 128, 130, 132, 170, 178, , 206, 200, 204, *passim*, – receptio speciei, 114

sperma, 168, 172, 184, 186, 194

spiritus, 62, 66, 68, 70, 72, 96, 114, 140, 144, 172 – animalis, 68, –gignitiuus, 172, – uitalis, 88

statua, 102

subiectum, 42, 46, 48, 54, 104, 106, 112, 120, 122, 126, 130, 132, 154

substancia, 40, 58, 68, 88, 116, 122, 124, 128, 140, 142, 154, 156, 158, 160, 170, 190

substancialis, 58, 90, 106, 158, 160, 188

superficies, 128

superfluitas, 126, 152, 170, 182

superfluum, 126, 150, 170

suppleo, – supple, 102, 104, 122, 152

susceptibilis, 128 – susceptibile, 128, 130, 132

talpa, 176, 180, 188

temperamentum, 114, 156, 164, 188

tempus, 50, 52, 54, 58, 60, 78, 82, 94, 114, 116, 120, 132, 172, 176, 178, 180, 182, 192, 194, 196

terra, 56, 92, 120, 146, 160, 164, 188, – terre nascentia, 56, 66

terrestris, 56, 158, 162

terrenus, 66

terreus, 142, 162, 164

testiculus, 184

testudo, 138

torrida, 188

tropicus, 188

uasa, 136

uene, 64, 66, 138

uigilia, 46, 58, 74, 76, 84, 86

uigilo, 84

uilis, 204, 206

uinum, 58, 96

uiolencia, 136, 138

uir, 184, 186, – occasionatus, 186

uirtus, 42, 58, 86, 88, 112, 116, 156, 170, 184, 186, 192, 202, 208, animalis, 86, 88, 138, –concupiscibilis, 64, digestiua, 68, 168, 182, – motiua, 64, naturalis, 66, 86, 88, – spiritualis, 62, 64, 66, 68, 88, – uirtutes actiue, 92, – sensitiue, 154

uita, 84, 94, 96, 104, *passim*, – prima, 40, – celi, 42, 44

unctuositas, 164

unctuosus, 96

universus, 204

utilitas, 202, 204

uoluntas, 112

uoluntarius, 44, 46, 152, 204

uox, 144

uter, 164

yems, 94, 106, 186

zirbus, 162, 164

Index to Introduction

Index nominum

Albert the Great, 14, 27
Alpharabi, 17
Al-Razi (Rasis), 16, 25
Ammonius, 14
Anaxagoras, 32
Aristotle, 14, 15, 16, 18, 19, 20, 21, *passim*
Augustine, 11
Averroes, 10, 11, 15, 26, 29, 30, 33
Avicenna, 11, 30
Baeumker, Clemens, 36
Bartholomaeus Anglicus, 27
Boethius, 11, 14
Cathars, 34
Constantine the African, 16, 28
Costa ben Luca, 30
Dator formarum, 29
Donati, Silvia, 14
Ebbesen, Sten, 15
Empedocles, 21, 32
Frederick II, Emperor, 11, 12, 27, 28, 34
Fruendenthal, Gad, 21
Galen, 10, 16, 25, 27
Gauthier, René-Antoine, 13
Haly Abbas, 16
Heidegger, Martin, 9

Ibn Zaur (Avensoreth), 33
Isaac Israeli, 16
Leophantes, 32
Manfred, King, 33
Michael Scot, 34
Montecassino, 11
Montpellier, 10
Moses ben Solomon, 11
Nicholaus Peripateticus, 16, 28
Peter Calo, 12
Peter of Spain, 14, 16
Proclus, 17
Richard FitzRalph, 10
Rilke, Rainer Maria, 9
Robert Grosseteste, 30
Robiglio, Andrea, 12
Salerno, 10
Thomas Aquinas, 10, 11, 12, 13
University of Naples, 11, 12, 34
Urso of Salerno, 28
Vincent of Beauvais, 27
Walter of Burley, 15
William of Moerbeke, 16
William of Tocco, 11, 12, 13

Index rerum

barnacle geese, 27
biotechnology, 9
birds of prey, 35

brain, 27, 29
catamenia, 21
climate, 32

INDEX TO INTRODUCTION

corruption, 30, 31
death, 9, 24
decay, 22
elements, 28, *passim*
elephant, 24
environment, 23, 33
eternity, 23
evil, 33
heart, 26, 27, 31
heat, 25, 27, *passim*, 31
humidity, 26, *passim*
illumination, 30
insects, 32
intellect, 30
logic, 13
magneticism, 33
naturalism, 11, 18
natural philosophy, 12

nature, – universal, 35
necessity, – material, 35
opposition, 31
original sin, 9
plants, 24, 32
providence, 34
reproduction, 32
semen, 31
sexual difference, 23, 32
sleep, 28
soul, 14, 16, 17, 20, 21, 23, 24, 26, 27, 28, 29, 30, 33, 35
spiritus, 21, 22, 25, 26, 27
transhumanism, 9
tropisms, 33
viator, 9
vital heat, 21, 22, 23, 26, 27
women, 33